# RESETTLEMENT

# RESETTLEMENT

*Uprooting and Rebuilding Communities in Newfoundland and Labrador and Beyond*

EDITED *by*

ISABELLE CÔTÉ *and* YOLANDE POTTIE-SHERMAN

ISER Books

LIBRARY AND ARCHIVES CANADA CATALOGUING IN PUBLICATION
Title: Resettlement : uprooting and rebuilding communities in Newfound-
land and Labrador and beyond / edited by Isabelle Côté and Yolande
Pottie-Sherman.
Other titles: Resettlement (St. John's, N.L.)
Names: Côté, Isabelle, 1981- editor. | Pottie-Sherman, Yolande, 1984- editor.
Series: Social and economic papers ; no. 37.
Description: Series statement: Social and economic papers ; no. 37 |
Includes bibliographical references and index.
Identifiers: Canadiana (print) 20200277006 | Canadiana (ebook)
20200277200 | ISBN 9781894725682 (softcover) | ISBN 9781894725811
(EPUB) | ISBN 9781894725835 (PDF)
Subjects: LCSH: Migration, Internal—Newfoundland and Labrador. | LCSH:
Migration, Internal. | LCSH: Newfoundland and Labrador—Social
conditions.
Classification: LCC HB1990.N4 R47 2020 | DDC 304.809718—dc23

Cover image: "Resettlement" by Kumi Stoddart
Cover design: Alison Carr
Page design and typesetting: Alison Carr
Copy editing: Richard Tallman

Published by ISER Books
Institute of Social and Economic Research
Memorial University of Newfoundland
PO Box 4200
St. John's, NL A1C 5S7
www.hss.mun.ca/iserbooks/

Printed in Canada
26 25 24 23 22 21 20    1 2 3 4 5 6 7 8

# CONTENTS

# LIST OF FIGURES

# CONTRIBUTORS

**STEVEN ARNFJORD** holds a Ph.D. in Sociology and is currently an Associate Professor and Chair of the Department of Social Sciences at the University of Greenland in Nuuk, Greenland. He has published extensively on social policy, social work, housing insecurity and homelessness, and the history of social welfare in Greenland. Dr. Arnfjord also leads NoINI, an advocacy group for people living without housing in Nuuk, Greenland.

**HANNAH BARRY** holds an International Bachelor of Arts (Honours) degree in Political Science and Communication Studies from Memorial University of Newfoundland. To date, she has largely focused her work on African affairs, completing fieldwork in both Ghana and Tanzania. Academically, her specializations include the politicization of food during armed conflict and the role that corruption plays in the protraction of civil war. Originally from St. John's, Hannah now lives in Zimbabwe, where she works as a Junior Professional Consultant with the United Nations World Food Programme (WFP).

**JULIA CHRISTENSEN** is an Associate Professor in Geography and a Canada Research Chair in Northern Governance and Public Policy at Memorial University of Newfoundland in St. John's. She has published extensively on northern and Indigenous housing and social determinants of health, including her 2016 edited volume with University of Manitoba Press, *Indigenous Homelessness: Perspectives from Canada, Australia and New Zealand* and her 2017 book with University of British Columbia Press, *No Home in a Homeland: Indigenous Peoples and Homelessness in the Canadian North.*

ISABELLE CÔTÉ is an Associate Professor in the Department of Political Science at Memorial University of Newfoundland. She received her Ph.D. in Political Science from the University of Toronto and was a postdoctoral fellow at KITLV (Royal Netherlands Institute of Southeast Asian and Caribbean Studies) in Leiden. Her research investigates the role of demographic factors in general, and internal migration in particular, on intra-state conflict and contentious politics in East and Southeast Asia and more recently in Western democracies. She has co-edited *People Changing Places*, a volume on "Sons of the Soil" conflict (Routledge, 2018).

REBECCA LEDREW is an M.A. student in Geography at Memorial University. Her expertise is in the field of human geography, with a particular interest in the socio-cultural aspects of sustainability, urban and rural planning, heritage, and adaptive reuse. She is currently working on her thesis, which focuses on peripheral stories of the circular economy and for which she recently completed research in Canada, the Netherlands, and Scotland.

TINA LOO is a historian at the University of British Columbia, where she teaches and writes about the environment and Canada. A member of the Royal Society of Canada, she is the author of a

number of award-winning books and articles about subjects ranging from wildlife conservation and the impacts of hydroelectric
development to forced relocation in Canada. She has also written
for *Canada's History* (formerly *The Beaver* magazine) and is co-editor
of the *Canadian Historical Review*. Her most recent book is *Moved
by the State: Forced Relocation and Making a Good Life in Postwar
Canada* (University of British Columbia Press, 2019).

NICOLE MARSHALL is an SSHRC postdoctoral fellow in political
theory at the University of Toronto. Anticipating the loss of a series of small island states to rising sea levels, her current work
explores the concept of political loss for climate migrants, particularly as it relates to the continuation of citizenship and rights
outside of the traditional state. She completed her Ph.D. at the
University of Alberta where her research mapped international
law, migration policy, and the ethics of climate migration.

YOLANDE POTTIE-SHERMAN is an Assistant Professor in the Department of Geography at Memorial University of Newfoundland
and a specialist in the study of human migration. She completed
her Ph.D. in Geography at the University of British Columbia,
and was a postdoctoral fellow in Geography at Dartmouth College.
Her research centres on the political economy of migration, community change, and local responses to migration, particularly in
the American Rust Belt and Atlantic Canada. She also co-leads the
Adaptive Cities and Engagement Space, a research collective at
Memorial University promoting social justice and inclusivity in
smaller cities and communities.

**GEORGE WITHERS** was born in Rock Harbour, an isolated Placentia West inshore fishing community of 150 souls. He graduated from Memorial University with a B.Ed. (1969), B.A., (1972), M.Ed. (1983), M.A. (2009), and Ph.D. (2016). He began a high school teaching career at Bell Island and St. John's, and retired from Prince of Wales Collegiate in 1999. At age 59 he enrolled in graduate school and fulfilled a dream of completing a doctorate in history.

# ACKNOWLEDGEMENTS

Research for this book was supported by a Harris Centre Applied Research Grant and by the Smallwood Foundation at Memorial University. We are also grateful for the support of of the office of the Vice President (Research) at Memorial University, which provided funding through the Scholarship in the Arts program, as well as Memorial's Publication Subvention Program to aid in the publication of the present work.

Special thanks to ISER Books academic editor Fiona Polack, managing editor Alison Carr, and copy editor Richard Tallman, who helped bring our manuscript to fruition. We also thank Rebecca Wilton, Mira Raatikainen, Lauren Onsom, Rachel Lutz, Hannah Barry, and Rebecca LeDrew for their work as research assistants on this project, and Charlie Conway for providing cartographic support. We also wish to thank Hannah Loeder for her help with the index and Philip Hiscock for his advice on the spellings of place names.

We gratefully acknowledge the permission to reprint material that was previously published. Parts of Isabelle Côté and Yolande Pottie-Sherman's Chapter 4 appeared in Côté and Pottie-Sherman, "The Contentious Politics of Resettlement Programs: Evidence from

Newfoundland and Labrador, Canada," *Canadian Journal of Political Science* 53, no. 1 (2020): 19–37 and are reprinted with permission.

Finally, we would like to express our gratitude to the contributors who provided helpful comments on the project's direction at the "Resettlement in Global Context Symposium" held in St. John's at the Atlantic Political Science Studies Association conference in October 2018. It has been a true pleasure to collaborate with such a generous and insightful group of scholars.

# CHAPTER 1

## Resettlement in Newfoundland and Labrador in Comparative Perspective

YOLANDE POTTIE-SHERMAN,
ISABELLE CÔTÉ, *and* REBECCA LEDREW

### COMMUNITIES DEBATE CLOSURE

In February of 2019, the remote community of Little Bay Islands off the northern coast of the island of Newfoundland voted unanimously in favour of resettlement.[1] After years of decline, the permanent shuttering of the town's crab processing plant (and major employer) had galvanized debate about its viability. The vote was the last and final step of the provincial government's Community Relocation Policy: in December of 2019, essential services to the community were cut, with each resident to receive a buyout package of $250,000 ($270,000 for families). The process has been long and controversial, and a previous vote on the matter in 2015 had failed by less than half a percentage point. Opinions on the Community Relocation Policy (CRP) have been bitterly divided in Little Bay Islands and Newfoundland and Labrador more broadly, with some viewing the resettlement of isolated communities as an absolute necessity for both the provincial economy and the welfare of its rural citizens, and others seeing it as a coercive dismantling of outport culture.[2]

Contemporary resettlement projects around the world are contending with many of the same issues raised in Little Bay Islands. In January of 2017, residents of Isle de Jean Charles, Louisiana, were also considering the terms of their resettlement. Having lost 98 per cent of its land area in the last 50 years, the state of Louisiana identified the narrow island in the Gulf of Mexico as a "resettlement zone."[3] The Isle de Jean Charles resettlement project represents the culmination of a process that has unfolded over two decades, as Indigenous groups on the island have asserted claims for tribal recognition and environmental protection from the state of Louisiana and the United States federal government.[4] This voluntary resettlement project has been contentious. Some residents do not want to leave or are unsure about relocating, and commentators have criticized the state government's efforts to meaningfully involve all residents of the island in the process.[5] The cost and slow nature of the relocation process have also raised questions concerning the government's financial commitment to resettlement.[6] Its projected cost is $100 million — well beyond the US$48 million allocated by the US Department of Housing and Urban Development. Popular media have labelled the community as abandoned by the "first climate change refugees," a narrative that ignores the layered vulnerabilities facing Isle de Jean Charles, including oil exploration, out-migration, and the failure of the federal government to recognize tribal sovereignty.[7]

Though these two contexts are very different, they involve common issues: how can resettlement projects — whether led by state actors or communities — meaningfully include the people affected by them? How can we reconcile the layers of mobility and immobility that may engender rifts within communities debating relocation? Perhaps most importantly, the real cost of resettlement goes far beyond the monetary value of the assets left behind. What is the true cost of resettlement and how can resettlement debates be reframed to recognize the social and cultural importance of places? This book takes up these questions by examining resettlement projects in Newfoundland and Labrador in critical, comparative perspective.

## THIS BOOK

Our goal here is to place Newfoundland and Labrador's ongoing experiences with resettlement in conversation with the broader field of resettlement studies. This field of study focuses on the dynamics of planned population movements, and takes stock of the causes and consequences of resettlement programs as well as the actors and policies involved.[8] As a starting point, we employ Vanclay's definition of resettlement as:

> the comprehensive process of planning for and implementing the relocation of people, households, and communities from one place to another for some specific reason, together with all associated activities, including: (a) provision of compensation for lost assets, resources, and inconvenience; and (b) the provision of support for livelihood restoration and enhancement, re-establishment of social networks, and for restoring or improving the social functioning of the community, social activities and essential public services.[9]

In other words, resettlement is a process that begins before and continues long after communities or individuals move. It is distinct from other forms of relocation because it involves relatively permanent, organized movement by an entire community.[10] Ideally, too, resettlement involves appropriate compensation and the mechanisms and resources for those who are uprooted to start anew or rebuild communities elsewhere.

In this introductory chapter, we start with a brief overview of Newfoundland and Labrador's resettlement experience before advocating for a critical, comparative approach to resettlement studies in order to better understand the multi-dimensional agendas that underlie resettlement projects, their governance structures, their potential benefits and harms, as well as their global span. Next, we highlight the four overarching themes of this edited volume: (1) the layered, historical legacies of colonialism, dispossession, and (re)resettlement; (2) the agency and legitimacy of the various actors involved in resettlement schemes, including government officials, academics, religious leaders, and non-state actors; (3) resistance and resilience; and (4) the role of resource and extractive development in resettlement. We conclude with an overview of the book.

## RESETTLEMENT IN NEWFOUNDLAND AND LABRADOR

Resettlement in Newfoundland and Labrador officially refers to the government-sponsored relocation of rural settlements that began in 1954, five years after Newfoundland joined the Canadian Confederation.[11] These programs aimed at centralizing its rural population and stimulating economic growth. From 1954 to 1977, under the leadership of Joseph R. Smallwood, resettlement programs in Newfoundland and Labrador involved the relocation of some 29,614 individuals (or 4,094 households) to 77 "growth centres."[12] These programs were modernization projects, and ideologically intertwined with many other post-World War II "state manipulations of communities of largely uneducated people."[13]

Architects of high-modernism believed in training rural people for work in urban centres and in supporting large-scale, capitalized production in primary industries. Newfoundland's resettlement (particularly its second phase, the Fisheries Household Resettlement Program; see Withers, Chapter 3) was a type of state-sponsored centralization that aimed to move rural populations to growth-pole communities where increased development was expected to generate spin-off industries. Smallwood's centralization plan dovetailed with his goal to modernize the fisheries, targeting the inshore and subsistence fishers he viewed as impediments to fisheries' modernization (symbolized by frozen-fish processing and capacity to compete with offshore foreign factory trawlers).[14] State planners not only believed economic change was necessary, but also that outport people's attitudes and habits needed transformation. By the late 1970s, resettlement had become a "lightning rod" for discontent in Newfoundland, and for the next thirty years, it was anathema to politicians.[15] Yet the program was not without its successes. Blake notes that by 1972, more than 95 per cent of the population had access to road connections and electricity, and increased and varied economic opportunities offered many rural residents good year-round employment.[16]

Official accounts of resettlement, which begin with the 1954 centralization policy, belie the far longer history of human displacement in Labrador and the island of Newfoundland as a result of European activity.[17] Settler colonialism is a distinct form of colonialism involving the purposeful physical displacement of Indigenous peoples from their lands in the interests of settlers and as "a method of asserting ownership over land and resources."[18] By the early sixteenth century, Britain had staked its claim to the island of Newfoundland, the traditional territory of the Beothuk and Mi'kmaq, a claim that would have disastrous consequences for these populations as permanent settlement from the British Isles unfolded over subsequent centuries.[19] Pre-Confederation, there are numerous examples of the deliberate relocation of Indigenous communities in both Newfoundland and Labrador. Some of these relocations had geopolitical agendas: in the 1940s, Innu and Mi'kmaw people were forced to move from their traditional lands to make way for the wartime construction of Canadian and United States air bases at Goose Bay and Stephenville, respectively.[20] Other relocations, such as that of the Labrador Mushuau Innu from Davis Inlet to Nutak in 1948, were carried out on the grounds of encouraging Innu "self-sufficiency." For the Mushuau Innu, this was only the first of multiple socially and culturally destructive relocations they would experience from 1948 to 2002, before they were resettled in Natuashish as part of the federal government's Labrador Innu Comprehensive Healing Strategy.[21]

With Confederation, the federal government, the province, and other actors including Moravian missionaries began withdrawing services from Inuit settlements north of Nain, effectively forcing their southern migration.[22] This process of withdrawal culminated with the closure of communities in Nutak in 1956 and Hebron in 1959, when the provincial government abruptly shuttered the town stores and missionaries closed their missions, forcing the relocation of the Inuit who resided there.[23] These injustices were important motivations in the 1973 formation of the Labrador Inuit Association, which ultimately secured the 2004 Labrador Inuit Land Claims Agreement and created the Nunatsiavut Government.[24] In 2005, the province formally apologized for the closure of Nutak and Hebron, acknowledging that "the closures were made without consultation" with those communities and that as "a result of the closures, and the way they were carried out, the Inuit of Nutak and Hebron experienced a variety of personal hardships and social, family and economic problems."[25] Furthermore, since the 1970s, a series of hydroelectric and mining projects in Labrador, including the Churchill Falls dam in 1972, mining at Voisey's Bay, and most recently, the Muskrat Falls project, must also be understood within the long series of development-induced displacements of Indigenous peoples in Newfoundland and Labrador, in Canada, and beyond.

Over the last decade, resettlement has once again come to the forefront of political debate in the province, revived by subsequent shifts in its resource economy. The collapse of northern cod stocks in the early 1990s prompted a moratorium that put 35,000 fishers and plant workers out of work, inducing acute and ongoing out-migration and decline across the province's coastal communities.[26] After the moratorium, a transition to shellfish mitigated some of the disruptions (for example, by retrofitting former fish plants for use in crab processing), but with geographically uneven and precarious impacts. The rush to retrofit and build new crab processing plants resulted in extreme competition for crab, prompting a spatial reorganization of the relationships between fishers and crab buyers.[27] These shifts have once again raised the question of community closure, as communities like Little Bay Islands have more recently seen their fish plants close for good.

The CRPs reflect the government's desire to minimize the costs associated with providing services to remote communities by offering struggling remote communities compensation for community closure (see Côté and Pottie-Sherman, Chapter 4).

Newfoundland Studies scholars have underscored the significance of resettlement to the history, culture, and politics of Newfoundland and Labrador.[28] Our aim with this book is not to re-open old wounds and rehash old debates. As the archives adviser at The Rooms (the province's major cultural gallery) noted recently, every generation "needs different things from the past."[29] We find this advice especially resonant in the case of resettlement: what Newfoundland and Labrador has learned about community closure — the controversies, the opportunities, the commemorations — provide crucial testimony for governments and communities around the world that are weighing such a decision. Further, scholars in this field have not yet adequately addressed the province's new phase of resettlement (2009–present) in which resettlement has been carried out at the request of communities, implemented to mitigate the fiscal mismatch between shrinking populations and infrastructure costs.

## WHY TAKE A COMPARATIVE APPROACH?

Resettlement programs in Newfoundland and Labrador represent only a small sample of ongoing or potential resettlement schemes around the world. Taking a more global view of resettlement allows us to better unpack the main rationales, actors, structures, and potential costs and benefits that underlie resettlement projects.

First, contemporary resettlement projects have many guises, intersecting with many of the major forces reshaping global relationships in the twenty-first century, from economic development to geopolitics and climate change.[30] Development-induced displacement and resettlement — like that experienced by the Labrador Innu when their traditional lands were flooded by the Churchill Dam project in 1972 — occurs when individuals, households, or communities are directly or indirectly displaced by development projects, including hydro power and resource extraction ("mine- or dam-induced" resettlement), infrastructure construction (bridges, roads, and railway-induced resettlement), or large-scale agriculture (known as "land grab-induced" resettlement).[31] Many of the world's largest population resettlement schemes have accompanied the construction of new transportation and energy infrastructure,[32] including the 1.4 million people who were relocated to make way for the Three Gorges Dam in China.[33] Turkey's Ilusu Dam, the largest hydro project ever undertaken in Turkey, impacts roughly 3 million people dispersed across five provinces in Anatolia.[34] In Bangladesh, the Jamuna multi-purpose bridge development connecting the western and eastern halves of Bangladesh affected roughly 16,500 households totalling 100,000 people.[35] Agricultural development, too, continues to be a major driver of economic-oriented resettlement projects such as in Ethiopia, where the government's "villagization" program, begun in 2010, resettled nearly all of the rural population of Gambella state to make larger pieces of land available to lease for large-scale commercial agricultural development.[36]

In both Global North and South, urban resettlement schemes have also accompanied "world class" city ambitions.[37] In the lead-up to the 2014 FIFA World Cup and 2016 Summer Olympics, Rio de Janeiro's municipal government embarked on a project of state-sponsored gentrification and growth acceleration. This project relocated people away from the places where the government planned to build infrastructure for these events and was decried as a "social cleansing" project.[38] While the intentions of these projects may be development-oriented, the people typically displaced have been ethnic minorities or the urban poor.[39] In this way, these projects share commonalities with the "slum clearance" urban renewal projects that were carried out in North America, including in St. John's, Newfoundland, during the mid-twentieth century. Sarah Manning has recently drawn parallels between development agendas in the Global South and Newfoundland and Labrador's resettlement policy, writing that "the agenda for economic development that played out in Newfoundland, linked to perceptions of outport life as primitive or backward, closely resembles the neoliberal development agenda forced on many post-colonies in the Global South after the end of formal British colonialism."[40]

Resettlement schemes have often been geopolitically motivated or conflict-induced. During China's Cultural Revolution (1966–75) and Cambodia's Khmer Rouge regime (1975–78), for example, urban people were sent to be "re-educated" in the countryside in an effort to eradicate their so-called pro-bourgeois or intellectual thinking.[41] In other non-democratic states, including the former Soviet Union, Laos, and Turkey, "undesirables" (e.g., prisoners), "enemies of the state," "troublemakers," and "risky" minorities were moved to improve national stability and cohesion.[42] During more recent conflicts, states and armies have used resettlement schemes to remake territory and exert control over their populations,[43] including the Sudanese government's forcible relocation of millions of ethnically African and non-Muslim groups throughout two civil wars.[44] Resettlement has also been requested by communities that find themselves in areas of territorial dispute, such as the Guatemalan community of Santa Rosa. Located in the disputed "Adjacency Zone" with Belize, the village requested to relocate to Guatemalan territory in 2008.[45]

Many communities worldwide are now weighing resettlement in the face of climate change due to sea-level rise, warming temperatures, and extreme weather.[46] Given their unique geographical features, islands are particularly vulnerable to evolving environmental conditions (Marshall, Chapter 7). As a result, several small island nations have recently devised demographic strategies to address these issues.[47] In Fiji, the village of Vunidogoloa asked to be resettled after a series of catastrophic weather events that made the village uninhabitable.[48] In Kiribati, rising sea levels pose a significant threat to the future existence of the country in its current location. The relocation process has begun — with the government initiating a "migration with dignity" policy for the relocation of its citizens to other countries.[49] In the Arctic, environmental changes are having a significant impact on northern communities due to rising sea levels and melting sea ice and permafrost.[50] But, as Marshall argues in Chapter 7, Indigenous peoples in Canada and the United States will have less control over climate-induced resettlement due to the nature of sovereignty within settler colonialism. Sea-level rise and melting sea ice have already significantly impacted many Alaskan villages built on permafrost and low-lying areas close to the coast or rivers, including Shishmaref and Newtok.[51] These current challenges must also be understood as produced by settler colonialism. As Kyle Powys White notes, the "colonial strategies that sought to missionize, educate, and render sedentary Indigenous peoples in the Arctic, replacing the Indigenous institutions with settler ones," have today limited the ability of communities, including Shishmaref, to adapt to environmental hazards.[52] Further, Strauss et al. predict that relocation induced by climate change will be necessary for 414 communities in the United States alone by 2100.[53] Such relocations are part of a much broader set of environmental or climate-induced migrations spurred by deforestation, natural disasters, or conservation initiatives spanning both inland and coastal contexts around the globe.[54]

While resettlement schemes may be classified as economically, politically, or ecologically induced, they often have overlapping motivations. Warner argues that the ongoing dispersal of Kurdish villages in Anatolia for Turkey's Ilusu Dam project (since 1997) is driven by hydro wars with neighbouring Iraq and Syria and the government's desire to curb Kurdish mobility across these borders, as much as it is about hydropower development.[55] Similarly, in Rwanda, climate change was used as an official justification for resettling people away from the Gishwati mountainous forest after a 2007 flood. Yet, Gebauer and Dovenspeck also emphasize that resettlement furthers the Rwandan government's agenda of modernizing agriculture and protecting the country's natural resources.[56] Along similar lines, writing about small Pacific island states, Connell argues that a history of migration in combination with ongoing hardship has encouraged these states to co-opt a climate change narrative of rising sea levels in order to engender sympathy in an environmentally conscious public.[57]

Despite the considerable attention paid to the political economy of resettlement globally, few scholars acknowledge that resettlement may also stem from governments' desire to minimize the costs associated with providing services to remote communities, as in the case of Newfoundland and Labrador's Community Relocation Policies. Loo labels this approach "neo-resettlement" to emphasize the role of neo-liberalism as a key driver.[58] While other commentators note that rural communities elsewhere may be weighing community closure due to population decline or neoliberal restructuring, we are unaware of any other government (national or subnational) that has adopted this type of policy.[59] This, in itself, is surprising, given the declining economic and political weight of rural areas worldwide.

Second, a complex multi-scalar regulatory landscape governs resettlement projects globally, involving the United Nations (i.e., the UN Guiding Principles on Business and Human Rights), national governments (and subnational ones) and their distinct laws and procedures for eminent domain and due process, international lending institutions and their standards (the World Bank and the International Finance Corporation), non-state actors including academics, religious leaders, and NGOs, as well as the resettlement project teams themselves.[60]

Many institutions, scholars, and practitioners argue that resettlement projects *can* benefit communities when guided by a human rights framework.[61] One key principle of this framework is that impacted communities — including vulnerable groups — must have the ability to participate meaningfully in the process at all stages, from planning to implementation to monitoring. Before resettlement planning begins, alternatives should always be considered, and people should retain access to heritage sites in their community. Overarching policy should acknowledge that resettlement projects may result in economic displacement, where people are displaced because of changes wrought by the project itself (i.e., pollution, loss of livelihood, housing costs). In light of these important repercussions for the host region, it is particularly noteworthy that local host communities rarely have the ability to participate in resettlement planning. The lack of consultations with the host communities is

not only in effect in authoritarian states like China;[62] it is also exhib-
ited in Louisiana, where plans to relocate the remaining 60 households of the Biloxi-Chitimacha-Choctaw band were thwarted by a
community nearby the chosen town site, which blocked the sale of
property to Isle de Jean Charles residents.[63] Finally, another principle is that resettlement projects must improve the livelihoods of the
relocated community. In this light, compensation must be appropriate, and must include both "land-for-land" arrangements and
monetary compensation. In other words, effective resettlement ne-
cessitates comprehensive, strategic, and sustained government
support to aid those affected in the transition.[64]

Despite many calls among experts for a "people centred"[65] approach to resettlement, adherence to these best practices is often
undermined by expediency or budgetary concerns. Around the
world, resettlement projects fail to engage communities properly
or to consider adequately the people who have already been displaced prior to implementation. More often than not, they also
underestimate the true cost of resettlement; as Vanclay notes,
"not everything is fungible."[66] How can one put a value on
non-monetized things like the loss of culture and ties to "place"?
And if such loss is not recognized as legitimate, how can it be deserving of restoration?

Because of this, no matter their scale, no matter how voluntary, and no matter how perfectly resettlement projects ascribe to
human rights norms, they can still cause harm. The stressors induced by resettlement are multi-dimensional and may occur at all
stages of the process.[67] Their impacts and benefits are highly variegated by access to economic, social, or cultural capital, by interests, and by investment and access to land and property and ties
to landscape.[68] Thus:

some people may benefit from being resettled, or at least from the project triggering the resettlement (e.g. through access to employment or business opportunities). Others may lose things they value and/or cherish dearly (e.g. memories, particular landscapes, sacred sites), for which no amount of remuneration can compensate.[69]

By focusing on resettlement in Newfoundland and Labrador in comparative perspective, this volume underscores four overarching common themes: (1) the layered, historical legacies of colonialism, dispossession, and (re)settlement; (2) the agency and legitimacy of the various actors involved in the resettlement process, whether government officials, academics, religious leaders, or non-state actors; (3) the simultaneous dynamics of resistance and resilience; and (4) the role of resource dependency and extractive development in resettlement.

## 1. Legacies of Colonialism, Dispossession, and (Re)Settlement

Resettlement schemes have often been used as a tool of human territoriality, with human populations reorganized to serve expansionist goals, consolidate control, and rationalize territory.[70] Some states, such as China and Indonesia, have relocated populations to claim sovereignty over newly integrated territories like Tibet and Papua, respectively.[71] In South Africa, under apartheid, non-white South Africans were moved to government-prescribed and -administered Bantustans in the late 1970s as part of "an attempt to rationalize the detached pieces of African occupied areas within delineated Bantustan boundaries."[72] An understanding of many contemporary resettlement projects begins with an understanding of colonialism, as such plans have often involved the forcible displacement or centralization of marginalized people — national minorities or Indigenous peoples — for territorial control, legitimized by ideological superiority.

Post-war Canadian resettlement projects have occurred in both urban and rural contexts, along all three coasts. In most cases, these projects involved sovereignty, modernization, or conservation goals, often targeting Indigenous populations who, displaced for centuries through myriad colonial mechanisms, have also more recently been the targets of explicit relocation initiatives.[73] The Canadian government often carried out disruptive post-war resettlement schemes under the pretense of acting in the best interests of Indigenous peoples in Canada.[74] One such case involved the Sayisi Dene First Nation community, whom the state forcibly relocated to Churchill in 1956 from their traditional lands in northern Manitoba and the southern Northwest Territories.[75] The abrupt shift from a semi-nomadic life to a sedentary way of life and the loss of access to traditional means of subsistence introduced layers of social dislocation. As Ila Bussidor and Üstün Bilgen-Reinart write, the resettlement marked "the beginning of two decades of destruction and suffering. During our time at Churchill, nearly a third of the Sayisi Dene perished — many from alcohol abuse and violence. For my people, the impact of the relocation had the same effect as genocide."[76] In the 1970s, 300 remaining members left Churchill to rebuild a new community and commenced a long process of seeking redress in the form of a relocation claim from the provincial and federal governments, finally established in 2010 and 2016.[77]

As the Sayisi Dene story illustrates, any discussion of resettlement in Canada must also be informed by an understanding of settler colonialism and its structures of territorial dispossession, which also produced treaties, the reserve system, and Indian residential schools.[78] The Canadian government designed treaties to take control of large areas of land while the reserve system restricted the mobility of Indigenous peoples and set the terms of their economic and political participation.[79] From 1879 to 1986, the residential school system removed Indigenous children from their families and traditional lands, placing them in church-run, government-funded schools apart from their families, communities, and cultures — a system that constituted "cultural genocide."[80] As a settler colonial country, Indigenous–non-Indigenous relations in Canada continue to be structured by the legal and practical norms established by European colonialism.

The 1996 Report of the Royal Commission on Aboriginal Peoples documents the series of relocations of Indigenous peoples in the twentieth century. Some of these forced movements were development-oriented, involving the relocation of communities to allow for industry or agriculture, such as the 1930s removal of the Métis from Ste. Madeleine, Manitoba, under the Prairie Farm Rehabilitation Act. There is also a substantial history of relocation related to conservation efforts and park creation in Canada involving Indigenous dispossession.[81] Many of these projects had administrative goals and aimed to centralize Indigenous populations across the country and administer government programs and services, and included the relocation of the Mi'kmaq to Isakson or Shubenacadie from 20 locations around Nova Scotia; in British Columbia, the Gwa-Sala and 'Nakwaxda'wx; and in Labrador, the Mushuau Innu of Davis Inlet and the Inuit from Hebron.[82]

Among the best-known of these projects, the Inuit Resettlement Project uprooted Inuit families from Inukjuak, Quebec, and Baffin Island's Pond Inlet to High Arctic settlements in Resolute

Bay (Cornwallis Bay) and on Ellesmere Island (Grise Fiord) in the 1950s to shore up Canada's control over and sovereignty claims to the High Arctic.[83] Such policies have had enduring legacies. As the Royal Commission on Aboriginal Peoples underscores, the High Arctic relocation project should be viewed as "part of a broader process of dispossession and displacement, a process with lingering effects on the cultural, spiritual, social, economic, and political aspects of people's lives."[84] The enduring consequences of settler colonialism have crucial implications for any future resettlement claims that may be made by Indigenous groups in Canada due to environmental change (see Marshall, Chapter 7).

In the United States, contemporary questions of relocation are predominantly affecting Native American and Native Alaskan communities, a pattern that reflects similar legacies of dispossession and forced migration. As Verchick argues, this pattern is "not a coincidence. Native people have rarely been able to choose the location in which they're currently living."[85] Writing about the Isle de Jean Charles resettlement project, Maldonado et al. argue that efforts to help the tribal communities adapt to sea-level rise must acknowledge that they fled to isolated parts of the Louisiana coastline in the nineteenth century to survive the Indian Removal Act and the U.S. government's forcible relocation of Indigenous people.[86] Similarly, in Alaska during World War II the US government forcibly relocated the Aleut in Alaska, and elsewhere aimed to concentrate Indigenous peoples around schools to prevent nomadic migration.[87] Research with the Isle de Jean Charles community, however, illustrates that settler colonialism is an often unacknowledged dimension of the "layering of disasters" that render places uninhabitable.[88] These legacies of forced displacement of Indigenous communities must be considered in light of proposals to "manage" the retreat of entire communities away from the coasts of Alaska and Louisiana.[89]

Globally, the breadth and depth of the social impacts of resettlement on Indigenous peoples have often been ignored while the legacies of previous resettlement projects are often not addressed.[90] Such legacies can profoundly impact the affected communities. Gilbert Islanders within the Republic of Kiribati, for example, are today contending with the realities of climate-change resettlement, alongside relatively recent memories of previous colonial resettlements. In the 1930s, British colonial authorities resettled Gilbert Islanders to the previously unsettled Phoenix Islands, a largely political manoeuvre done under the guise of mitigating overcrowding. However, the move placed the Islanders in far greater danger due to the arid conditions and high risk of drought in the Phoenix Islands. By the 1950s, many residents begged the authorities to be moved.[91] This case, like that of Isle de Jean Charles, illustrates how histories of forced migration cannot be separated from contemporary attitudes towards climate-induced relocation.

The historical legacies of such "layered resettlement" were made obvious in the cases of Indigenous resettlement in Canada (see Loo, Chapter 2, and Marshall, Chapter 7). In Greenland (see Christensen and Arnfjord, Chapter 5), the post-war Danish centralization policy entailed the closure and resettlement of targeted settlements, and under Home Rule (autonomy from Denmark) resettlement continues to be used as both an overt and passive instrument to encourage urbanization. Such histories of colonial uprooting have had profound consequences for Indigenous peoples and also shape contemporary debates about resettlement.[92]

## 2. The Agency and Legitimacy of State and Non-State Actors

A second important theme of this book concerns the role of government officials, academics, experts, and non-state actors in resettlement projects. Who is ultimately at the reins? With what outcomes? When resettlement has been government-led or managed, the question of voluntarism has been a contentious one. What appears to be a purely voluntary decision may contain elements of coercion.[93] In fact, the distinction between voluntary and involuntary resettlement is often a false dichotomy.[94] Authorities may label a resettlement voluntary in order to abrogate their responsibilities to the population and may choose to call another move involuntary in order to justify the use of force. Conversely, the role of authorities in successful resettlement where little choice is presented to those relocating is crucial to the success of the project. From their comparison of "voluntary" poverty alleviation resettlement in China and the "involuntary" resettlement associated with the Three Gorges Dam project, Wilmsen and Wang conclude that the voluntary program was more successful due to its emphasis on people-centred practices, including sustained support in helping those resettling to establish permanent communities. However, the picture was far more nuanced than a simple voluntary/involuntary split, as even within the involuntary scenario, resettlers had some choice as to where to relocate and Chinese authorities have learned to incorporate some of the successful practices from the voluntary program into the Three Gorges framework. How actors behave within these contexts is also profoundly instructive as local decision-making can shape the outcome of resettlement even within politically restrictive climates.

More often than not, resettlement programs are initiated, organized, and funded by state actors — national government officials as in Greenland (see Christensen and Arnfjord, Chapter 5) or subnational government workers as in Newfoundland and Labrador and Quebec (see Loo, Chapter 2), or by both (see Withers, Chapter 3).Yet, what this volume makes clear is that a variety of non-state actors are also instrumental to resettlement projects, some of whom exercise a surprisingly high degree of agency and autonomy. As Loo demonstrates, academics working through Memorial University played an important role in guiding Newfoundland's first resettlement programs, a partnership that was sometimes controversial. While many scholars were sympathetic to outport residents, thus putting them at odds with the government, some were not. Academic expertise was also brought to bear in Quebec, where "an army of 75 researchers from Laval University" came up with a development plan for eastern Quebec that included the consolidation of the rural population (Loo, Chapter 2). This reliance on expert knowledge has in turn pushed out local Indigenous knowledge of the land, and silenced the relationship between people and place that this knowledge was built on (Marshall, Chapter 7). Other non-state actors have also played a role in leading resettlement programs. Looking at early resettlement in Newfoundland and Labrador, Withers, in Chapter 3, underscores how the clergy and religious leaders could determine the fate of a remote outport by closing the school or the church, thereby shaping attitudes towards resettlement. In Ireland, for instance, a small grassroots organization called Rural Resettlement Ireland has relocated hundreds of Dubliners to rural counties (Barry and Côté, Chapter 6), whereas in Greenland the non-profit sector stepped in to provide programs and services for the housing insecure, newly resettled population (Christensen and Arnfjord, Chapter 5). While the small, voluntary, and bottom-up approach of these organizations gave them the flexibility that larger state programs would not have possessed; they also lacked the legitimacy, deep pockets, and institutional infrastructure that would come with being an organ of the state.

## 3. Resistance and Resilience

A large body of literature examines the resistance and contentious politics surrounding resettlement schemes in non-democratic and democratizing states.[95] With limited room for debate, control over the media, and full access to extensive financial and material resources, non-democratic states are particularly well positioned to organize population movements to promote their interests. The quasi-unfettered ability of such states to resettle large segments of their populations in turn constrains the ability of those affected by resettlement to exercise agency and control over whether or where they relocate.[96]

But authoritarian states are not the only regime type that has relied on population resettlement to promote their respective agendas: democratic states have also done so over the years, fostering contention in the process. For instance, in India, the world's largest democracy, mass displacements alienated already vulnerable people from their natural sources of sustenance, resulting in stiff resistance and even violent agitations against the developmentalist policy of the Indian state.[97]

Lestrelin argues that resettlement is fundamentally a "joint process" of de-territorialization and re-territorialization. The former process involves the uprooting of a population and their dislocation from the territory in which they resided, while the latter entails the relocation of the population to a new location with its own norms and socio-economic dynamics. Resistance to resettlement, including "passive non-compliance, footdragging, and deception," should be understood, then, as a form of counter-territorialization. As Lestrelin shows, villagers in Ban Lack Sep and Ban Done Kang in Laos have been able to resist government territorialization schemes.[98] Despite a coercive state with frequently detrimental policies, local actors engage in acts of everyday resistance and form empowering, dynamic social alliances that link various actors, institutions, and practices to present a challenge to state power. Community affiliations may have been much stronger than anticipated and override participation in state goals. Despite being separated by geographical distance, members of the original community may still engage in alliances to circumvent state-sanctioned regulations.

Along similar lines, Li et al.'s study of China's displaced farmers also illustrates bottom-up "creative resistance" to involuntary resettlement schemes. Farmers displaced by the state's reappropriation of collective agricultural land for urban development who move to transitional communities in the buffer zone between urban and rural areas maintain their rural lifestyles within their new communities. As these environments are not often amenable to such practices, the resettlers transform their spatial environments through "dynamic replacement, addition, superposition and permanent replacement." Such practices represent "creative resistance from the bottom up [to] the structure enacted by authority."[99]

The chapters of this volume continue in the same vein and highlight how, even though they may take place in democratic countries and are being touted as "voluntary," resettlement projects may contain elements of coercion (see Côté and Pottie-Sherman, Chapter 4). As we noted above, authorities may label a resettlement project voluntary to renege on their responsibilities to the population and may choose to call another move involuntary to justify the use of force. More important is the degree to which the voluntary resettlement program incorporates people-centred practices into its mandate.[100] Resettlement can never be considered fully voluntary when national or subnational governments invoke eminent domain.[101] Even when resettlement is voluntary, Lyall cautions, observers must not lose sight of the potentially coercive practices by the state, nor should they ignore the legacies of oppression and disenfranchisement that may have led to certain kinds of decision-making.[102]

## 4. Resources, Extractive Development, and Resettlement

The state of the Newfoundland fishery looms large in any discussion of resettlement, and the global literature on resettlement also reflects natural resource development and its boom-and-bust resource geographies (see Withers, Chapter 3; Côté and Pottie-Sherman, Chapter 4).

From the Amazon to the Gulf of Mexico to the Arctic, the opening up of new spaces of oil extraction are also fuelling resettlement projects. Ecuador's Millennium Communities Resettlement scheme (comunidad del Milenio) involves the relocation of Indigenous Kichwa people displaced from the Amazon by oil exploration and development to a series of master-planned communities.[103] The policy emerged in response to sustained Kichwa resistance to oil development efforts by the state-owned oil company, Petroamazonas, in Sucumbios province.[104] After failed attempts to form an Indigenous-run oil company and a month-long period of armed resistance against Petroamazonas in 2008, Kichwa residents ultimately agreed to resettle to so-called Millennium Communities, which would be built and paid for by the oil company. The first of these communities was completed at Playas de Cuyabeno in 2013. Designed by Petroamazonas engineers, its aesthetic mimicked the organization of the oil fields themselves. Andrade argues that the project reflects a broader "colonial matrix" in Ecuador that seeks to rationalize Indigenous communities, first through violence, and then later through social control, including the erasure of traditional architectural styles and spiritual spaces. Three other Millennium Communities have since been built (Pañacocha, Cofán Dureno, and Ciudad Jardín) and the government of Ecuador has vowed to build 200 more as part of its initiative for sustainable development and urbanization in the Amazon, although efforts have been slowed by slumping oil revenues.[105]

Climate change-induced rises in sea level have made retreat the only adaptation available for some coastal communities and small island states (Marshall, Chapter 7). Extractive development in the Gulf of Mexico has also been a double-edged sword for low-lying coastal communities like Isle de Jean Charles. In addition to the burning of fossil fuels impacting sea-level rise through greenhouse gas emissions, which cause rising temperatures that lead to melting ice sheets and ocean thermal expansion,[106] offshore oil development has also involved the dredging of wetlands to create canals for the oil industry. These efforts, for example, have increased the vulnerability of Isle de Jean Charles to storm surges and coastal erosion, making the area more susceptible to catastrophic flooding.[107] Sea-level rise and canal dredging have led to saltwater intrusion and amplified the impact of frequent hurricanes and flooding. Oil and gas exploration in the Gulf beginning in the 1960s disrupted the tribe's subsistence fishing and trapping-centred livelihood on the Louisiana coast via routine and dramatic oil spills in the Gulf of Mexico.[108] The nature of work opportunities in extractive industries undermined social cohesion, as "working 'on the clock' restricts the flexible time available for community residents to be able to participate in time-honored practices of reciprocity and mutual aid."[109] Additionally, regulatory changes in the Louisiana fishery disrupted the communities' access to oyster beds for subsistence, which they now must lease (including from oil companies).[110] In short, global oil development has contributed to combinational vulnerabilities driving the Isle de Jean Charles need for resettlement.[111] These overlapping difficulties resulted in out-migration and a threat to the people's way of life. As Peterson and Maldonado (2016: 348) note, Isle de Jean Charles' vulnerability must therefore be understood as "socially constructed," and considered in the context of a "long-standing foundation of extractive-industry driven economic and political forces that more often place communities in harm's way."[112] Similar socio-economic vulnerabilities are also displayed in Greenland (Christensen and Arnfjord, Chapter 5) and in the Canadian Arctic (Marshall, Chapter 7).

Recent literature on global resettlement processes leaves us with a more nuanced understanding of the phenomenon, illustrating that resettlement projects must be understood as products of the confluence of unique circumstances. Resettlement schemes often involve multi-layered agendas and competing interests, which frequently disadvantage those without a strong enough voice to counter the will of powerful authorities. Where challenges to power have been successful, local actors have frequently developed cohesive networks unified around a common goal. Moreover, challenges to official agendas can come in small, quotidian acts of resistance, which include maintaining practices and relationships from the original communities. Resettlement, then, may be seen to include human and cultural aspects as much as economic and political dimensions. Success can only come through a thorough consideration of all the factors in play and sustained engagement with those affected.

## OVERVIEW

While all resettlement programs are, to a certain degree, ingrained in their historical, social, and economic particularities, in this book we highlight points of connection, arguing that much is gained by placing Newfoundland and Labrador's resettlement projects in conversation with other contemporary resettlement cases. To do so, we adopt a multi-disciplinary approach, with nine contributors drawn from the fields of geography, history, law, and political science. Part I focuses on resettlement in Newfoundland and Labrador. Chapter 2 (Loo) contextualizes Newfoundland's resettlement history within "travelling rationalities" of community development, drawing parallels between Newfoundland and Labrador, the Arctic, and eastern Quebec. Chapter 3 (Withers) explores the agency of coastal communities during the Newfoundland Fisheries Household Resettlement Program (FHRP) from 1965 to 1975. In Chapter 4, Côté and Pottie-Sherman focus on the more recent Community Relocation Policies (CRPs) from 2009 to 2018, approaching the process as a negotiation of the right to "stay" (or relocate).

Part II examines resettlement in Greenland, Ireland, and Canada's Arctic. We highlight these cases because of their geographical proximity to Newfoundland and Labrador, but also because they allow us to explore layered histories of resettlement and vulnerability and the role of different kinds of actors in resettlement projects in Global North democracies. Beginning with

Chapter 5, Christensen and Arnfjord review historical and contemporary processes of state-sanctioned resettlement and urbanization in the Greenlandic context, showing how resettlement projects in Greenland shape the pathways to homelessness experienced in particular by vulnerable young people and women. Then, using the case of Rural Resettlement Ireland, Barry and Côté ask in Chapter 6 how the politics around such a project change when resettlement emerges from the bottom up, suggesting that NGO-led voluntary resettlement might provide a useful way of mitigating both housing crises and rural demographic decline.

Finally, in Chapter 7, Marshall focuses on the ethical challenges surrounding climate change resettlement of Indigenous people in the Canadian Arctic. Marshall argues that sovereignty is a contextually specific concept and must be examined in Canada in connection to settler colonialism (and, hence, resting on the control/subjugation of Indigenous peoples). Contemporary (and future) climate change/environmentally induced resettlement cannot be addressed ethically without acknowledging that Arctic Indigenous communities do not have the same kind of (sovereign) autonomy to seek protection as do small island states. Marshall adopts a "capabilities approach" to show how settler-colonial notions of autonomy undermine the Inuit's ability to be recognized as legitimate climate migrants.

**NOTES**

1   "Little Bay Islands Votes Unanimously to Resettle," *CBC News*, 14 Feb. 2019.
2   "Resettlement and Amalgamation Don't Have to Be Dirty Words, Says Financial Planner," *CBC News*, 28 Nov. 2017; Glen Whiffen, "Newfoundland and Labrador's Forced Resettlement a Historic Injustice, Brothers Say," *The Telegram*, 15 Dec. 2017.

3    Madaline King, "A Tribe Faces Rising Tides: The Resettlement of Isle de Jean Charles," *LSU Journal of Energy Law and Resources* 6, no. 1 (Fall 2017): 300.

4    Adam Crepelle, "The United States First Climate Relocation: Recognition, Relocation, and Indigenous Rights at the Isle de Jean Charles," *Belmont Law Review* 6, no. 1 (2019): 1–39.

5    Ibid.

6    King, "A Tribe Faces Rising Tides," 295.

7    Victoria Herrmann, "America's First Climate Change Refugees: Victimization, Distancing, and Disempowerment in Journalistic Storytelling," *Energy Research & Social Science* 31 (2017): 205–14.

8    Although the term "resettlement" is often applied to the movements of refugee populations (e.g., the UN Refugee Agency), we focus instead on the resettlement of *internal* migrants within their country's borders.

9    Frank Vanclay, "Project-induced Displacement and Resettlement: From Impoverishment Risks to an Opportunity for Development?" *Impact Assessment and Project Appraisal* 35, no. 1 (2017): 6.

10    King, "A Tribe Faces Rising Tides."

11    Maritime History Archive, "'No Great Future': Government Sponsored Resettlement in Newfoundland and Labrador since Confederation" (Memorial University, 2004), https://www.mun.ca/mha/resettlement/.

12    Ralph D. Matthews, "The Smallwood Legacy: The Development of Underdevelopment in Newfoundland 1949–1972," *Journal of Canadian Studies* 13, no. 4 (1978): 98.

13    At mid-century, urban renewal schemes were uprooting urban populations across Canada in the name of modernity. In St. John's, a "slum clearance" agenda mandated the resettlement of poor urban communities from 1950 to 1966. This was not an isolated case, as many other perceived "problem" settlements were destroyed in North American and European cities, including the African-Canadian community of Africville, Nova Scotia, and Hogan's Alley, British Columbia, which have become symbols of the disruption wrought by urban renewal in Canada as well as the

racial ideology underlying the high modernist "planners' gaze."
Likewise, on the Gaspé Peninsula in eastern Quebec, people were
relocated in an effort to eliminate poverty and create a "Just Society"
based on people living a good life, fulfilling their potential as
individuals (Loo, Chapter 2). Raymond B. Blake, *Lions or Jellyfish:
Newfoundland–Ottawa Relations since 1975* (Toronto: University of
Toronto Press, 2015); Tina Loo, *Moved by the State: Forced Relocation
and Making a Good Life in Postwar Canada* (Vancouver: University of
British Columbia Press, 2019); Jennifer J. Nelson, *Razing Africville:
A Geography of Racism* (Toronto: University of Toronto Press, 2009);
John Phyne and Christine Knott, "Outside of the Planners' Gaze:
Community and Space in the Centre of St. John's, Newfoundland,
1945–1966," *Sociology of Home: Belonging, Community, and Place in
the Canadian Context* (2016): 167; George Withers, *Engineering
Demographic Change: State Assisted Resettlement of Newfoundland
Inshore Fishing Communities in the Smallwood Era* (submitted to
Provincial Historic Sites Commemoration, Feb. 2012).

14  Blake, *Lions or Jellyfish*; Miriam Wright, *A Fishery for Modern Times:
The State and the Industrialization of the Newfoundland Fishery,
1934–1968* (Toronto: Oxford University Press, 2001).

15  Blake, *Lions or Jellyfish*.

16  Ibid.

17  Susan M. Manning, "Contrasting Colonisations: (Re)storying
Newfoundland/Ktaqmkuk as Place," *Settler Colonial Studies* 8, no. 3
(2018): 314–31.

18  Chelsea Vowell, *Indigenous Writes: A Guide to First Nations, Métis &
Inuit Issues in Canada* (Winnipeg: Portage & Main Press, 2016), 16.

19  Manning, "Contrasting Colonisations."

20  FemNorthNet, *Displaced from the Land. Resource Development in
Northern Communities: Local Women Matter #5* (Ottawa: Canadian
Research Institute for the Advancement of Women, 2016).

21  Aušra Burns, "Moving and Moving Forward: Mushuau Innu
Relocation from Davis Inlet to Natuashish," *Acadiensis* 35, no. 2
(2006): 64; Indigenous and Northern Affairs Canada, "Relocation
of the Mushuau Innu of Davis Inlet to the New Community of

Natuashish" (2007), https://www.aadnc-aandc.gc.ca/eng/11001000 18932/1100100018933.

22  Peter Evans, "Abandoned and Ousted by the State: The Relocations from Nutak and Hebron, 1956–1959," in *Settlement, Subsistence, and Change among the Labrador Inuit*, eds. David C. Natcher, Lawrence Felt, and Andrea Procter (Winnipeg: University of Manitoba Press, 2012), 86.

23  Ibid.

24  FemNorthNet, *Displaced from the Land.*

25  Government of Newfoundland and Labrador, "Government of Newfoundland and Labrador Apologizes to Relocatees" (2005), https://www.releases.gov.nl.ca/releases/2005/exec/0122n03.htm.

26  Charles Mather, "From Cod to Shellfish and Back Again? The New Resource Geography and Newfoundland's Fish Economy," *Applied Geography* 45 (2013): 402–09.

27  Reade Davis and Kurt Korneski, "In a Pinch: Snow Crab and the Politics of Crisis in Newfoundland," *Labour/Le Travail* (2012): 119–45.

28  Blake, *Lions or Jellyfish*; Maura Hanrahan, *Uncertain Refuge: Lectures on Newfoundland Society and Culture* (St. John's: Breakwater Books, 1993); Noel Iverson and Ralph Matthews, *Communities in Decline: An Examination of Household Resettlement in Newfoundland* (St. John's: ISER Books, 1968/1979); Jeff A. Webb, *Observing the Outports: Describing Newfoundland Culture, 1950–1980* (Toronto: University of Toronto Press, 2016).

29  Mary Ellen Wright, cited in Sarah Smellie, "Digging Through Quidi Vidi History Taught Me a Lot about Hidden Treasures in Our Archives," *CBC News*, 1 Aug. 2018.

30  Vanclay, "Project-induced Displacement and Resettlement."

31  Christopher McDowell, ed., *Understanding Impoverishment: The Consequences of Development-induced Displacement*, vol. 2 (New York: Berghahn Books, 1996); Andreas Neef and Jane Singer, "Development-induced Displacement in Asia: Conflicts, Risks, and Resilience," *Development in Practice* 25, no. 1 (2015): 601–11.

32  Filippo Menga, "Hydropolis: Reinterpreting the Polis in Water Politics," *Political Geography* 60 (2017): 100–09; Pham Huu Ty,

A.C.M. Van Westen, and Annelies Zoomers, "Compensation and Resettlement Policies after Compulsory Land Acquisition for Hydropower Development in Vietnam: Policy and Practice," *Land* 2, no. 4 (2013): 678–704.

33  Gorild Heggelund, "Resettlement Programmes and Environmental Capacity in the Three Gorges Dam Project," *Development and Change* 37, no. 1 (2006): 179–99.

34  Behrooz Morvaridi, "Resettlement, Rights to Development and the Ilisu Dam, Turkey," *Development and Change* 35, 4 (2004): 719–41.

35  The figures for displacement by the Jamuna project are debated. Syed Al Atahar, "Development-driven Forced Displacement and Compensation-based Resettlement: Experiences from the Jamuna Multi-Purpose Bridge Project," *Development in Practice* 24, 2 (2014): 258–71.

36  William Davison, "Ethiopia's 'Villagisation' Scheme Fails to Bear Fruit," *The Guardian*, 22 Apr. 2014, https://www.theguardian.com/global-development/2014/apr/22/ethiopia-villagisation-scheme-fails.

37  Sejal Patel, Richard Sliuzas, and Navdeep Mathur, "The Risk of Impoverishment in Urban Development-induced Displacement and Resettlement in Ahmedabad," *Environment and Urbanization* 27, no. 1 (2015): 231–56.

38  Fernanda Sánchez and Anne-Marie Broudehoux, "Mega-Events and Urban Regeneration in Rio de Janeiro: Planning in a State of Emergency," *International Journal of Urban Sustainable Development* 5, no. 2 (2013): 132–53.

39  Al Atahar, "Development-driven Forced Displacement"; Leopoldo J. Bartolome, "Forced Resettlement and the Survival Systems of the Urban Poor," *Ethnology* 23, 3 (1984): 177–92; Morvaridi, "Resettlement, Rights to Development and the Ilisu Dam, Turkey"; Ty et al., "Compensation and Resettlement Policies."

40  Manning, "Contrasting Colonisations."

41  Kosal Path and Angeliki Kanavou, "Converts, Not Ideologues? The Khmer Rouge Practice of Thought Reform in Cambodia, 1975–1978," *Journal of Political Ideologies* 20, no. 3 (2015): 304–32.

42   Ian G. Baird and Bruce Shoemaker, "Unsettling Experiences:
     Internal Resettlement and International Aid Agencies in Laos,"
     *Development and Change* 38, no. 5 (2007): 865–88; Terry Martin, *The
     Affirmative Action Empire: Nations and Nationalism in the Soviet Union,
     1923–1939* (Ithaca, NY: Cornell University Press, 2001); Morvaridi,
     "Resettlement, Rights to Development and the Ilisu Dam, Turkey."

43   Bart Klem, "The Political Geography of War's End: Territorialisa-
     tion, Circulation, and Moral Anxiety in Trincolmalee, Sri Lanka,"
     *Political Geography* 38 (2014): 33–45; Nigel Parsons and Mark B.
     Salter, "Israeli Biopolitics: Closure, Territorialisation and Govern-
     mentality in the Occupied Palestinian Territories," *Geopolitics* 13, no.
     4 (2008): 701–23.

44   Jok Madut Jok, *War and Slavery in Sudan* (Philadelphia: University
     of Pennsylvania Press, 2010).

45   Janelle Conaway, "A New Home," *Americas* 60, no. 2 (2008): 53.

46   Michael Cernea and Julie Maldonado, eds., *Challenging the Prevail-
     ing Paradigm of Displacement and Resettlement* (New York: Routledge,
     2018); A. de Sherbinen et al., "Preparing for Resettlement Associated
     with Climate Change," *Science* 334, no. 6055 (2011): 456–57; Karen
     E. McNamara and Helene J. Des Combes, "Planning for Community
     Relocations due to Climate Change in Fiji," *International Journal for
     Disaster Risk Science* 6, no. 3 (2015): 315–19.

47   M.M. Naser, *Assessing the Evidence: Migration, Environment, and
     Climate Change in Papua New Guinea* (Grand-Saconnex, Switzer-
     land: International Organization for Migration, 2015), 11.

48   K.E. McNamara and H.J. des Combes, *Planning for Community
     Relocations due to Climate Change in Fiji* (Grand-Saconnex, Switzer-
     land: International Organization for Migration, 2015).

49   K.E. McNamara, "Cross-border Migration with Dignity in Kiribati,"
     *Forced Migration Review* 49 (2015): 62.

50   L.C. Hamilton, K. Saito, P.A. Loring, R.B. Lammers, and H.P.
     Huntington, "Climigration? Population and Climate Change in
     Arctic Alaska," *Population and Environment* 38, no. 2 (2016): 115–33.

51   Ibid.

52   Kyle Powys Whyte, "Is It Colonial Déjà Vu? Indigenous Peoples

and Climate Injustice," in *Humanities for the Environment: Integrating Knowledges, Forging New Constellations of Practice*, eds. J. Adamson and M. Davis (New York: Routledge, 2016), 88–104; Elizabeth Marine, "The Long History of Environmental Migration: Assessing Vulnerability Construction and Obstacles to Successful Relocation in Shishmaref, Alaska," *Global Environmental Change* 22, no. 2 (2012): 374–81.

53   Benjamin H. Strauss, Scott Kulp, and Anders Levermann, "Carbon Choices Determine US Cities Committed to Futures Below Sea Level," *Proceedings of the National Academy of Sciences* 112, no. 44 (2015): 13508–13.

54   C. Gebauer and M. Doevenspeck, "Adaptation to Climate Change and Resettlement in Rwanda," *Area* 47, no. 1 (2015): 97–104.

55   J. Warner, "The Struggle over Turkey's Ilısu Dam: Domestic and International Security Linkages," *International Environmental Agreements: Politics, Law and Economics* 12, no. 3 (2012): 231–50.

56   Gebauer and Doevenspeck, "Adaptation to Climate Change."

57   John Connell, "Losing Ground? Tuvalu, the Greenhouse Effect and the Garbage Can," *Asia Pacific Viewpoint* 44, no. 2 (2003): 89–107; John Connell, "Last Days in the Carteret Islands? Climate Change, Livelihoods and Migration on Coral Atolls," *Asia Pacific Viewpoint* 57, no. 1 (2016): 3–15.

58   Tina Loo, "'The Government Game:' Resettlement Then and Now," *Canadian History and Policy, Active History*, 16 June 2013, http://activehistory.ca/2013/06/the-government-game-resettlement-then-and-now/; see also John C. Kennedy, *Encounters: An Anthropological History of Southeastern Labrador* (Montreal and Kingston: McGill-Queen's University Press, 2015).

59   Michael Isaac Stein, "Moving a Louisiana Town Out of the Path of Climate Change," *CityLab*, 24 Jan. 2018; Vanclay, "Project-induced Displacement and Resettlement."

60   Vanclay, "Project-induced Displacement and Resettlement."

61   King, "A Tribe Faces Rising Tides"; Gerry Reddy, Eddie Smyth, and Michael Steyn, *Land Access and Resettlement: A Guide to Best Practice* (Sheffield, UK: Greenleaf, 2015); Lidewij van der Ploeg and Frank

Vanclay, "Challenges in Implementing the Corporate Responsibility to Respect Human Rights in the Context of Project-induced Displacement and Resettlement," *Resources Policy* 55 (2018): 210–22.

62  Isabelle Côté, "Horizontal Inequalities and Sons of the Soil Conflict in China", *Civil Wars* 17, no. 3 (2015): 357–78.

63  King, "A Tribe Faces Rising Tides."

64  Kevin Lo, Longyi Xue, and Mark Wang, "Spatial Restructuring through Poverty Alleviation Resettlement in Rural China," *Journal of Rural Studies* 47 (2016): 496–505; Brooke Wilmsen and Mark Wang, "Voluntary and Involuntary Resettlement in China: A False Dichotomy?" *Development in Practice* 25, no. 5 (2015): 612–27.

65  Gezahegn Zewdie, Abebe, and Jan Hesselberg, "Community Participation and Inner-city Slum Renewal: Relocated People's Perspectives on Slum Clearance and Resettlement in Addis Ababa," *Development in Practice* 25, no. 4 (2015): 560; Wilmsen and Wang, "Voluntary and Involuntary Resettlement in China."

66  Vanclay, "Project-induced Displacement and Resettlement."

67  Reddy, Smyth, and Steyn, *Land Access and Resettlement*; Thayer Scudder, *The Future of Large Dams: Dealing with Social, Environmental and Political Costs* (London: Earthscan, 2005).

68  King, "A Tribe Faces Rising Tides."

69  Vanclay, "Project-induced Displacement and Resettlement," 3.

70  Klem, "The Political Geography of War's End"; Peter Vandergeest and Nancy Lee Peluso, "Territorialization and State Power in Thailand," *Theory and Society* 24, no. 3 (1995): 385–426.

71  Greg Rohlf, "Dreams of Oil and Fertile Fields: The Rush to Qinghai in the 1950s," *Modern China* 29, no. 4 (2003): 455–89.

72  Luvuyo Wotshela, "Territorial Manipulation in Apartheid South Africa: Resettlement, Tribal Politics and the Making of the Northern Ciskei, 1975–1990," *Journal of Southern African Studies* 30, no. 2 (2004): 318.

73  Julia Christensen, "Our Home, Our Way of Life: Spiritual Homelessness and the Sociocultural Dimensions of Indigenous Homelessness in the Northwest Territories (NWT), Canada," *Social & Cultural Geography* 14, no. 7 (2013): 804–28; Pamela D. Palmater, "Genocide,

Indian Policy, and Legislated Elimination of Indians in Canada,"
*Aboriginal Policy Studies* 3, no. 3 (2014): 27–54.

74  Paulette Regan, *Unsettling the Settler Within: Indian Residential
Schools, Truth Telling, and Reconciliation in Canada* (Vancouver:
University of British Columbia Press, 2010), 79.

75  Ila Bussidor and Üstün Bilgen-Reinart, *Night Spirits: The Story of
the Relocation of the Sayisi Dene* (Winnipeg: University of Manitoba
Press, 1997).

76  Ibid., 4.

77  Sayisi Dene First Nation, Relocation Settlement Trust, http://
sdfntrust.ca/history/.

78  Glen Sean Coulthard, *Red Skin, White Masks: Rejecting the Colonial
Politics of Recognition* (Minneapolis: University of Minnesota Press,
2014); Patrick Wolfe, "Settler Colonialism and the Elimination of
the Native," *Journal of Genocide Research* 8, no. 4 (2006): 388.

79  Caroline Desbiens and Carole Lévesque, "From Forced Relocation
to Secure Belonging: Women Making Native Space in Quebec's
Urban Areas," *Historical Geography* 44 (2016): 91; James S. Frideres,
Madeline A. Kalbach, and Warren E. Kalbach, "Government Policy
and the Spatial Redistribution of Canada's Aboriginal Peoples," in
*Population Mobility and Indigenous Peoples in Australasia and North
America*, eds. John Taylor and Martin Bell (New York: Routledge,
2004), 96.

80  The Truth and Reconciliation Commission (TRC) found that the
residential schools and their practices of uprooting children and
forcibly separating them from Indigenous language, customs, and
traditional lands, along with systematic abuse, constituted "cultural
genocide." TRC, *Honouring the Truth, Reconciling for the Future:
Summary of the Final Report of the Truth and Reconciliation Commission of Canada* (Winnipeg: Truth and Reconciliation Commission of
Canada, 2015), 1.

81  Desirée Valadares, "Dispossessing the Wilderness: Contesting
Canada's National Park Narrative," in *Cultural Contestation:
Heritage, Identity and the Role of Government*, eds. Jeroen Rodenberg
and Pieter Wagenaar (London: Palgrave Macmillan, 2018), 139–53;

Theodore (Ted) Binnema and Melanie Niemi, "'Let the Line Be Drawn Now': Wilderness, Conservation, and the Exclusion of Aboriginal People from Banff National Park in Canada," *Environmental History* 11, no. 4 (2006): 724–50; Mark David Spence, *Dispossessing the Wilderness: Indian Removal and the Making of the National Parks* (New York: Oxford University Press, 1999).

82  Royal Commission on Aboriginal Peoples (RCAP), *Final Report*, vol. I, *Looking Forward, Looking Back*, Chapter 11, "Relocation of Aboriginal Communities" (Ottawa: RCAP, 1996), http://caid.ca/RRCAP1.11.pdf.

83  Shelagh D. Grant, "Errors Exposed: Inuit Relocations to the High Arctic, 1953–1960," *Documents on Canadian Arctic Sovereignty and Security*, no. 8 (2016); RCAP, *Final Report*, vol. 1, "The High Arctic Relocation. Summary of Supporting Information," http://publications.gc.ca/collections/collection_2018/aanc-inac/Z1-1991-1-41-3-1-eng.pdf.

84  RCAP, *Final Report*, vol. 1, Chapter 11.

85  Robert Verchick, cited in Michael Isaac Stein, "How to Save a Town from Rising Waters," *CityLab*, 24 Jan. 2018, https://www.citylab.com/environment/2018/01/how-to-save-a-town-from-rising-waters/547646/.

86  Julie K. Maldonado et al., "The Impact of Climate Change on Tribal Communities in the U.S.: Displacement, Relocation, and Human Rights," *Climatic Change* 120, no. 3 (2013): 601–14.

87  Karen Hesse, *Aleutian Sparrow* (New York: Margaret K. McElderry Books, 2005).

88  Lowlander Center, Isle de Jean Charles Resettlement (2018); Kristina J. Peterson and Julie K. Maldonado, "When Adaptation Is Not Enough: Between the 'Now and Then' of Community-led Resettlement," in *Anthropology and Climate Change: From Actions to Transformations*, eds. S.A. Crate and M. Nuttal (New York: Routledge, 2016), 336–72.

89  Nicole Marshall, "Forced Environmental Migration: Ethical Considerations for Emerging Migration Policy," *Ethics, Policy, & Environment* 19, no. 1 (2016): 1–18; Liz Koslov, "The Case for

Retreat," *Public Culture* 28, no. 2 (2016): 359–87.

90 Vanclay, "Project-induced Displacement and Resettlement."

91 Eberhard Weber, "Only a Pawn in Their Games? Environmental (?) Migration in Kiribati — Past, Present and Future," *DIE ERDE — Journal of the Geographical Society of Berlin* 147, no. 2 (2016): 153–64.

92 Ibid.

93 Isabelle Côté and Yolande Pottie-Sherman, "The Contentious Politics of Resettlement Programs: Evidence from Newfoundland and Labrador, Canada," *Canadian Journal of Political Science* 53, no. 1 (2020): 19–37.

94 Wilmsen and Wang, "Voluntary and Involuntary Resettlement in China."

95 T. Martin, *The Affirmative Action Empire: Nations and Nationalism in the Soviet Union, 1923–1939* (Ithaca, N.Y.: Cornell University Press, 2001); Brooke Wilmsen and M. Webber, "Mega Dams and Resistance: The Case of the Three Gorges Dam, China," in *Demanding Justice in the Global South*, eds. J. Grugel, J. Singh, L. Fontana, and A. Uhlin (London: Palgrave Macmillan, 2017), 69–98.

96 Côté, "Horizontal Inequalities and Sons of the Soil Conflict in China."

97 Mahendra P. Lama, "Internal Displacement in India: Causes, Protection and Dilemmas," *Forced Migration Review* 8 (2000), https://www.fmreview.org/accountability-and-displacement/lama; R.N. Sharma, "Changing Facets of Involuntary Displacement and Resettlement in India," *Social Change* 40, no. 4 (2010): 503–24.

98 Guillaume Lestrelin, "Rethinking State–Ethnic Minority Relations in Laos: Internal Resettlement, Land Reform, and Counter-territorialization," *Political Geography* 30, no. 6 (2011): 311–19.

99 Yuhang Li, Hans Westlund, Xiaoyu Zheng, and Yansui Liu, "Bottom-up Initiatives and Revival in the Face of Rural Decline: Case Studies from China and Sweden," *Journal of Rural Studies* 47 (2016): 506–13.

100 Wilmsen and Wang, "Voluntary and Involuntary Resettlement in China."

101 King, "A Tribe Faces Rising Tides."

102 Angus Lyall, "Voluntary Resettlement in Land Grab Contexts:

Examining Consent on the Ecuadorian Oil Frontier," *Urban Geography* 38, no. 7 (2017): 958–73.

103 Matthew Bozigar, Clark L. Gray, and Richard E. Bilsborrow, "Oil Extraction and Indigenous Livelihoods in the Northern Ecuadorian Amazon," *World Development* 88 (2016): 125–35; Michael A. Uzendoski, "Amazonia and the Cultural Politics of Extractivism: Sumak Kawsay and Block 20 of Ecuador," *Cultural Studies* 32, no. 3 (2018): 364–88.

104 Alejandra Espinosa Andrade, "Space and Architecture of Extractivism in the Ecuadorian Amazon Region," *Cultural Studies* 31, 2 (2017): 307–30.

105 Lyall, "Voluntary Resettlement in Land Grab Contexts"; Japhy Wilson and Manuel Bayón, "Millennium Cities: Staging the Origins of Twenty-first Century Socialism," Working Paper #7, CENEDET, Feb. 2016, https://cenedet.files.wordpress.com/2015/11/cenedet-wp7.pdf.

106 Aimee B.A. Slangen, John A. Church, Cecile Agosta, Xavier Fettweis, Ben Marzeion, and Kristin Richter, "Anthropogenic Forcing Dominates Global Mean Sea-Level Rise Since 1970," *Nature Climate Change* 6 (2016): 701–05.

107 Julie K. Maldonado, "A Multiple Knowledge Approach for Adaptation to Environmental Change: Lessons Learned from Coastal Louisiana's Tribal Communities," *Journal of Political Ecology* 21, no. 1 (2014): 61–82.

108 Peterson and Maldonado, "When Adaptation Is Not Enough."

109 Ibid., 342.

110 Julie K. Maldonado, "Everyday Practices and Symbolic Forms of Resistance," in *Hazards, Risks, and Disasters in Society*, eds. Andrew E. Collins, Samantha Jones, Bernard Manyena, and Janaka Jayawickrama (Waltham, MA: Elsevier, 2015), 203.

111 Maldonado, "A Multiple Knowledge Approach."

112 Peterson and Maldonado, "When Adaptation Is Not Enough," 348.

# PART I:

RESETTLEMENT IN NEWFOUNDLAND
AND LABRADOR

# CHAPTER 2

## *Development's Travelling Rationalities: Contextualizing Newfoundland Resettlement*

TINA LOO

*'Twas in the year of 'sixty-six, the date I won't forget.*
*The Government plan was sent around, I can see the paper yet.*
*"Sign it if you want to or reject it if you like.*
*The rules and regulations, they're there in black and white." . . .*

*Smallwood he got on the air, each word he spoke seemed great:*
*"Haul up your punts and dories! Destroy your stage and flake!*
*I'm moving you away from here, employment sure you'll find,*
*And you won't regret the day you left those outports far behind."*

*When fifty percent of the people the Government plan did sign*
*The other fifty had no choice, 'twas go or be left behind;*
*We moved in all directions, all around our native coast,*
*And bid good-bye to our home-sweet-homes, the places we*
*cherished most.*

*After we resettled, everything seemed pretty odd*
*Us independent fishermen, we could not find a job. . . .*
*I'm an employee at the Waterford, I'm lucky, sure, myself,*
*That I didn't end up a patient from the blow below the belt.*

— Anthony Ward, "The Blow Below the Belt"[1]

## INTRODUCTION

Anthony Ward's song is just one of many pieces of popular culture generated by Newfoundland's resettlement program. Over a decade, more than 20,000 people were moved from the province's small coastal outports under its auspices, often against their wills, in an effort to improve their lives (see Figure 2.1). The academic writing on resettlement explores the workings of the program itself or examines it in the context of federal–provincial relations and the modernization of the fishery.[2] In contrast, novelists, songwriters, and visual artists focus on the trauma of displacement, communities torn apart by the decision to stay or go, and the lingering sense of loss. For them, resettlement was fundamentally unfair, a "blow below the belt."[3]

But "the Government plan" involved much more than uprooting people: resettlement was both a welfare measure and a technique of economic, social, and political development aimed at modernizing Newfoundlanders as well as Newfoundland. As Yolande Pottie-Sherman, Isabelle Côté, and Rebecca LeDrew note in their introduction to this volume, resettlement is a process that begins before and continues long after people actually move. The state did not just displace people and destroy their "home-sweet-homes" to centralize the population; its agents also rebuilt community. Doing so was crucial to achieving the goal of development;

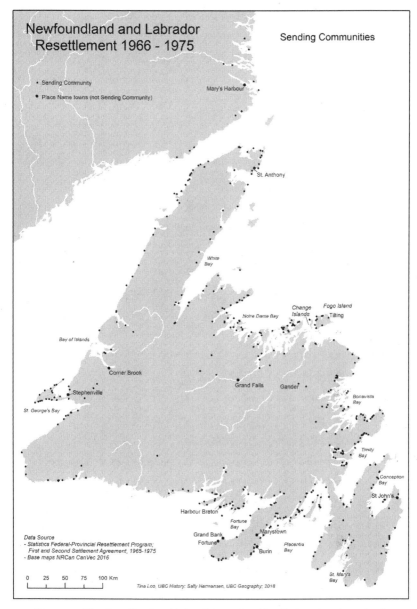

**Figure 2.1.** Newfoundland and Labrador communities that sent and received resettled people, 1965–1975. Map by Sally Hermansen.

namely, to "help people help themselves" by inculcating "the capacity to aspire."[4] Whether it was through local improvement committees or co-operatives, Newfoundlanders would learn to imagine a collective future and work together to realize it.

What happened in Newfoundland was not unique. The same development ideas and tools used there were deployed in other parts of Canada — both earlier and contemporaneously — to alleviate poverty. Informed and implemented by experts, centralization through forced relocation and citizen participation were the "travelling rationalities" of development, both international and domestic. They were techniques applied irrespective of the particularities of place and people to achieve similar ends. In Canada, that meant "a good life" for all, as Pierre Trudeau put it in 1968.

The future prime minister believed in equality of opportunity premised on equal access to social services across the country. Significantly, however, he framed it in more expansive terms, arguing "every Canadian has the right to a good life whatever the province or community he lives in."[5] A good life was a secure and prosperous one. More fundamentally, however, it was one in which people could realize their potential as individuals. A good life was thus framed in terms of a liberal order.

As we will see, in Newfoundland and elsewhere in Canada, forced relocation and the larger plan of development extended the reach of the state and intensified its power, helping to create particular political subjectivities that were crucial to the liberal project of rule. The connections between forced relocation, development, and the production of citizens by the state are what distinguish Newfoundland resettlement in the 1960s and 1970s from its twenty-first century iteration.

In what follows, I discuss Newfoundland resettlement, linking the movement of people to efforts to develop the province. In doing so, I examine the ideas and techniques that characterized modernization, showing how they were informed by social scientific knowledge and aimed at problematizing and transforming local cultures and, specifically, people's relationships to place and each other. Both the ideas and the techniques used to develop Newfoundland were common to initiatives undertaken by the state to address poverty and underdevelopment in Canada's North and in eastern Quebec. Regardless of where it pursued its project of improvement, the state did not act alone. It relied and drew upon outside expertise, enrolling universities and their personnel to the cause of making a good life. In Newfoundland, the Canadian North, and eastern Quebec these non-state actors played a crucial role in planning, implementing, and assessing resettlement.

## CENTRALIZATION THROUGH FORCED RELOCATION: ONE SOLUTION TO MANY PROBLEMS

According to political scientist Timothy Mitchell, "fields of analysis often develop a convention for introducing their subject."[6] The convention politicians, policy-makers, and social scientists adopted to explain Newfoundland's poverty and the challenges of addressing it was its history and settlement pattern. As Provincial Economist Robert Wells observed in 1960, "[i]t has long been realized that social and economic development in Newfoundland has been retarded because our population is scattered around 6,000 miles of coastline in some 1,144 settlements."[7] Centuries of participating in the cod fishery meant that the majority of Newfoundlanders lived in thousands of small coastal villages — outports — many of which were accessible only by sea. With the inshore fishery in decline by the mid-twentieth century, commentators like Minister of Community and Social Development William Rowe considered such a settlement pattern "obsolete" and increasingly detrimental to Newfoundlanders' standard of living and social security.[8] Many outports lacked electricity, running water, and reliable access to medical services and education. Providing such basic services to communities that for the most part had fewer than 500 people was an expensive proposition for a poor province.

Consolidating the population seemed to be the answer: before it embarked on the Fisheries Household Resettlement Program in 1965, the province implemented a more modest relocation initiative to accomplish just that. Intended largely as a welfare measure and aimed at shutting down entire communities with "no great future," Premier Joey Smallwood's Centralization Program offered households in communities where everyone agreed to leave a maximum of $600 to move to places of their own choosing. From 1954 to 1965, approximately 8,000 people from 115 communities availed themselves of the funds.[9]

Saving money wasn't the only benefit of bringing people to services rather than services to people. Centralizing the population was also meant to generate revenue. By consolidating people in "growth centres" the state would create labour forces of sufficient size to attract the kind of capital investment that could spur employment, prosperity, and modernization. The joint federal–provincial resettlement program offered Newfoundlanders greater financial incentives to move and lowered the bar to qualify for it. Instead of all households in a given community having to agree, the program set the requirement at 90 per cent, then 80 per cent, and eventually funded the moves of individual households. In return for these increased funds, the Fisheries Household Resettlement Program (1965–70) and Community Consolidation Program (1970–75) attempted to direct those who moved under its auspices to particular kinds of places deemed by the government to have better economic and social prospects.

The key idea underpinning Newfoundland's resettlement program — that centralizing populations would spur investment and economic growth — was based on the work of French economist François Perroux (1903–87). Challenging classical economic theory, Perroux argued growth was irregular and concentrated around "growth poles" rather than spread evenly through space. While they occurred naturally, growth poles could also be created by concentrating investment at particular locations — or at least that was the thought. Investment was usually in the form of fiscal support to "propulsive" industries that would drive regional development, but in practice it could also take other forms. As John B. Parr points out, government could bring people to work as well as work to people.[10]

Perroux's theory became a mainstay of regional development around the world in the 1960s and 1970s, and was particularly popular in Newfoundland. As geographer Michael Staveley observed, "[r]arely in North America was there such an overt confluence of academic analysis and applied public policy as in the Canadian province of Newfoundland," where its resettlement program was premised on growth pole theory.[11]

In translating Perroux's theory — or their reading of it — into policy, federal and provincial government bureaucrats had to identify places where the prospects for growth were great. This was no easy task, particularly when there was very little in the way of granular economic or social statistics for Newfoundland. The shifting number of communities the government designated as eligible to receive resettlers and the varying terminology used to describe these communities speak to its struggle to succeed in its resettlement project. There were "designated major fishery growth centres," "other portions of major fishery growth centres," "suitable communities within community distance of a major fishery growth centre," and "other fishery growth centres." As the resettlement program evolved, it funded moves to "other growth points," "other advantageous locations involving additional land costs," and "any area with improved circumstances for widows, retired and incapacitated persons."[12]

The "Isolation Criteria Program" undertaken by the federal Department of Regional Economic Expansion in the late 1960s is also evidence of Newfoundland's illegibility. It was an attempt to categorize the province's communities according to their educational, medical, and communications facilities. When weighted and taken together, these factors measured a given community's isolation and hence its residents' eligibility to move under the resettlement program. While information on seven census districts was compiled, the project does not appear to have ever been completed.[13]

Based on a theory whose originator never intended it to be applied, and in the absence of comprehensive economic and social data and a set of explicit criteria to judge the suitability of receiving and sending communities, Newfoundland's resettlement program nevertheless went ahead. Thousands tried to take advantage of the "shifting money," so many, in fact, that in the first years of its operation the number of requests sometimes outstripped the capacity of the program's yearly budget to accommodate all of them. Of the more than 20,000 people who moved, 85 per cent did so between 1966 and 1971.[14]

The process of resettlement was meant to ensure that New-foundlanders themselves decided whether to stay or go. It seemed straightforward enough: to start, at least half of the residents in a community had to attend a public meeting called to discuss resettlement (see Figure 2.2). If those in attendance passed a resolution indicating they were in favour of moving — the 50 per cent Anthony Ward refers to in his song — they then chose three community members to serve on a committee whose task was to

**Figure 2.2.** Robert Wells, Department of the Attorney General, discussing resettlement with Diver [Dover] residents, August 1961. Credit: Bob Brooks, Library and Archives Canada, National Film Board fonds, e011177532.

circulate a petition in support of resettlement. If it garnered signatures from 90 per cent of households, or later, 80 per cent, and
those signatures were verified, the committee was then empowered to begin negotiations with the province.[15]

The dynamics of such a process left many residents feeling
resettlement was anything but voluntary or democratic despite
the government's insistence that it was. In part, its coerciveness
lay in the fact that public meetings, voting, and petitions were not
part of outport political culture. As the anthropologists and sociologists working at Memorial University's Institute of Social and
Economic Research (ISER) were learning, in these small face-to-
face communities people avoided direct confrontation, including
the kind that was invited by a public meeting and a vote. In addition,
Newfoundlanders' recent experience with the formal democratic
process was not very deep or wide. There were few incorporated
communities, which meant few people had experience with municipal elections. As well, between 1934 and 1949, an appointed
Commission of Government administered the British colony's
affairs. Moreover, the Commission itself came to an end as a result of two divisive referendums on Newfoundland's constitutional
future in 1948 that likely did little to convince outporters of the
productive qualities of open debate.[16]

Whatever its role in maintaining social peace, it was precisely
this reluctance to engage in public discussion about their collective futures that, in the view of many outsiders, made outports
immune to change and kept them impoverished. If the province
were to prosper, its people had to be made modern, not just its
economy. In fact, the latter depended to a great extent on the former. While the process Newfoundlanders undertook in deciding
to resettle — the public meetings, voting, and petitions — may

have had some pedagogical effect in that regard, simply moving people did little to change their attitudes and behaviour, much less guarantee their prospects would improve.

Expert intervention was required to better their chances of achieving a good life. Through its Institute of Social and Economic Research (ISER) and its Extension Department, Memorial University of Newfoundland was a key player in the state's efforts to continue the process of development that had started with forced relocation. Funded partly by the federal government, ISER generated social scientific knowledge about Newfoundland and Newfoundlanders and assessed the operation of the resettlement program, while Extension engaged directly in the work of modernizing outport residents.[17]

The anthropologists associated with ISER were at the forefront of problematizing rural culture for policy-makers, something Joey Smallwood considered an obstacle to the province's progress. "Is it not true that we have been intensely, bitterly individualistic?", he asked. "Have we not failed almost completely in the one virtue that the modern world has made absolutely essential: the ability and desire to co-operate to achieve a commonly desired end?"[18]

His shiny new university, itself a symbol of progress and modernity, would help guide the province's development. ISER had been created in 1961 out of a more general concern on the part of the Atlantic Provinces Economic Council about underdevelopment in the region and the lack of basic research to inform policy. Could it be, one Council member wondered, that "the devotion to traditional ways of life and the shunning of innovation" lay at the root of the region's poverty?[19] Only expert analysis would tell.

To that end, as historian Jeff A. Webb discusses, one of ISER's first initiatives was to fund seven ethnographies of "typical" outport

communities. Because Memorial had no doctoral program, between 1965 and 1968 ISER recruited graduate students in anthropology from prestigious universities in the United States and
United Kingdom who were looking for a fully-funded research
trip and a ready-made dissertation project. Why should they consider coming? Because, as the Institute's first director, anthropologist Ian Whitaker, told prospective applicants, "Newfoundland is
the Canadian province which is undergoing the greatest sociological transition and therefore offers wonderful material to the social scientist."[20] Specifically, what was on offer to these students
was a chance to examine first-hand a society undergoing the transition from primitive to modern.

For Whitaker, who embraced an evolutionary model of social
change, the Newfoundland outport was a peasant society, one that
was largely unchanged until the mid-twentieth century. This was
an assumption, not a hypothesis to be tested by the graduate students who took up his offer. Louis Chiaramonte, who worked with
Margaret Mead at Columbia University, wrote his supervisor when
he arrived at the southwest coast outport Whitaker sent him to.
Francois was "self-contained" and "relatively isolated," he reported,
a place "as close as you can come to fulfilling the social scientist's
dream of an ideal society." Looking back, James Faris, one of Jack
Goody's students at Cambridge, admitted that his assumption
about the primitive character of Lumsden North, the community
he had been sent to on the northeast coast, had led him to over-
emphasize the "exotic" and folkloric aspects of rural society.[21]

The St. John's *Evening Telegram* reported on Faris's work, taking
exception to what it considered its more fanciful claims. "A settlement in Newfoundland where men are afraid to go into the woods
because of fairies? Where midwives are regarded as witches?

Where malformed children are 'done away with'?"[22] Outport people may have had their outport ways, but, the newspaper implied, Faris's characterization of them bordered on the Brothers Grimm.

Despite this criticism, the portrait of rural Newfoundland provided by ISER's scholars remained largely intact and unchallenged at the time. Their reports revealed outports to be egalitarian, intensely individualistic places made livable by a set of social rules that minimized open disagreement and confrontation. On Fogo Island, for instance, Cato Wadel reported that "one does not talk publicly about controversial topics; every man has a right to an opinion, and one man's opinion is as good as another; one does not give advice to one's neighbour; to do so can be regarded as questioning a man's ability to think for himself."[23] James Faris and Melvin Firestone — another of Whitaker's recruits — made similar observations of other places, noting that people preferred to withdraw in the face of potential conflict and adopt a relatively permissive attitude about how people conducted themselves.[24]

In addition to these outport ethnographies, ISER also produced two contemporary assessments of the resettlement program by sociologists Noel Iverson and Ralph Matthews and economists A. Leslie Robb and Roberta Edgecombe Robb. While the Robbs's report was favourable, revealing that nearly two-thirds of the people who moved between 1965 and 1967 were "generally satisfied" with the outcome, Iverson and Matthews were more critical.[25] They decried "the almost total lack of preparation, on the part of government, industry, and reception communities to receive the migrants and to assist them in adjusting to their new surroundings and help them find work."[26] Sympathetic to the difficulties encountered by the people they interviewed, Iverson and Matthews suggested ways to make the resettlement program run more efficiently.[27]

Newfoundland was not unique in putting the social sciences, and particularly anthropology, at the service of the state, or in problematizing culture and identifying cultural transformation as the key to modernization. In Canada, social scientific knowledge was also implicated in forced relocation and development schemes in the central Arctic and eastern Quebec.

As in Newfoundland, an economic and environmental crisis in the central Arctic led the state to intercede more directly in the region's development. The collapse of the fur trade in Arctic fox, combined with a decline in the population of barren ground caribou on which many Inuit depended, led to widespread misery, starvation, and, ultimately, to intervention by the federal government. Having relocated the Ahiarmiut, a group of inland Inuit, back on to the land and away from white settlement twice in the early 1950s to prevent what it feared was a growing dependency on "handouts," the Department of Northern Affairs and National Development was forced to move them again when starvation struck at the end of the decade. This time, however, instead of relocating them to places where wildlife was thought to be more plentiful, it sent them to settlements on the west coast of Hudson Bay; specifically, Eskimo Point (Arviat) and Rankin Inlet (Kangiqtiniq). The Ahiarmiut were joined there by other inland Inuit from Garry Lake, people who had also been relocated by Northern Affairs because of starvation. In addition to these inland peoples, Rankin Inlet also housed Inuit from other Arctic coastal communities who were sent or drawn there to work at the North Rankin Nickel Mine. Underground operations started at what was then the most northerly hard rock mining operation in the world in 1953, one that relied on local labour to keep costs down.[28]

These relocations signalled the end of what Frances Abele

called Ottawa's "state of nature" policy, that is, a policy premised on leaving Inuit to provide for their own welfare as bureaucrats argued they always had — ignoring the fact that the context in which they did so had changed profoundly as a result of capitalism and colonialism.[29] In its place, Northern Affairs began a process of turning "Arctic migrants" into "Arctic villagers," as David Damas puts it.[30] The starvation experienced by the Inuit in the central Arctic merely reinforced the efforts he discusses to sedentarize and urbanize Inuit, a project that came along with the extension of the Canadian welfare state north.

Centralizing the Inuit population was an important foundation for northern development. As in Newfoundland, the government lacked the necessary knowledge on which to base policy. To address the deficit, Ottawa created the Northern Coordination and Research Centre (NCRC) in 1954, an organization that managed studies on the region and funded scholarly research, including that by anthropologists.[31] In the central Arctic, the NCRC supported work examining the inland Inuit generally and the impact of industrial wage labour on them at the North Rankin Nickel Mine. When it closed in 1962, leaving Inuit without a significant source of paid work, anthropologists and anthropological knowledge were again brought to bear in sending these men and their families to other mining communities in the Canadian North and tracking how they fared.[32]

In discussing the Inuit of the central Arctic, anthropologists identified the challenges confronting their participation and integration in a modern, industrial North. Inuit had never lived in permanent settlements, much less in groups that extended beyond the family and were multicultural. While they had participated in the commercial fur trade, they were not accustomed to being governed by the clock or the rigid hierarchies of an industrial workplace. Like outport Newfoundlanders, Inuit were reluctant to assert themselves, particularly to their Euro-Canadian bosses. For Walter Rudnicki, head of Northern Affairs' Welfare Division, overcoming Inuit diffidence, something that had been reinforced by colonialism, was crucial to developing the North. His focus and that of his colleagues was on building Inuit capacity — not in addressing other obstacles to development like the racism they encountered.[33]

Like Newfoundlanders and Inuit, the people of rural eastern Quebec also suffered under the heavy burden of tradition, or so the province's planners believed. Although they also lived in small, face-to-face communities, these were not egalitarian. Social and political power resided with the clergy, lawyers, and members of the merchant class. Rather than actively participate in civic matters, ordinary people tended to defer to their judgment: their primary affiliations were to family and parish.[34]

Many believed such attitudes contributed to the region's underdevelopment. The Lower St. Lawrence, Gaspé, and Îles-de-la-Madeleine region was Quebec's poorest, but its poverty was hidden from view by its distance from urban centres and its geography. In the post-war period, its residents made their living as they had for generations, through a mixture of small-scale farming, logging, and fishing. Few had specialized or modernized their agricultural and forestry practices or chose to participate in the offshore fishery. The population of 325,000 was dispersed, with nearly half living in settlements of less than 1,000 people, most of which were projected to shrink.

When Jean Lesage's Liberals were elected in 1960 on a platform of change and then re-elected in 1962, promising to make people *maîtres chez nous* — masters of their own house — eastern Quebec became visible in a way it had not been since the 1930s, when there were efforts to colonize the area. Unlike previous governments, this one was committed to using the power of the state to make Quebec modern. *Rattrapage*, or catching up, was the order of the day: not only would the provincial government institute policies meant to help Quebec achieve the level of social security and prosperity enjoyed by the rest of Canada, but it would also address disparities within the province. Through a federal–provincial agreement struck in 1963, it channelled funds acquired under the Agricultural Rehabilitation and Development Act (ARDA) to the Bureau d'aménagement de l'Est du Québec (BAEQ). Independent of the state, BAEQ's mandate was to come up with a development plan for the region.

As was the case in Newfoundland and the North, academic expertise was brought to bear on the task of *rattrapage*. Over the next three years an army of 75 researchers, drawn largely from Laval University and representing the physical, biological, and social sciences, turned their attention to understanding the region's natural and human resources. The result was a 10-volume, 2,000+ page report containing 231 recommendations. Most called for the modernization of agriculture, forestry, fishing, and mining, as well as measures that would improve transportation and communication in the region and establish opportunities for adult education.[35]

Perhaps the best-known and certainly most controversial recommendations drew on François Perroux's growth pole theory and called for the consolidation of the rural population. BAEQ's consultants estimated that 85 "marginal localities" would be closed and a total of some 60,000 people forced to move (see Figure 2.3).[36] It seemed that Quebecers would become masters of their own house by forcing some people out of theirs — and changing their attitudes and behaviours.

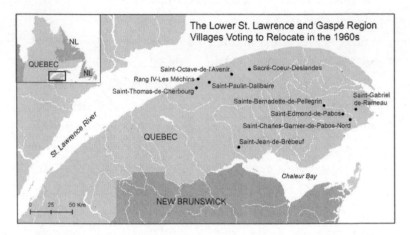

**Figure 2.3.** Communities affected by resettlement in eastern Quebec. Although BAEQ estimated that 85 communities would be closed in eastern Quebec, only these 10, comprising about 2,000 people, were relocated.[37] Map by Sally Hermansen.

## COMMUNITY DEVELOPMENT: INSTILLING A CAPACITY TO ASPIRE

While anthropologists and sociologists had identified the cultural barriers to modernization, the actual work of making the people of Newfoundland, the central Arctic, and eastern Quebec modern fell to a different group of experts, those trained in community development. Despite working in these divergent contexts, all believed that the key to "helping people help themselves" was to encourage and structure their involvement in discussions and decision-making about matters of collective interest to the communities they lived in. Along with centralization through forced relocation, citizen participation was the key to development, a tool so powerful it could transform cultures and re-create community. In Newfoundland, the Extension Department at Memorial University was central to community development.[38] Established in 1959, its mandate was to deliver adult education, particularly to rural Newfoundland, using locally based fieldworkers whose knowledge of people and place enhanced their effectiveness. While economic development had been a key part of Extension's mandate, with the appointment of its second director in 1964 the department's commitment to instigating social change became much more explicit.[39]

Donald Snowden brought his experience working on northern development with the federal government to Newfoundland. Influenced by his involvement with the Inuit, as well as the growing critiques of top-down modernization that were then emerging internationally, Snowden came to believe that Extension had to pursue a different kind of development, one that cultivated political expression and not just economic growth. Looking back on Extension's work in the 1960s and 1970s, Snowden's colleague and successor as director, Tony Williamson, considered development was about facilitating citizen participation. "Just as men have a right to food, they also have a right to speak, to know, to understand the meaning of their work, to take part in public affairs and to defend their beliefs," Williamson argued, quoting a 1975 Dag Hammarskjöld Foundation report to describe Extension's rationale.[40]

At Northern Affairs, Snowden had been instrumental in establishing co-operatives in the Arctic as a way to teach Inuit who were new to community living to govern themselves. By running a business that was accountable to local shareholders, Inuit learned about loans, amortization on capital, and dividends.

Equally importantly, they learned how to participate using the particular practices of democratic governance like open discussion and debate, voting, and secret ballots. They were able students: the first Inuit-run co-operative was established in Arctic Quebec in 1959. Five years later, there were 19, and by 1970 northern co-ops handled over $2.5 million in sales of goods and services yearly, returning close to $1.25 million to members in the form of salaries, purchases from members, and patronage dividends.[41]

While it is easy to see co-operatives as instruments of assimilation, disciplining Inuit to capitalist and Western democratic norms and forms, they were more than that. They were competition for the Hudson's Bay Company, which had enjoyed a virtual monopoly in many settlements, and they kept money in the community. Snowden and Northern Affairs also saw them as tools of self-government and decolonization. As he told Edith Iglauer of the *New Yorker*, "I don't believe that the government is infallible, and the co-ops make it possible for the Eskimos to give us hell."[42] Asked later about what he thought he had accomplished at Northern Affairs, Snowden singled out co-operatives, institutions that allowed people to live in the region and govern their own lives in a changing world. "[They] now know they can continue to live where home is for them and that they can do this through their own efforts. They know THEY can make decisions . . . ."[43] The Inuit interviewed about their participation agreed, arguing co-ops gave them "a way to regain some of the control [over our lives] we previously had." Others went further, pointing out their long-term political consequences; according to former Inuit politician Thomas Suluk, co-ops were "underground governments" that provided the foundation for a "pan Inuit solidarity that had no historic precedent."[44]

The successful introduction of co-operatives in the North was what brought Snowden to Newfoundland and, eventually, to Extension. The only way rural Newfoundland would have a future was if rural Newfoundlanders were also empowered to take charge of their own affairs. Extension used a variety of different tools to do so, many of which aimed to provide people with the information on which they could make decisions. Because Snowden and his colleagues believed the poor were poor in part because they lacked the knowledge necessary to improve their own situations, Extension's resident fieldworkers acted as resource people, informing rural Newfoundlanders of government programs and educational opportunities they could take advantage of; they organized workshops and conferences on subjects of local interest; and they provided advice on establishing co-operatives.

Neither those working for Extension nor those in government considered community development contrary to resettlement. Donald Snowden attended the quarterly meetings of the federal–provincial Resettlement Committee and his Extension Department offered training for resettlement fieldworkers. The provincial department charged with administering resettlement was the Department of Community and Social Development. Its section heads, including the Director of Resettlement, met regularly. On those occasions, the director, Kenneth Harnum presented his report in concert with those of his colleagues, men charged with implementing leadership training and local initiatives programs, with no sense of inconsistency.[45]

An official from the federal Department of Fisheries — which represented Ottawa in the first resettlement agreement — offered the clearest statement about the relationship between relocation and community development: in his view, encouraging people to participate in governing their affairs would allow them to make better decisions about their future, whether that was to stay or go. "Nobody on the [Resettlement] Committee seems to be aware of such a thing as community development work to convince people to move out," wrote Guy Lemieux in 1966. "And they require an 80% approval by people to close down a community. With proper community action and adequate financial incentives, there should be no trouble."[46]

As Snowden and his fieldworkers discovered, simply arming people with information was not enough to instigate the kind of community action necessary to bring about the social change they felt was needed. There were cultural barriers that prevented rural Newfoundlanders from participating in their own governance. Before they could run a co-op or a school board or a local development committee, they would have to overcome their reluctance to air issues that had the potential to be controversial. This fear of open disagreement was borne partly of sectarian differences and a lack of experience with formal democratic processes. More fundamentally, however, it was due to concerns about the social consequences of open disagreement.

Through a partnership with the National Film Board of Canada (NFB), which had a mandate to do films on poverty, Extension embarked on an experiment aimed at overcoming these silences and ultimately transforming Newfoundlanders' relationships with each other. Both organizations believed that film could assist in "communication for social change" by helping people see themselves and their neighbours in a different way. By revealing their frustrations and fears as well as their challenges and triumphs to each other, films could expose common ground for collective action.[47]

In consultation with Extension, filmmaker Colin Low chose Fogo Island as his subject. At the time, about 60 per cent of its population of nearly 5,000 was on welfare, the island's merchants had shut down operations, and some people were considering taking advantage of the government's resettlement program or leaving Newfoundland entirely. Despite repeated attempts, earlier efforts to establish a co-operative on the island had failed.[48] Fogo Island was at a crossroads and islanders had three choices: according to Premier Joey Smallwood, they could drift, resettle, or develop the island so they could stay. The filming would help residents decide which path they would take.[49]

Shot over a five-week period in the summer of 1967, using a local crew and featuring local people speaking for themselves, the 27 films were meant to forge community and spur collective action in a troubled place. Islanders were involved in making the films, they saw them with their neighbours, and they listened to and participated in discussions about them afterwards, facilitated by Low and Fred Earle, the Extension fieldworker. The conventional wisdom about the Newfoundland Film Project, as it was dubbed, is that it was a success: the "cool" medium of film allowed people from the island's 10 communities to speak their minds and be heard publicly by their neighbours for perhaps the first time. Through watching the films and talking about them, they discovered that, whatever their differences, they faced common problems and may even have had common views on how to solve them. They may have been Catholic, Anglican, or Salvationist; residents of Joe Batt's Arm, Seldom, or Tilting — to name a few of the island's outport communities — but they could also come together as Fogoites to form a shipbuilding co-operative and a non-sectarian school board that could serve the educational needs of the entire population more effectively.[50]

Not only did the films forge horizontal ties among islanders, but they also created vertical ones between provincial politicians and their constituents. After seeing a film featuring islanders discussing their views on the fishery, Minister Aidan Maloney and his colleagues agreed to respond on film.[51] Similarly, when the federal government announced it would shut down radiophone service on the Labrador coast, Extension fieldworker Tony Williamson, Snowden's colleague and his successor as director, filmed Labradorians voicing their concerns and screened it for an audience that included Eric Kierans, the federal minister in charge, as well as a vice-president of Bell Canada and other bureaucrats. Kierans, too, agreed to respond on video and later reflected on how seeing and hearing Labradorians had changed his perspective; it had peopled and humanized a coastline that he had previously thought of only in terms of distances and population.[52]

While the "Fogo Process" came to be used in development work around the world, its power lay less in the capacity of film to act as a "mirror," as Colin Low argued, and more in the ability of the filmmakers to shape what the audience saw. The community "consensus" revealed in the films was something that the NFB's Colin Low and Extension made, rather than found. As I have discussed elsewhere, the films celebrated a particular set of values central to community development — risk-taking, independence, co-operation, forthrightness, and non-sectarianism — and amplified the voices of a particular group of islanders, namely, members of its Improvement Committee and, more generally, those we might call respectable.[53]

In terms of spurring collective action, the selective focus of the films didn't matter. Assessing their impact in 1969, Cato Wadel concluded that "[t]he major change that has occurred on Fogo Island would seem to be that some people from all the settlements are committed to an island-wide community. Together, these individuals form a sizable group although they are a minority."[54]

As Wadel's observation suggests, successful community development was about more than imparting values. It also involved cultivating connections, that is, multiple scales of affiliation among local people. In this case, it meant getting enough of them — "some people from all the settlements" — to commit to "an island-wide community." Successful community development did not so much depend on individuals abandoning their allegiances to family, faith, and place, as it did on placing them in the context of new ones — to region, province, and nation. In short, community development work was about remaking community, reconfiguring it for modern times. According to Tony Williamson, outport Newfoundlanders "have a very great difficulty in seeing beyond their own community, their own harbour, their own bay." Extension's task was "to help people assess their situation, not only in terms of their community, but in terms of the region, of the province and the country as a whole" and to act.[55]

But action was a matter of organization as well as affect. It was one thing for rural Newfoundlanders to feel they were members of a more encompassing body politic, and quite another to translate that sense of connection into concrete action. We can get some idea of how the state did so in the development efforts it undertook in eastern Quebec, where it used a number of techniques to inculcate different scales of political affect and give them institutional form. Indeed, before Low and Snowden set to work on Fogo, BAEQ produced films in partnership with the NFB, as well as shows for radio and television, and a newspaper, all to convince people of the necessity of modernization and their direct participation in it.[56]

But perhaps the most powerful way BAEQ instilled eastern Quebecers with the capacity to aspire and translated those aspirations into institutional form was how it structured the planning process. From the start, BAEQ insisted its regional development plan would be people-centred, the outcome of citizen participation. Indeed, it considered the participation of residents of the Lower St. Lawrence, Gaspé, and Îles-de-la-Madeleine in creating a plan for their region crucial, as important as the plan itself.[57]

To that end, BAEQ encouraged people to form local development committees to discuss challenges, set goals, and undertake specific tasks like creating inventories of resources. As in Newfoundland, its fieldworkers were crucial to eliciting and facilitating such participation. They were trained in *animation sociale*, a pedagogy aimed at encouraging people to see themselves as experts about their own situation and how to change it. The *animateur* or facilitator was meant to be *homme sans projet*, someone with no particular agenda except to help the group articulate its own needs and how to meet them.

*Animation sociale* had its origins in the work Dominican priest Louis-Joseph Lebret (1897–1966) did in helping to organize the fishermen of St-Malo in the 1930s, work that would be the foundation for his belief in the need for a "human-centred economy," that is, one that served people's needs. With François Perroux of growth pole fame, he went on to found the Économie et Humanisme (Economy and Humanism) movement in 1941, suggesting that both men believed high modernism and planning on a human scale were not enterprises at odds with each other. After the war Lebret became involved in international development, work that led to an invitation to join the Vatican Council and ultimately to play a key role in drafting *Populorum Progressio, On the Development of Peoples*, an encyclical issued by Pope Paul VI in 1967 that expressed his concern over growing inequality. Borrowing directly from Lebret's writings, Paul VI argued "the development we speak of here cannot be restricted to economic growth alone. To be authentic, it must be well rounded; it must foster the development of each man and of the whole man" (s. 14).

BAEQ's "animateurs" aimed to foster the political development of eastern Quebecers, instilling in them a capacity to aspire beyond the locales in which they lived. When the work of its local committees reached a certain stage, BAEQ arranged for representatives from each of them within particular geographic zones to meet with their counterparts to discuss their interests and to come up with a plan of action. It then formed zonal committees that would do the same thing, with the goal of coming up with recommendations for the region as a whole.

The way BAEQ facilitated and structured participation was meant to have a disciplinary effect. *Animation sociale* and the committee and consultation structure it put in place were aimed at giving people — some people at least — a way of seeing their economic interests in relation to those of their neighbours and the region as a whole, and to expose them to the process of negotiating among those different scales to come up with a plan that would serve the needs and aspirations of everyone. Indeed, BAEQ's planners also intended this structure of participation to have a life beyond the planning process: it was meant to serve as the structure for a new regional government.

In helping people to help themselves it was all too easy for community development workers to slip into telling them what to do. In his work with Northern Affairs, Donald Snowden worried Inuit were establishing co-operatives just because they had been told to do so. Some of BAEQ's *animateurs* were equally conscious of imposing their wishes on eastern Quebecers. Roger Guy found it impossible to find a balance between facilitating open discussion and shaping the conversation to certain ends. He quit when it became evident that his job was to get people to buy into a program of development designed by BAEQ's experts, not one that reflected local needs and desires. To him, the revolutionary potential of *animation sociale* had been stifled. Under BAEQ, development had become a technocratic exercise, not a democratic one.[58]

Guy might have been surprised to learn that some of the experts enrolled in the state's project of development felt similarly disillusioned. Ralph Matthews's experience assessing resettlement in Newfoundland made him conscious of the dangers of putting academic expertise at the service of the state. The problem was not that governments ignored experts like him; it was that they took them surprisingly seriously. "Contrary to the popular belief that government sponsored research reports remain unread on bureaucrats' shelves, we found an amazing willingness among federal and provincial officials to both read our reports and implement our suggestions," he noted. "Thus, our conclusion that the 'means' of the resettlement program were inadequate was taken as an impetus to change these 'means.' As a result of these changes, the resettlement process was actually speeded up, and more people than ever before were encouraged (and likely felt coerced) to resettle."[59] Researchers needed to remember that the "employers of sociologists are most often the policymakers rather than the people directly affected by their policies." Above all, they needed to "take a more activist role," interrogating the values embedded in public policy and their own.[60]

## CONCLUSION

In the post-war period, the Canadian state moved people to consolidate geographically scattered populations and in so doing deliver social services and the opportunities they provided more effectively. Centralization via forced relocation went hand in hand with a larger project of development aimed at alleviating poverty and modernizing rural peoples. University-based experts were central to this project. Anthropologists and sociologists deployed their expertise to understand and transform rural cultures. By facilitating participation, community development workers sought to do nothing less than to reconfigure rural peoples' relationships and expand their political and cultural horizons, creating new solidarities and subjectivities. Such an expansive view was the key to achieving a good life; individuals could only realize their potentials if they had an awareness of the possibilities, ones, as Extension's Tony Williamson observed, that lay beyond their own communities, harbours, and bays.

Seeing development's travelling rationalities at work in Newfoundland in the 1960s and 1970s, as well as their disciplinary effect, provides a perspective from which to consider the province's efforts to again encourage communities to close. The 2009 Community Relocation Policy (CRP) has been characterized as resettlement redux, and in many ways it is, particularly in the emphasis given to the voluntary nature of moving and the coercive effects of such voluntarism: now, as in the 1960s and 1970s, resettlement is meant to be "community-initiated and community driven."[61] And now, as then, the voluntarism has created tensions among neighbours as people discuss what to do.[62]

But whereas resettlement and development previously served a liberal order, the CRP seems to be serving a neo-liberal one. Kevin O'Reilly of St. Brendan's captured some of the distance New-foundlanders and Canadians have travelled in the 60 years since the first federal–provincial resettlement agreement. Reflecting on the current push for relocation being brought to bear on the island community, he observed "[t]here's no way to defend your home, you know, if they look at you as an expense."[63]

In the 1960s and 1970s resettlement and development in Newfoundland, the central Arctic, and eastern Quebec were about more than a budgetary bottom line. They were forms of disciplinary power exercised in the name of a particular vision of social justice, namely, eliminating poverty and creating a Just Society based on people living a good life, fulfilling their potential as individuals. As problematic as that vision may have been, it was based on an expansive understanding of the state's responsibilities to its citizens. It is that understanding that seems lacking in the CRP now.

## NOTES

1   In Genevieve Lehr, ed., *Come and I Will Sing You: A Newfoundland Songbook* (Toronto: University of Toronto Press, 1983), 15–16. Lehr notes that "Waterford" was Waterford Hospital, a mental health institution in St. John's, Newfoundland.

2   The key academic works on resettlement in Newfoundland and Labrador are Raymond Blake, *Lions or Jellyfish: Newfoundland–Ottawa Relations since 1957* (Toronto: University of Toronto Press, 2015), Chapters 3 and 4; Noel Iverson and D. Ralph Matthews, *Communities in Decline: A Study of Household Resettlement in Newfoundland* (St. John's: Memorial University of ISER Books, 1968); George Withers, "Reconstituting Rural Communities and Economies: The Newfoundland Fisheries Household Resettlement Program, 1965–1970" (PhD dissertation, Memorial University of Newfoundland, 2016); Miriam Wright, *A Fishery for Modern Times: The State and the*

*Industrialization of the Newfoundland Fishery, 1934–1968* (Toronto: Oxford University Press, 2000), Chapter 7. The Newfoundland and Labrador Heritage website also features a number of useful articles on resettlement. These include ones on "Centralization," "Outports," "The Resettlement Program," "Resettlement," "The Second Resettlement Program," "Was Resettlement Justified?" and "Rural Depopulation." See https://www.heritage.nf.ca.

3    For instance, see Michael Crummey, *Sweetland* (Toronto: Doubleday, 2014); Katherine Lochnan, ed., *Black Ice: David Blackwood Prints of Newfoundland* (Vancouver: Douglas & McIntyre, 2011); and Scott Walden, *Places Lost: In Search of Newfoundland's Resettled Communities* (Toronto: Lynx Images, 2003).

4    Arjun Appadurai, "The Capacity to Aspire: Culture and the Terms of Recognition," in *Culture and Public Action*, eds. Vijayendra Rao and Michael Walton (Stanford, CA: Stanford University Press, 2004), 59–84.

5    Pierre Elliott Trudeau, *Federalism and the French Canadians* (New York: St. Martin's Press, 1968), 147.

6    Timothy Mitchell, *Rule of Experts: Egypt, Techno-Politics, Modernity* (Berkeley: University of California Press, 2002), 210.

7    Robert Wells, *Report on Resettlement in Newfoundland* (St. John's, 1960), 5. Provincial Archives of Newfoundland and Labrador (PANL), GN 34/2, box 29, file 12/62/1E.

8    William N. Rowe, "The Newfoundland Resettlement Program: A Case Study of Regional Development and Social Adjustment" (Harrison Liberal Conference, Harrison Hot Springs, BC, 21–23 Nov. 1969), 6.

9    "Centralization," Newfoundland and Labrador Heritage website, https://www.heritage.nf.ca/articles/politics/centralization.php.

10   John B. Parr, "Growth-pole Strategies in Regional Economic Planning: A Retrospective View — Part 1, Origins and Advocacy," *Urban Studies* 36, no. 7 (1999): 1200.

11   "Travelling rationality" is from David Craig and Doug Porter, *Development Beyond Neoliberalism: Governance, Poverty Reduction, and Political Economy* (London: Routledge, 2006). Michael Staveley,

"Resettlement and Centralisation in Newfoundland," in *Policies of Population Distribution*, eds. John W. Webb, Arvo Naukkarinen, and Leszek A. Kosinski (Oulu, Finland: Geographical Society of Northern Finland for the International Geographical Union on Population Geography, 1981), 160.

12    Maloney to Robichaud, 22 Jan. 1968, 2, Library and Archives Canada (LAC), RG 124, vol. 133, file 168-N5, part 6; Minutes of Meeting of the Fisheries Household Resettlement Subcommittee, 17 July 1967, 2-4, PANL, GN 34/2, file 12/62/1A, vol. 1.

13    Department of Regional Economic Expansion (DREE), *Summary Description: Isolation Criteria Program, Newfoundland and Labrador Unincorporated Communities* (Ottawa: DREE, Nov. 1970).

14    The numbers are calculated from DREE, *Statistics: Federal–Provincial Resettlement Program, Community Consolidation Program — First Resettlement Agreement (1965–1970) and Second Resettlement Agreement (1970–1975), Completed to April 30, 1975* (Ottawa: DREE, 1975).

15    The legislative framework (though not the details) were provided in An Act to Provide for the Resettlement of the People in Certain Parts of the Province, Statutes of Newfoundland, 1965, c. 48.

16    J.C. Crosby, "Local Government in Newfoundland," *Canadian Journal of Economics and Political Science* 22, no. 3 (1956): 332–46; Peter Neary, "Democracy in Newfoundland: A Comment," *Journal of Canadian Studies* 4, no. 1 (1969): 37–45; James K. Hiller, *Confederation: Deciding Newfoundland's Future, 1934–1949* (St. John's: Newfoundland Historical Society, 1998); Ralph Matthews, "The Sociological Implications of Resettlement: Some Thoughts on the Power and Responsibility of Planners," paper presented to the annual meeting of the Canadian Institute of Planners, Halifax, NS, 6 Aug. 1979, 8–11; Sean T. Cadigan, *Newfoundland and Labrador: A History* (Toronto: University of Toronto Press, 2009), Chapters 9 and 10.

17    Tina Loo, *Moved by the State: Forced Relocation and Making a Good Life in Postwar Canada* (Vancouver: University of British Columbia Press, 2019), Chapter 2; Jeff A. Webb, *Observing the Outports: Describing Newfoundland Culture, 1950–1980* (Toronto: University of

Toronto Press, 2015), Chapter 4; Jeff A. Webb, "The Rise and Fall of Memorial University's Extension Service, 1959–91," *Newfoundland and Labrador Studies* 29, no. 1 (2014): 84–116.

18  J.R. Smallwood, "Newfoundland To-Day," in *The Book of Newfoundland*, vol. 1, ed. J.R. Smallwood (St. John's: Newfoundland Book Publishers, 1937), 2.

19  Cited in Webb, *Observing the Outports*, 288.

20  Cited ibid., 278.

21  Cited ibid., 209, 225.

22  "Life in a Rural Fishing Community: 'You Can Never Tell about Strangers'," *Evening Telegram* (St. John's,), 24 Feb. 1967.

23  Cato Wadel, *Communities and Committees: Community Development and the Enlargement of the Sense of Community on Fogo Island, Newfoundland* (St. John's: Extension Service, Memorial University of Newfoundland, 1969), 56.

24  James C. Faris, *Cat Harbour: A Newfoundland Fishing Settlement* (St. John's: ISER Books, 1966), Part 3 and especially Chapter 11; Melvin M. Firestone, *Brothers and Rivals: Patrilocality in Savage Cove* (St. John's: ISER Books, 1967), Chapter 5.

25  A. Leslie Robb and Roberta Edgecombe Robb, *A Cost-Benefit Analysis of the Newfoundland Resettlement Program* (St. John's: Memorial University of Newfoundland Institute of Social and Economic Studies, 1969), 24.

26  Noel Iverson and D. Ralph Matthews, *Communities in Decline: An Examination of Household Resettlement in Newfoundland* (St. John's: ISER Books, 1968), 138.

27  Ralph Matthews, "Ethical Issues in Policy Research: The Investigation of Community Resettlement in Newfoundland," *Canadian Public Policy* 1, no. 2 (1975): 207.

28  Loo, *Moved by the State*, Chapter 2.

29  Frances Abele, "Canadian Contradictions: Forty Years of Northern Political Development," *Arctic* 40, no. 4 (1987): 312.

30  David Damas, *Arctic Migrants, Arctic Villagers: The Transformation of Inuit Settlement in the Central Arctic* (Montreal and Kingston: McGill-Queen's University Press, 2004).

31 V.F. Valentine and J.R. Lotz, "Northern Co-ordination and Research Centre of the Canadian Department of Northern Affairs and National Resources," *Polar Record* 11 (1963): 419–22.

32 Loo, *Moved by the State*, 40–41.

33 Ibid., 41–55.

34 Unless otherwise indicated, the information on relocation and development in eastern Quebec is drawn from Loo, *Moved by the State*, Chapter 3.

35 Bureau d'aménagement de l'est du Québec, *Plan de développement, région-pilote Bas-St-Laurent, Gaspésie et Îles-de-la-Madeleine, un projet ARDA*, cahiers 1–10 (Mont-Joli, QC: Bureau d'aménagement de l'est du Québec, 1966).

36 Métra Consultants Ltée, *Relocalisation de population dans l'Est du Québec* (Québec: Office de planification et de développement du Québec, 1970), 47, 18.

37 For more information on what happened in eastern Quebec and the local reaction to BAEQ's development plan, see Loo, *Moved by the State*, Chapter 3.

38 Webb, "The Rise and Fall of Memorial University's Extension Service."

39 Loo, *Moved by the State*, 79–80.

40 Tony Williamson, "Don Snowden, Participatory Communications and People-Centred Development," 26 Oct. 1998, H.A. Williamson Collection, Memorial University of Newfoundland Archives and Special Collections (MUNASC), Coll-347, file 3.07.054; *What Now — The 1975 Dag Hammarskjöld Report on Development and International Cooperation* (Uppsala: Dag Hammarskjöld Foundation), 27.

41 R.J. Wickware, "Northern Co-operative Development," paper presented to the NAACL annual meeting, St. John's, 5–8 July 1971, 1–2; Alexander Stevenson fonds, Price of Wales Northern Heritage Centre (PWNHC), N-1992-023, box 30, file 10.

42 Edith Iglauer, "Conclave at Frobisher — A Reporter at Large," *New Yorker*, 23 Nov. 1963, 192.

43 Snowden to Edith Hamburger, n.d. [appears to be in response to a letter from her dated 1 Nov. 1963], Donald Snowden fonds,

1961–64, LAC, MG 31 D 163, vol. 14, file 34: Northern Affairs, Miscellaneous. Emphasis in original.

44   Marianne P. Stopp, "The Inuit Co-operative Movement in Northern Canada, 1959–1968," in *The Amazing Power of Cooperatives: Texts Selected from the International Call for Paper Proposals*, eds. Marie-Joëlle Brassard and Ernesto Molina (Quebec: Sommet International des Coopératives, 2012), 625.

45   Directors Meeting No. 130, Department of Community and Social Development, 14 Sept. 1970, 4, PANL, GN 59/7/A, box 4, file 1.

46   Lemieux to Davidson, 28 July 1966, 1, LAC, RG 124, vol. 27, file 168-N5, part 1. Also see Memorandum from the Rural Development Branch (ARDA), Department of Forestry and Rural Development, to Interdepartmental Committee on Centralization of Newfoundland Communities, n.d., Appendix F, 4–5, Minutes of the Meeting of the Interdepartmental Committee on Centralization of Newfoundland Communities, 16 Nov. 1966, LAC, RG 124, vol. 27, file 168-N5, part 1.

47   Loo, *Moved by the State*, 81–82; Susan Newhook, "The Godfathers of Fogo: Donald Snowden, Fred Earle, and the Roots of the Fogo Island Films, 1964–1967," *Newfoundland and Labrador Studies* 24, no. 2 (2009): 171–97. The Fogo films were the first project in what would become the National Film Board of Canada's "Challenge for Change" program. On that, see Thomas Waugh, Michael Brendan Baker, and Ezra Winton, eds., *Challenge for Change: Activist Documentary at the National Film Board of Canada* (Montreal and Kingston: McGill-Queen's University Press, 2010).

48   Donald Snowden, "The Co-operative Movement in Newfoundland: An ARDA Study of Co-operative Organization from the Viewpoint of Industrial and Social Development" (prepared for the Government of Newfoundland by the Co-operative Union of Canada under the direction of Donald Snowden, 1965), 37.

49   Robert L. DeWitt, *Public Policy and Community Protest: The Fogo Case* (St. John's: ISER Books, 1969), 13.

50   Loo, *Moved by the State*, 82.

51   Newhook, "The Godfathers of Fogo," 188.

52  "An Interview with the Honorable Eric Kierans, Minister of Communications, and Memorial University of Newfoundland Extension Service on Communications on the Coast of Labrador," Ottawa, 4 Dec. 1970, 1, Fred Earle Collection, MUNASC, Coll-399, file 2.01.159.

53  Loo, *Moved by the State*, 83–85.

54  Wadel, *Communities and Committees*, 49. Emphasis in original.

55  [H.A. Williamson,] "Presentation to Fieldworkers by Anthony H. Williamson," n.d., 8. Fred Earle Collection, MUNASC, Coll-399, file 2.01.159.

56  Loo, *Moved by the State*, 106–08.

57  Unless otherwise noted the description of BAEQ's method of development is from ibid, 98-104.

58  Roger Guy, "Mon expérience d'animateur au BAEQ," in *Animation sociale, entreprises communautaires et coopératives*, ed. Benoit Lévesque (Laval: Éditions coopératives Albert Saint-Martin, 1979), 59–60.

59  Matthews, "Ethical Issues in Policy Research," 209–10.

60  Ralph Matthews, "Studying Social Planning: The Investigation of Community Resettlement in Newfoundland," presented to a conference on "The Researcher, the Community, and Social Policy," York University, 1 Mar. 1973, 15–16.

61  Newfoundland, Department of Municipal Affairs and Environment, "Community Relocation Policy, 2016," https://www.mae.gov.nl.ca/publications/relocation/Community_Relocation_Policy2016.pdf.

62  Isabelle Côté and Yolande Pottie-Sherman, "The Contentious Politics of Resettlement Programs: Evidence from Newfoundland and Labrador, Canada," *Canadian Journal of Political Science* 53, no. 1 (2020): 19–37.

63  Anna Maria Tremonti, "The Current," *CBC Radio*, 9 Nov. 2017.

# CHAPTER 3

*Not Just Pawns in a Board Game:*
*Local Actors in the Newfoundland Fisheries*
*Household Resettlement Program, 1965–1970*

GEORGE WITHERS

## INTRODUCTION

In this chapter, I explore the state-assisted evacuation of coastal communities in Newfoundland and Labrador (NL) under the Fisheries Household Resettlement Plan (FHRP) of 1965–70. In contrast to the focus on the "heavy-handedness" of external actors that has dominated so far the resettlement literature in the province,[1] I contend that coastal people were not pawns in a board game. They contested resettlement and negotiated moves: they wrote letters; circulated petitions; enlisted the aid of politicians, church leaders, Memorial University Extension Service, and the National Film Board; and called on the premier to provide the necessary infrastructure to develop local resources. The NL archival record is replete with evidence that coastal people pressured government to amend the resettlement agreement and approve moves that frustrated and contradicted the aims of the FHRP — so much so that by 1970, the resettlement tsunami that had swept people from the islands of Placentia Bay lost strength and governments in Ottawa and St. John's began to question the efficacy of using the blunt instrument of resettlement to reform rural economies.

This chapter starts with an overview of post-war economic development theories before moving on to the goals and methods of the FHRP. Then, it highlights the main critiques pertaining to the program, depicting life post-resettlement. Finally, it underscores the role of various social actors, including the churches, Memorial University Extension Service, the National Film Board, and the Salvation Army in both furthering — and sometimes hindering — the FHRP, providing a closer look at the resettlement process of the small community of Port Elizabeth.

## SITUATING THE FHRP IN POST-WAR ECONOMIC DEVELOPMENT LITERATURE

Modernization theory informed development projects throughout the Western world following World War II.[2] Ideologically, modernists shared a faith in the ability of capitalism, science and technology, and democratic governments to produce a better world for all. Modernization theorists proposed that people of underdeveloped regions must be freed from ignorance and superstition and converted into rational, productive citizens. Modernization required a social, psychological, cultural, and political makeover, "a multi-faceted approach involving changes in human thought and activity."[3] Children could be reformed through formal schooling while the minds of adults could be rehabilitated through socialization in factories in an urban setting. The shift from "traditional" to "modern" required members of society to throw off beliefs founded on superstition, fatalism, and emotionalism and replace them with an understanding of the world based in efficiency and science.[4]

The government-sponsored resettlement of Newfoundland outports, including the provincial Centralization Plan (1954–65) but especially the FHRP, was premised on the belief that an economy based on domestic commodity production could never provide producers with a decent standard of living. *The Newfoundland Fisheries Development Committee (1953) Report* (hereafter the Walsh Report) condemned the undercapitalized traditional inshore fishery on which 1,400 coastal communities depended.[5] The Walsh Commission agreed with the findings of previous reports that had urged governments to centralize the fishery in a dozen key ports and transfer surplus labour from the declining inshore fishery to the industrial offshore sector as soon as possible. It was time to free women and children from the backbreaking work of sun-curing fish and allow women to concentrate on homemaking and children to tend to their studies, while men would crew larger vessels, equipped with modern navigational and fish-finding technology, and take on the masculine role of breadwinner.

The governments of Newfoundland and Canada jointly agreed on a radical fisheries development program to end the cycle of illiteracy and dependence and to raise the incomes of fishers closer to the Canadian average, and central to that program was the FHRP, implemented in 1965. This joint federal–provincial resettlement program had two main goals: first, it aimed to move people from communities in decline to communities more favourable in terms of social services and modern amenities; and, second, it intended "to direct households from areas of unemployment and underemployment to growth centers with better opportunities for employment."[6] Conflict between economic and social policies of the many government departments involved with re-settlement created opportunities for householders to manipulate the program to personal advantage. For example, Employment Insurance regulations encouraged fishers to stay in the traditional fishery and others to return to it. It cemented the fishery as an occupation of last resort. High school graduates saw no future in it and migrated to urban centres.

While state planners devised and managed the FHRP, pres-sures to resettle came from many sources, including those with minimal capital investment in the community; the elderly and disabled who wanted to be near medical facilities or wished to re-unite with family elsewhere in the province; clergy who moved parish headquarters to the near mainland; university-trained teachers; and the merchants who turned migration into a busi-ness opportunity. The exodus of youth and the downgrading or cancellation of medical, education, and transportation services destabilized some settlements. Inquiries about relocation grants poured into the Premier's office before the federal and provincial Fisheries ministers had signed the agreement. Increased de-mands for services allowed government to frame centralization as a rescue mission. However, nearly half of resettlers chose to move to growth centres without changing occupations and into situa-tions where they were more underemployed and experienced a higher rate of unemployment than in the sending community.[7] Migration into industrial growth centres was so meagre that it caused Premier Joseph Smallwood to inform Prime Minister Les-ter Pearson that the goal of "transferring people from dependent status to productive employment" was at risk,[8] and that the target of moving 10,000 fishermen in a five-year period was unlikely to be met without a solution to the housing crisis.[9] A brief review of resettlement dynamics in communities of Placentia Bay will illustrate the challenges that ultimately brought the FHRP into disrepute by 1970.


## LIFE AFTER RESETTLEMENT

Contrary to a report by Deputy Minister of Community and Social Development Zeman Sametz and Director of Resettlement Ken Harnum that the great majority who moved to Arnold's Cove were "grateful to the government" and "wished they had moved long ago,"[10] the relocation of island communities into Arnold's Cove and Southern Harbour drew criticism from all quarters, including the children who were expected to benefit most from centralization (see Figure 3.1). Clergy, health officials, rural development officers, and the media described the horrific conditions that resulted from concentrating too many people into a region with limited resources and few modern amenities. The population of Arnold's Cove went from 200 to 1,000 between 1965 and 1967, without any advance preparations. The newcomers overcrowded roads, the school, church, and hall, and polluted the community well. The debacle created such a furor that the federal government funded a sociological study of resettlement of Newfoundland fishing communities while the province assigned two development officers to investigate problems in Placentia Bay. The researchers attributed much of the discontent to the competition for fishing space, a housing and schools' crisis, and the high rate of unemployment.[11]

The relocation of Placentia Bay communities to the Avalon Peninsula is an example of planning run amok. Health inspectors feared for the health and safety of settlers in unserviced subdivisions and children crammed into makeshift classrooms without

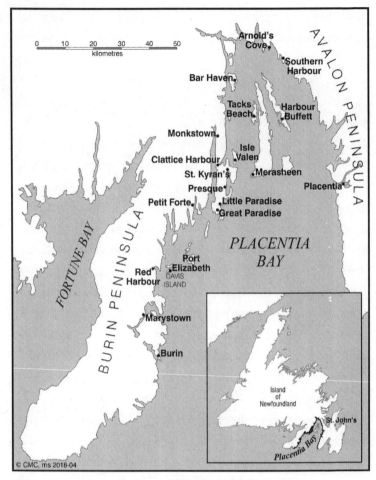

**Figure 3.1.** Main communities of Placentia Bay affected by the Fisheries Household Resettlement Program. Map by Charles Conway.

plumbing, adequate lighting, or ventilation. A polluted community well was the primary source of drinking water. Government directives to stop issuing permits-to-occupy to homeowners in subdivisions not connected to sewer mains had no effect. In 1968, 14 households lived in a subdivision without sanitation services.[12]

Despite the risks to health and safety, the Resettlement Committee continued to approve moves and leave housing to private developers.[13] J.L. Seymour of the Newfoundland and Labrador Housing Corporation advised the Resettlement Committee that unless it adopted a more orderly scheduling of moves and financed the relocation of schools, churches, halls, and recreation centres, they could expect "already deplorable conditions to worsen."[14] The Department of Education refused the school board's request for special funding for school construction in reception centres. The Education Minister advised the chairman that the schools' crisis was a by-product of resettlement and he was forwarding his request to the appropriate department. Iverson and Matthews reported that schools left behind in Tack's Beach and Harbour Buffett were superior to those children now attended in Arnold's Cove.[15] The bureaucrats had lost control over the pace and direction of centralization.

Satirist and journalist Ray Guy alleged that "real jobs [were] wasted and destroyed for imaginary jobs. And dole piled on dole." Guy declared that "the death of Harbour Buffett wasn't a sacrifice of the old Newfoundland for bringing in the new. It was senseless murder."[16] Another journalist, Ron Crocker, decried the senselessness of bringing 2,000 wage earners per year from areas of underemployment into centres already plagued by chronic unemployment — "that is what resettlement has done."[17] When this author asked Bruce Wareham, a former Harbour Buffett merchant, who operates the fresh fish processing plant at Arnold's Cove, what were his first impressions of Arnold's Cove, he replied it was the "arsehole of the world."[18]

The host of *W-5*, a CTV public affairs program, compared Arnold's Cove to a medieval town during the Black Death. The *W-5* report prompted the Anglican minister and some high school students, who had berated the government for the way resettlement occurred, to defend the town.[19] In letters to the *Evening Telegram* the priest and students accused *W-5* of focusing on mud and disease while ignoring the fact that 85 per cent of homes now had water and sewer connections and safe drinking water. Smallwood claimed the CTV report had erroneously portrayed his administration as a "criminal government" that was trying to "murder an unspoiled way of life."[20] He ranted that "only a fool or an ignoramus, or a complete romantic" could ignore the benefits of assisting people to move from a "primitive" existence and conclude it was wrong to do so. He alleged "economic" and "natural" forces had stimulated people to leave behind a primeval lifestyle where they eked out a living without benefit of radio, television, or roads while in a malnourished state. Smallwood believed resettlement was a way for coastal people to escape "Third-World" conditions and framed it as a civilizing mission. On the contrary, *Daily News* columnist Albert Perlin considered the removal of Tack's Beach to Arnold's Cove to be "one of the most badly planned ventures of its kind" and it made resettlement a "dirty word."[21]

A study of resettled schoolchildren at Arnold's Cove and Southern Harbour revealed that a high percentage had difficulty adjusting.[22] Half the sample said they had not wanted to move and that they preferred to return to the islands. Before the move they had worried about being separated from friends and starting over in a new school, but the arrival of old friends helped ease their minds. The majority of respondents said they enjoyed the movies and the dances and opined it would be hard to get used to living on the islands again. Nonetheless, some high school students expressed dissatisfaction with recreational facilities. Helen Best reminded the Minister of Community and Social Development, Bill

Rowe, that one of the objectives of the FHRP was to bring people from areas of disadvantage to areas with better services, especially education and recreation.[23] She alleged the only recreational areas available were a muddy parking lot and a bog. Rowe was not sympathetic, blaming the resettlers who "insisted on moving ... before adequate provision could be made for schools" for the debacle.[24]

Bureaucrats and fish plant managers could not convince the fishers of Tack's Beach of the efficacy of relocating to Burin, a major fisheries growth centre desperately short of labour. The fish plant manager advised householders to select a delegation to make an exploratory trip to the town and report back to the residents. Spokesperson Eric Bolt confirmed that there was employment in the plant and aboard trawlers and the school board promised to accommodate the children.[25] Countering these benefits were expensive housing, municipal taxes, and a more regulated way of life. The desire of older fishermen to stay in the inshore fishery tipped the scales in favour of Arnold's Cove. After 18 months of turmoil and repeated petitioning, the Resettlement Committee caved. Only six of 75 households relocated to an industrial fishing port. Home ownership had trumped a job.

Few Placentia Bay communities opted to move to major fisheries growth centres on the Burin Peninsula. They preferred to settle in unincorporated centres without changing occupation or lifestyle. The settlers soon discovered that so-called organized reception centres offered few services. Mrs. Henry Hickey of Southern Harbour wrote:

> We were moved to this dirty dive of Southern Harbour
> with not a drop of water of any kind always going around
> with a bucket trying to Beg [*sic*] a drop of water from the

few people here that got a drop and no one had very
much. There is six in my family after having Hipatitis
[*sic*] this winter from dirt of [*sic*] of the water .... Not a
drop of water to wash bed cloths [*sic*] not a drop to wash
your floors not a drop to flush the toilet and . . . some
people on this hill [have] no toilet.[26]

Earl Hickey opined:

My reason for moving [from Petite Forte to Southern
Harbour] was to get school for my children as I was told
there would be no school at Petite Forte. Mr. Premier I
may have made it better for my children as far as school
goes, but worse for myself and my wife. We have no water
and sewerage, my wife have [*sic*] to bring a pail across the
high road down to a beach where men are working, she
is getting fed up with it all. We have to go to a neighbor to
get a bucket of water to drink ....[27]

In a second missive to Smallwood he wrote "[it was] a terrible
mistake on someone's part to put people into places . . . to spend
the last of [*sic*] of his years in misery begging for a bucket of
water."[28] At Petite Forte he had had plenty of clean water and a
flush toilet.

The lack of counselling before and after shifting made moving
more traumatic than necessary. Relocatees, reared on the credit
system, overestimated the value of resettlement grants and underestimated the cost of launching, transporting, and setting up
houses in new environs. Twelve householders from St. Joseph's,
Placentia Bay who moved to Southern Harbour provide one example.

Having spent all their money on moving expenses, they had no means to pay for a lot purchased from a private landowner. For over a year they lived in a hostile community menaced by a landowner who threatened to evict them.[29] The settlers reported feeling a greater sense of isolation than in the old community.

The Resettlement Committee's decision to designate the Placentia area as a growth centre was politically motivated. It was a strategy by which community leaders hoped to reverse a downshift in the regional economy due to cutbacks at Canadian National Railway (CNR) and the American military base. The shrinking of the CNR coastal fleet was a consequence of resettlement. Now the Placentia East Association of Towns and Community Councils began to examine the new possibilities for development that the FHRP might present. The Association, together with their local government officials, persuaded the Resettlement Committee to designate the Placentia area a growth centre while offshore fish companies begged for workers.[30] The labour shortage was so dire Atlantic Fish Processors executives threatened to shut down operations at Marystown,[31] and Gus Etchegary, vice-president of Fishery Products, threatened to divert trawlers to mainland ports and cancel orders for three new trawlers if the Resettlement Division failed to direct settlers into Burin.[32] In the meantime, the FHRP assisted 200 fishers to migrate to a region with a shrinking economy. It is testament to how averse inshore fishers were to switching from the inshore to the offshore and the powerlessness of the state to direct them.

Like those who resettled to the isthmus of Avalon, resettlers experienced trauma. Elaine Duggan, a Memorial University graduate student, conducted a study of 27 resettled households at Placentia.[33] Seventy-five per cent of subjects surveyed said they were content to live out their lives in the old community if resettlement had not intervened. Respondents identified rumours of post office and school closures, reduction or discontinuance of coastal boat services, and the departure of clergy and merchants from the islands as push factors. Some reported feeling "real scared" when the merchant left. Their greatest concern was how to earn a living. Mrs. Loyola Pomeroy, formerly of Great Paradise, when she appeared on a CBC *Land and Sea* program, summed up those fears: "I mean to leave a place where you can earn plenty for your family and go to some place where you can't do that, it's frightening."[34] Unable to find alternate employment, parents took their children from school to return to abandoned fishing rooms to fish from April to November, thus jeopardizing their children's education. The alternative was to go on the dole. Duggan reported that 70 per cent of the study group felt they lived in a cold, unfriendly town, clustered in a welfare ghetto.[35] Ken Harnum, Director of Resettlement, expressed concern that independent fishers, who came from 21 different communities, were in danger of becoming chronic welfare cases and social outcasts unless the government invested in infrastructure in Placentia.[36]

The majority of movers had no desire to spend 10 days at sea on the icy deck of a trawler for uncertain returns, and fishers' attitude to plant work was that it was a "low paying, demeaning occupation fit only for women and children."[37] Plant managers and union executives signed contracts that kept men's wages low and women's earnings even lower. In 1969 a trimmer earned $55 for 54 hours of work in a fish factory. When management introduced an incentive program to increase productivity and reduce overtime, production workers' incomes declined by as much as $150 per month due to reduced hours.[38] Disgruntled workers from northern bays complained about conditions at Trepassey, one of eight major fisheries growth centres: "Plan to get out of this place in the spring and not coming back"; "can't save a cent — worst [*sic*] off than before [the move]"; "the water here is not fit to drink . . . and every family here have had children sick with diarrhea and vomiting"; "I'm satisfied with the [company] house now but it's not going to stay that way — it's poorly built"; and "we're working for nothing, just able to feed the family."[39] Some threatened to pay back resettlement grants and return home. The fieldworker attributed the unhappiness of the relocatees to their customary dependence on welfare and credit in the old community. He alleged the demoralized character of the settlers hindered their ability to adapt to a cash economy and the routine of industrial employment. Hence, the problems in Trepassey were more moral than economic. Bureaucrats, with a colonial mentality, preferred to attribute blame for the FHRP's shortcomings to the immoral character of the movers. The Interdepartmental Committee on Centralization of Newfoundland Communities' recommendation that a team of "social animators" and counsellors be sent to the outports to "prepare *these people* (italics added) sociologically and psychologically to live in large settlements where [they] would be strangers to their neighbours" was ignored.[40] Predictably, the "economic and pleasant settlements" envisioned by federal planners existed only in committee rooms.

At Harbour Breton newcomers competed with townspeople for jobs at BC Packers Ltd. Union president Lawrence Mahoney questioned the rationale for continuing to encourage outlying communities to settle in a town where there were sufficient workers to process all fish landed at the plant.[41] The union leader accused government of colluding with the company to maintain a pool of surplus labour to keep wages stagnant. Meanwhile, tensions mounted as the Resettlement Committee approved more moves into the town. The Anglican clergyman in Harbour Breton, Edward Marsh, cautioned Harnum to take a more systematic approach in evacuating nearby communities and to do so with as little inconvenience as possible.[42] Rev. Marsh highlighted the importance of reducing capital and social costs by relocating households and houses simultaneously. Although bureaucrats realized Harbour Breton had already exceeded its absorptive capacity, they continued to encourage the families of Grole, Miller's Passage, and Jersey Harbour to settle in the town. In 1971 Marsh informed the Minister of the Department of Regional Economic Expansion (DREE), Jean Marchand, that moving 700 persons into Harbour Breton had created an "unconscionable" rate of unemployment and created wretched conditions for every age group.[43] Reverend William Noel informed Marchand the situation would worsen if five additional communities were relocated to Harbour Breton in the next two years.[44] Marchand replied that he was very disturbed by the report of high unemployment and promised to review Harbour Breton's status as a growth centre. In a letter to Bill Rowe he strongly urged that the Resettlement Committee approve no more moves into Harbour Breton until school facilities were assessed.[45] The federal minister's response to the clergyman revealed the ability of the church to influence policy-makers at the highest level.

## THE ROLE OF THE CHURCH: USE OR ABUSE OF POWER?

Throughout Newfoundland and Labrador's history as a colony and a province, religious hierarchies have played an important role in

the affairs of state. Ministers of the Crown hired civil servants on
the basis of religion rather than merit. Sectarianism played a role
in general elections, and in 1948 clerics influenced the outcome of
referenda on Confederation. When the Newfoundland delegation
negotiated the Terms of Union with Canada, they entrenched the
denominational education system in the Canadian Constitution.
As chairs of local school boards, clergy could determine the fate of
remote outports by closing the school and/or the church. In 1957
Smallwood asked clerics to compile a list of "submarginal" settlements because he believed it was "of utmost importance" for
church leaders to favour the close-out of unviable communities.[46]
Sociologist R.L. Dewitt contended clergy shaped attitudes towards
resettlement on Fogo Island. Through his study he discovered that
religious leaders had more influence in determining choice of reception centres than government officials. The Anglican clergyman discussed moves with individual householders, chaired
meetings, and discussed resettlement in informal gatherings.[47]
He also advised high school graduates to leave Fogo Island. The
Catholic priest found himself at odds with his congregation when
he attempted to consolidate his parish. The United Church minister, a newcomer to the province, tried to remain neutral.

However, the decision not to compensate the churches for
what the governments called social capital disappointed clergy of
all faiths. The Anglican rector of Burin attacked the planners for
refusing to set aside a lot in the Marystown subdivision for a
church to accommodate resettlers.[48] The Anglican Diocesan Synod drew attention to the "human cost of resettlement" and appealed to government to extend special assistance to replace
churches, halls, and schools left behind.[49] An article in the Anglican *Newfoundland Churchman* portrayed resettlement planners as

"cold, callous, and hard-hearted" people who make empty promises to entice people to sign petitions and after the move the planners retreat to their offices where they "stick another pin in [the map] to signify the great achievement of creating another ghost town."[50]

The Anglican rectors of Grand Bank, Burin, and Harbour Breton described one incidence of callousness. They alleged that several Rencontre West families arrived in Grand Bank by coastal boat after dark without any accommodations or any official to greet them.[51] The party included "one mentally deficient woman, one half-blind woman, a man with one hand, and a woman seven months pregnant. They reprimanded the provincial minister for treating people as pawns in the "sinister game of resettlement." The 1969 Anglican Diocesan Synod passed a resolution asking government to establish a special fund for the elderly and the disabled and to conduct an in-depth assessment of growth centres.[52] The Diocesan Council for Social Services identified several concerns that governments should address: unemployment created by moving people to less viable areas; cost of housing; compensation for social capital (schools, churches, and halls); social dislocation; and counselling to help relocatees to adjust to a consumer society.[53] The Council advised against settling families in apartment blocks and row housing, fearing it would create ghettoes and stigmatize the settlers.

Mark Genge, rector of the Anglican parish of Burgeo, which included Ramea and Grey River, supported his parishioners' struggle to preserve, and improve, medical, transportation, communication, and educational services on the southwest coast. His attacks on centralization inflamed the people to such a degree that the district MHA advised Smallwood to postpone a scheduled visit to Burgeo. Genge was outraged by the release of "A Productivity

Study of the Frozen Fish Industry in Newfoundland" report that recommended dismantling and relocating the Burgeo and Gaultois fish plants to the Burin Peninsula.[54] He accompanied parishioners who took petitions to the Premier's office proclaiming Grey River was an ideal site for the inshore fishery and the people would not be forced out.[55] Genge summed up the position of the Anglican Church in a terse message to the Premier: "I appreciate your good intentions about relocating people, but I do disagree with your methods and philosophy."[56] He suggested a road connection to the Trans-Canada Highway would attract medical personnel and teachers and keep communities alive.

The Roman Catholic Archdiocese attempted to use the FHRP to assist in the centralization of parishes. Father Dennis Walsh advised Harnum that he could "hinder or further the cause, and it would be in the interests of all concerned for me to further the cause of centralization."[57] Father Philip Lewis of Merasheen urged Smallwood to take a more coercive approach. Lewis suggested it was unrealistic to expect 90 per cent of householders to move at once. He felt 40 or 50 per cent would be a more practical limit. Lewis recommended resettling Great and Little Paradise, Clattice Harbour, Presque, St. Kyran's, and Isle au Valen into the "more prosperous, industrious, community minded, and co-operative" town of Merasheen, a place with a fish plant and electricity, and a resident priest.[58] Success, he wrote, depended on appealing directly to the people, bypassing greedy merchants who spread false information about the program.[59] The priest's plans to use the FHRP to consolidate his parish failed and Merasheen declined. When Lewis's successor announced his departure and the schoolchildren could be accommodated in one classroom, the remaining families decided to leave.

Like Father Lewis, Father W.P. Collins endeavoured to consolidate his parish at Bar Haven. He appealed to Smallwood to construct a road, which would entice settlements in the region to move into Bar Haven, an island community in Placentia Bay. He envisioned Bar Haven as a growth centre and forwarded his case to Smallwood. The crux of his case was that Bar Haven had a 10-month fishing season, a herring packing plant, and few welfare cases.[60] The priest accused the government of subtly forcing the people to resettle elsewhere without any guarantee of employment. One week after Collins made this plea, the Resettlement Committee approved the evacuation of Bar Haven, mostly to the Placentia area.[61] The merchants, who Father Lewis had accused of spreading false information about resettlement to preserve their clientele, led the exodus from Bar Haven. The closure of Wadman Brothers, an important supplier and fish buyer in Placentia West, demoralized communities and weakened the regional economy. Shortly after Bar Haven voted to resettle, Wadman began transporting householders and houses out of surrounding communities.

On the northwest coast, two Catholic priests, Desmond McGrath and his predecessor, Father Murphy, were keen to consolidate the parish of Port au Choix.[62] McGrath attempted to dissuade the Power Commission from constructing a pole line and encouraged the Minister of Highways to cancel plans for a road to New Ferrole as part of a strategy to force them out. Murphy had allegedly threatened to close the community school and removed some furniture to another settlement to force people into Port au Choix, according to Catherine Hynes, a parishioner and resident of New Ferrole. Hynes lived in a new three-storey house with her husband and seven sons, who fished together and allegedly earned a good living. She vowed she would rather live on berries and fish in New Ferrole than move to Port au Choix. Hynes informed Smallwood: "We are not shifting out of it [New Ferrole] until God takes us . . . our parish priests are all for money in big settlements . . . ."[63] Harnum advised the MHA for St. Barbe district that the Resettlement Committee had discussed the case with the community council and "especially Father McGrath, who was involved with their decision-making," and the government supported the move.[64] However, the regional development officer for the northwest coast urged Harnum to proceed with caution owing to the lack of services and amenities and the attitude of the neighbouring outports towards the "backward" town.[65]

The United Church took a less overt stance than the Anglican and Catholic clerics. A report on resettlement presented to the May 1969 annual meeting of the Newfoundland Conference of the United Church of Canada provides some insight.[66] The report examined the effects of the FHRP on each age group and concluded that when one cohort moved it produced a domino effect. Wage earners relocated to enhance their children's education, and when the wage earners and their dependants moved, the elderly were forced to follow because the community could no longer maintain essential services. The presenters asked the Conference to be mindful of the social, spiritual, and material needs of each generation as they transitioned to a new way of life. They asked the Conference to take a proactive role in the planning phase and to be mindful not only of the needs of those who chose relocation but also of those who remained in the evacuated outport without benefit of church, school, communication, transportation, or medical services. The report urged governments to continue to provide essential services to evacuated communities, but at the same time asked government to extend and expand the FHRP.

The Conference believed resettlement presented an opportunity to make the Church more relevant in an increasingly secular world.[67]

In a meeting of resettlement planners, the town council, and clergy, the United Church minister at Burgeo asked the bureaucrats what their plans were for the southwest coast settlements. Rev. Burke reminded the bureaucrats of the need to ease the anxiety in south coast settlements by providing accurate information about CNR's plans for coastal boat services.[68] Burke, together with the Anglican rector and the town council, emphasized the need to explain the pros and cons of resettlement so that people could make rational decisions about their future. Burke claimed that rumours, if left unchecked, would demoralize communities at risk. On Fogo Island the United Church minister urged the Fogo Island Improvement Committee to organize co-operatives and encourage tourism as alternatives to resettling 12 communities outside Fogo Island.

Memorial University Extension Service and the National Film Board played an important role in saving Fogo Island (see Loo, Chapter 2), but without the participation of local groups their efforts would have come to naught. The clergy influenced congregations from the pulpit and joined development associations to promote new industries. The regional development officer credited the Fogo Island Improvement Committee for much of the social and economic progress that occurred. The Committee, initiated by the Catholic priest, organized conferences, workshops, and student exchanges, and lobbied the government for roads, a ferry service, a community park, improved medical facilities, and a regional high school. Through what became known as the "Fogo Process," Fogo Islanders forged a new sense of community and identity by working together as a unit.

Fogo Island was not the lone community to choose develop-ment. Lorne Hiscock, the Salvation Army officer at Monkstown, Placentia Bay, joined a group of women activists who led the fight to save a viable community. Monkstown was fortunate to have a diverse economy, potential for resource and tourism development, and an industrious population. In 1967 less than 50 per cent of adult males were fishermen. Others were employed in lumbering and boatbuilding. Fieldworkers recognized the potential for fish-eries diversification, expansion of sawmilling, and tourism, but concluded Monkstown would not survive without a road.[69] His-cock asked the Premier to add Monkstown to the list of reception centres and construct a road to the Burin Highway.[70] When Small-wood denied this request, the women engaged in a letter-writing campaign and circulated petitions.[71] Hattie and Laura May and Mrs. W. Butler insisted Monkstown was a viable, disease-free community with potential for tuna fishing in Paradise Sound and salmon fishing on three rivers.[72] They questioned why Port Eliza-beth had three publicly owned and operated diesel generators while Monkstown had none. Citing incompetence, they asked Smallwood to fire their MHA, Patrick Canning. Butler alleged Monkstown had a healthy, industrious population who had in-stalled private sewer systems and bought generators to electrify their homes.[73] The efforts of these women and the Salvation Army officer paid off. Monkstown survived into the twenty-first century.

In the district of White Bay North, a charismatic Apostolic Faith pastor and businessman, Booth Reid, dominated spiritual and secular life in Hooping Harbour, a fishing village of 200 souls. Initially, Reid determined the best strategy to save his fol-lowers from the perils of resettlement was to use his political con-nections to lobby for generators, local road improvements, and a community stage. He believed that when these services were in place, he could convince the Resettlement Committee to designate Hooping Harbour a reception centre. MHA Edward Roberts was sympathetic but could not convince Canadian National Telegraph (CNT) and the Department of Highways that Hooping Harbour residents were adamantly opposed to moving and in the meantime were entitled to rudimentary services.[74] When the Department of Highways refused to build a road connection to the Roddickton highway and CNT refused to improve telecommunications, Reid decided locals would control the exodus and move Hooping Harbour as a unit, to Bide Arm. There they would build a new town. The self-styled modern-day Moses chaired the local resettlement committee, constructed a barge at public expense, hired boats to transport houses and stages, and built a community with water and sewer services and a new church and school. The moving project employed relocatees to build the barge, transport houses, and construct a dam and infrastructure to meet the needs of a modern town. To avoid criticism for creating a new community, the government documents referred to Bide Arm as "Englee North," indicating it was a part of Englee, a growth centre located 20 kilometres away. The move from Hooping Harbour to Bide Arm is a prime example of the powerlessness of governments to direct people into designated growth centres.

## SETTLING ON FORBIDDEN GROUND: THE PORT ELIZABETH-RED HARBOUR MOVE

By the late 1960s, resistance to state-sponsored migration had intensified. The release of the Iverson and Matthews report on the FHRP prompted journalists to add "murder," "blitzkrieg," and "genocide" to the resettlement lexicon. Port Elizabeth, a community of 300 persons located on Davis Island, Placentia Bay, had a corps of highly capitalized fishermen with strong attachment to place and occupation.[75] To preserve social relationships, maintain access to familiar fishing grounds, and preserve their investments in boats and gear, 50 families insisted on moving as a unit to Red Harbour, a place evacuated in 1965. Donald Jamieson, MP for Burin-Burgeo, urged the Resettlement Committee not to list Port Elizabeth as a sending community. Jamieson described it as a viable community with a council, a school with a reputation for scholarship, and a highly capitalized fishery concentrated in the hands of a dozen industrious fishers. Nonetheless, the population dwindled with the departure of youth, the hospital ship no longer visited, and Fishery Products withdrew its floating fresh fish plant.

Once the people accepted resettlement as inevitable, the merchant, the community council, and the United Church minister, together with 46 successful fishers, agreed to move to Red Harbour, a previously resettled community near the Burin Highway. Here they would resettle as a single entity, live in relocated houses, worship together as a congregation, attend classes in a reconstructed school, and fish the same grounds, utilizing gear valued at over $600,000.[76] Rev. Gerald Sacrey feared that if governments insisted on moving them into an industrial centre, all gear and equipment would become redundant and industrious fishers might drift into dependence. Since the merchant, H.E. Senior and Son, agreed to re-establish his business in Red Harbour, life could continue with minimal disruption. Port Elizabethans believed they had the industry and character to thrive in a reconstructed community.[77] Neighbouring fishing communities, who depended on Senior's, circulated a petition calling on government to support the move. The chair of Local 150 of the Federation of Fishermen notified Harnum that if Willard Senior was denied permission to re-establish his business at Red Harbour, the fishing grounds between Petite Forte and Port Elizabeth would be abandoned.[78]

Bureaucrats in the Departments of Community and Social Development and Municipal Affairs were diametrically opposed to permanent occupation of evacuated outports.[79] They described the move as "counterproductive" and "contrary to the aims of the regional plan and the resettlement programme."[80] After repeated appeals to Port Elizabethans to resettle to Marystown and Burin, the Director of Resettlement informed Deputy Minister Sametz he was convinced 40 families would resettle nowhere other than Red Harbour. He assured his deputy minister he had "personally made every effort to persuade the people [to move] to some other centre."[81] On 7 May 1969 the provincial cabinet approved the move on strict terms. The province would make available the government barge to transport houses, but would not assume responsibility for providing water and sewer systems, electrification, telephone, telegraph, or school bus services; enactment of these services would be left to the community council to negotiate with the various departments and agencies.[82] When resettlement commenced in July, Port Elizabeth was not a designated sending community, nor was Red Harbour a reception centre. On 6 November 1969 Canada's Fisheries Minister designated "Riverview" a reception centre for the region. During the winter families towed fishing premises across the strait, built wharves, and readied gear and vessels for the fishery.

## CONCLUSION

Underpinning post-World War II regional development projects was a philosophy that people needed to be helped, that is, they could not progress without the intervention of external agents. Development experts and policy-makers shared an ideology that portrayed rural populations as inferior to urban populations. In this light, the FHRP was a gendered and colonial development scheme designed to eradicate an underclass of citizens by removing them from physical environments. While post-1950s Newfoundland and Labrador resettlement programs precipitated one of the greatest human migrations in Canadian history, the FHRP was not as coercive as the eviction of Japanese Canadians from the west coast during World War II, the Ojibway from Riding Mountain National Park in 1936, the settlement of Inuit from northern Quebec into the High Arctic in the 1950s, or the bulldozing of Africville in Nova Scotia in the 1960s. Nonetheless, the attachment of descriptors like "murder" and "blitzkrieg" to the program creates the impression it was highly coercive.[83] Indeed, coercive pressure to move came from many sources: from Smallwood, overzealous bureaucrats, former residents, commuters, clergy, municipalities, and corporate executives, among other sources.

Rumours of curtailment of transportation, communication, and medical and education services demoralized communities, but they did not herd up, mill about, and wait for the opportunity to stampede. They were actors in their own history. Individuals and communities travelled paths they felt advantageous to them. Some stated they moved to a place they considered a nice place to live. Others followed neighbours in an effort to preserve social connections. Resilient outports rejected the findings of state-sponsored commissions that undervalued the pluralistic economy of rural regions and exaggerated the benefits of the industrial economy. The reports ignored class differences and overlooked the character of the people. Attachment to homes and fondness for an unregulated lifestyle along with a distaste for mortgages, rent, and taxation diminished the desire to abandon a centuries-old way of life to move into a structured industrial cash economy centred on fish factories and, possibly, greater reliance on government handouts.

What this also reveals is that mobility, no matter how voluntary, is never costless, even when houses, schools, and churches, along with the people, are transported simultaneously and free of charge. Left behind are the memories of a specific way of life that could only exist in a particular environment. Resettlement planners overlooked the importance of home ownership and underestimated attachment to place and occupation. Inshore fishers were jacks-of-all-trades and travelled long distances to find jobs, but they treasured the knowledge that they had a home and occupation to come back to. Besides, when ascribing a "cost" to resettlement, planners often only accounted for incomes from cod fishing and ignored the earnings from lobster, pelagic, salmon fisheries, as well as the various types of in-kind incomes from hunting and gathering berries or firewood. Indeed, as development expert Donald Savoie has advised planners, they must be sensitive to the subjects' attachment to place, and a "general sense of belonging and of knowing how to behave in a particular society" should be considered.[84]

## NOTES

1    See, for example, Ralph Matthews, "The Outport Breakup," *Horizon Canada* 102 (1987): 2438–43; Fred Earle to Cato Wadel, 27 Sept. 1968, 2.01.155, Fred Earle Papers, Archives and Special

Collections (ASC), MUN, quoted in Jeff A. Webb, *Observing the Outports: Describing Newfoundland Culture, 1950–1980* (Toronto: University of Toronto Press, 2015), 304.

2   For more on economic development theories influencing early resettlement programs, see Pottie-Sherman, Côté, and Ledrew, Chapter 1; Loo, Chapter 2.

3   Dean C. Tipps, "Modernization Theory and the Comparative Study of Societies," *Comparative Studies in Society and History* 15, no. 2 (1973): 200.

4   Timmons Roberts and Amy Hite, eds., *From Modernization to Globalization: Perspectives on Development and Social Change* (Malden, MA: Blackwell Publishers, 2000), 4.

5   Canada and Newfoundland, *Newfoundland Fisheries Development Committee Report* (St. John's: Queen's Printer, 1953).

6   See the Newfoundland Fisheries Household Resettlement Agreement (1965) in A.G. Stacey Collection, Coll. 065, file 1.05.001, ASC, Memorial University.

7   William Rowe to Rev. Reuben Hatcher, 3 Dec. 1970, GN39/1, S349, PANL.

8   Smallwood to Pearson, 12 Jan. 1967, J.R. Smallwood Collection, Coll. 075, file 3.10.078, ASC, MUN.

9   Memorandum Re: The Newfoundland Fisheries Development Programme. J.R. Smallwood Collection, Coll. 075, file 3.10.078, ASC.

10   Harnum to F.W. Rowe, 16 Jan. 1967, GN39/1, Box 125, file S32, PANL.

11   Lance C. Shirley and Donald W. Burry, "Placentia Bay Study, May–June 1967," GN39/1, file S83, PANL. See also Noel Iverson and Ralph Matthews, *Communities in Decline: An Examination of Resettlement in Newfoundland* (St. John's: ISER, 1968).

12   J.T. Allston, Director of Urban and Rural Planning, to Norman Ash, Chairman of the Local Improvement District, Arnold's Cove, 26 Feb. 1968. GN39/1, Box 35, file S2, PANL.

13   J.M. Graham, H. Powell, and O. Bowering, "Health Inspection Division Report, 15 April 1969," GN39/1, Box 125, file S2, PANL.

14 J.L. Seymour, "Report on Housing," submitted to the Federal–
   Provincial Advisory Committee of the Fisheries Household
   Resettlement Programme Annual Meeting, 11–12 June 1969,
   Minutes, Appendix G, 67–71, A.G. Stacey Collection, Coll. 065, file
   1.04.004, ASC, Memorial University.
15 House to Harnum, 21 Nov. 1967, GN39/1, Box 125, file S2, PANL.
16 Ray Guy, "Left Behind by Scavengers," *Evening Telegram*, 12 Sept.
   1969, 2.
17 Ron Crocker, "Resettlement Report Reveals Some Old Themes,"
   *Evening Telegram*, 17 Nov. 1970.
18 Bruce Wareham in conversation with the author, Nov. 2018.
19 Letter to Editor, *Evening Telegram*, 18 Apr. 1969; House to Harnum,
   11 Apr. 1969, GN39/1, Box 125, file S2, PANL.
20 J.R. Smallwood, "Budget Speech," 30 Apr. 1969, J.R. Smallwood
   Collection, Coll. 075, file 3.10.078, ASC, Memorial University.
21 Wayfairer, *Daily News*, Apr. 1966, GN39/1, Box 125, file S64, PANL.
22 Peter M. Godfrey, "The Impact of Resettlement on Children: Study
   of the Effects of Resettlement on Children Relocated to Arnold's
   Cove," unpublished study, Memorial University, 1970.
23 Helen Best to William N. Rowe, 23 Sept. 1970, GN39/1, Box 125,
   file S2, PANL. Best was a former resident of Tack's Beach.
24 Rowe to Debbie Williams, 22 Nov. 1970, GN39/1, Box 125, file S2,
   PANL. Williams moved to Arnold's Cove from Woody Island.
25 Eric Bolt to Joseph Moulton, 16 Mar. 1966, GN39/1, Box 126, file
   64, PANL.
26 Hickey to Smallwood, 24 Feb. 1968, GN39/1, Box 126, file S60, PANL.
27 Earl Hickey to Smallwood, 19 May 1970, J.R. Smallwood Collection,
   Coll. 075, File 1.29.016, ASC, MUN.
28 Earl Hickey to Smallwood, 2 May 1971, J.R. Smallwood Collection,
   Coll. 075, file 1.29.019, ASC, MUN.
29 See Southern Harbour Community File, Box 126, file S60, PANL.
30 F.W. Rowe, Minister of Community and Social Development, to
   G.A. Frecker, 15 May 1967. As of 1 April 1967, the newly created
   Department of Community and Social Development (C&SD) took
   control of the FHRP.

31 Zeman Sametz, Deputy Minister, C&SD, to Aidan Maloney, Minister of Fisheries and C&SD, "Re: Marystown Community Development," 8 Jan. 1968, GN39/1, Box 130, file S263, vol. 1, PANL.

32 Augustus Etchegary to Harnum, 27 June 1967, GN39/1, Box 126, file S55, PANL.

33 M. Elaine Duggan, "Resettlement of the Isolated Newfoundland Community" (Memorial University, Centre for Newfoundland Studies, 1970).

34 Hal Andrews, "Back to the Islands," *Land and Sea*, Canadian Broadcasting Corporation, Television Archives, St. John's, NL.

35 Duggan, "Resettlement of the Isolated Newfoundland Community," 46–50.

36 Harnum to Sametz, 5 Mar. 1969, GN39/1, Box 126, file S70, PANL.

37 John Mannion, *Point Lance in Transition* (Toronto: McClelland and Stewart, 1974), 52.

38 L.N. Woolfrey to Harnum, Nov. 1969, GN39/1, Box 126, file S71, PANL.

39 "Memo: Re: Trepassey," L.N. Woolfrey to Harnum, n.d., GN39/1, Box 126, file S71, PANL.

40 Raymond Blake, *Lions or Jellyfish: Newfoundland–Ottawa Relations Since 1957* (Toronto: University of Toronto Press, 2015), 129.

41 Lawrence J. Mahoney to A.C. Warnell, 29 Oct. 1968, J.R. Smallwood Collection, Coll. 075, 1.19.006, ASC, Memorial University.

42 Edward Marsh to Harnum, 26 Feb. 1968, GN39/1, Box 130, file S261, PANL.

43 Jean Marchand to Bill Rowe, 7 Jan. 1971, GN39/1, Box 130, file S261, PANL

44 Rev. William Noel to Jean Marchand, 12 Jan. 1971, GN39/1, Box 130, file S261, vol. 2, PANL.

45 Marchand to Rowe, 7 Jan. 1971, GN39/1, Box 130, file S261, PANL.

46 J.R. Smallwood Collection, Coll. 075, file 3.10.003, ASA, Memorial University.

47 R.L. Dewitt, "Attitudes toward Resettlement on Fogo Island," in *Perspectives on Newfoundland Society and Culture*, ed. Michael Sterns (St. John's: ISER, 1974), 54–57.

48  Owen Coffin to William Rowe, 15 July 1969, GN39/1, Box 125, file
    S5, PANL.

49  R.L. Seaborn, "Bishop's Charge to Synod, 1969." See Herbert
    Pottle, *Dawn Without Light* (St. John's: Breakwater, 1979), 58.

50  O.W.C., "Viewpoint," *Newfoundland Churchman*, Sept. 1970, 2.

51  R. Hatcher to William Rowe, 19 Oct. 1970, GN39/1, file S349,
    PANL.

52  "Resettlement," *Newfoundland Churchman*, July 1969, 5.

53  "Synod Sees Need for Improvement in Resettlement Programme,"
    *Newfoundland Churchman*, Sept. 1971.

54  "A Productivity Study of the Frozen Fish Industry in Newfound-
    land," Ibucon Resources, 1968.

55  Frank Young to Smallwood, 19 Sept. 1967, J.R. Smallwood
    Collection, Coll. 075, file 1.05.022, ASC.

56  Mark Genge to Smallwood, 22 Oct. 1967, J.R. Smallwood Collec-
    tion, Coll. 075, file 1.05.022, ASC.

57  Denis P. Walsh to Harnum, 29 Mar. 1967, GN39/1, Box 128, file
    S168, PANL.

58  Philip J. Lewis to Ross Young, Newfoundland Fisheries Develop-
    ment Authority, 6 Apr. 1965, GN39/1, Box 125, file S11, PANL.

59  Ibid.

60  W.P. Collins to Harnum, 22 Nov. 1965, GN39/1, Box 125, file S95,
    PANL.

61  A.G. Stacey to Harnum, 3 Dec. 1965, GN39/1, file S95, PANL.

62  E.P. Nugent, "Report on Northern Peninsula Visit, July 15–18,
    1969," GN39/1, Box 131, file S356, PANL.

63  Catherine Hynes to Smallwood, 7 Mar. 1967, GN39/1, Box 128, file
    S162, PANL.

64  Harnum to James Chalker, 26 June 1969, GN39/1, Box 128, file
    S162, PANL.

65  L. Woolfrey to Harnum, "Report on Visit to Northern Peninsula,
    December 1968," GN39/1, Box 131, file S280, PANL.

66  "Reports: The Forty-Fifth Meeting of the Newfoundland Confer-
    ence of the United Church of Canada," 20–23 May 1969, Box 19,
    WY100, 1967–1972, United Church Archives. St. John's.

67  George Withers, "Reconstituting Communities and Economies" (PhD thesis, Memorial University, 2016), 232.

68  Memo "Re: K. Garland's Visit to Burgeo April 6th–7th, 1970," GN39/1, Box 128, file S186, PANL.

69  Donald Burry and Lance Shirley, "Placentia Bay Study (1967)," GN39/1, File S83, PANL.

70  Lorne Hiscock to Smallwood, 9 Nov. 1965, J.R. Smallwood Collection, Coll. 075, file 1.30.023, ASC, Memorial University.

71  Smallwood to Hiscock, 23 Nov. 1965, J.R. Smallwood Collection, Coll. 075, file 1.30.023, ASC.

72  Hattie and Laura May to Smallwood, 25 Aug. 1966, J.R. Smallwood Collection, Coll. 075, file 1.30.024, ASC.

73  Mrs. W. Butler to Smallwood, 6 June 1969, J.R. Smallwood Collection, Coll. 075, File 1.30.023, ASC.

74  Roberts to J.A. Donich, Superintendent CNT, 30 June 1966, Edward M. Roberts Collection, Coll. 078, file 2.01.026, ASC.

75  Withers, "Reconstituting Rural Communities and Economies," 10.

76  Gerald Sacrey to Harnum, 19 Oct. 1968, GN39/1, file S140, PANL.

77  J.M. Roberts, Manager NLHC, Marystown Office, to A. Vivian, Chair of NLHC, 3 Jan. 1968, GN39/1, file S140, PANL.

78  John J. Lake to Harnum, 26 Oct. 1968, GN39/1, file S140, PANL.

79  Zametz to J.G. Channing, Deputy Minister of Provincial Affairs, 14 Nov. 1968, GN39/1, file S140, PANL.

80  J.T. Allston to H.U. Rowe, 6 Dec. 1968, GN39/1, file S140, PANL.

81  Harnum to Sametz, 5 Feb. 1969, GN39/1, file S140, PANL.

82  W.N. Rowe to Community Council, 14 Feb. 1969. GN39/1, Box 128, file S140, PANL.

83  Guy, "Left Behind by Scavengers."

84  Donald J. Savoie, *Regional Economic Development: Canada's Search for Solutions* (Toronto: University of Toronto Press, 1992), 10.

# CHAPTER 4

## Should We Stay or Should We Go?
## Mobility, Immobility, and Community Closure
## in Newfoundland and Labrador, 2009–2018[1]

ISABELLE CÔTÉ *and* YOLANDE POTTIE-SHERMAN

> *I think the government doesn't really know themselves if they*
> *want to do a wholesale relocation of outport Newfoundland or*
> *not, I think these are all test cases, every one, and this is, this is*
> *another test case and they're just gauging it as they go.*
>                           — Interview, Little Bay Island homeowner, 2018

Our focus in this chapter is on Newfoundland and Labrador's
(NL) Community Relocation Policies (CRPs) from 2009 to today,
which revived the resettlement issue to mitigate the high cost of
servicing remote communities whose populations were shrinking. These CRPs represented an important departure from earlier
resettlement schemes in NL, thanks to the requirement that relocation be "community-initiated and community-driven," requiring
all communities interested in obtaining government assistance
to relocate to pass through a four-stage process ending with a

**Table 4.1** NL communities that have applied for CRP since 2009

| | Year Process Initiated | Population | Appeal | Savings - Costs: Estimated Net Savings |
|---|---|---|---|---|
| **Gaultois** | 2015 | Approximately 130 (as of Oct. 2016) | None | Did not reach that stage |
| **Grand Bruit** | 2007 | 31 residents (as of 2009) | None | N/A |
| **Little Bay Islands** | 2011 | 61 residents (as of 2016) | 18 appeals (2015 vote)<br><br>35 appeals (2018 vote) | Estimated $6,848,100 in net savings over 20 years |
| **McCallum** | 2014 | 79 residents | None | Did not reach that stage |
| **Nippers Harbour** | 2013 | 46 residents | None | Estimated costs of relocation surpassed estimated savings over 20 years by $4.4 million |
| **Round Harbour** | 2010 | 2 permanent residents, 4 commercial property owners | 1 (to win rights to stay put in Round Harbour) | Estimated $1,349,000 in net savings over 20 years |
| **Snook's Arm** | 2013 | 10 residents (as of 2016) | | Estimated $294 in net savings over 20 years |
| **William's Harbour** | 2013 | 26 residents (as of 2015) | 12 appeals | Estimated $10,796,000 in net savings over 20 years |

community vote.[2] These steps have proven so stringent that only three communities have so far relocated under the new program: Grand Bruit (in 2010), the southeastern Labrador community of William's Harbour (in 2017), and, most recently, Little Bay Islands, in December 2019.[3] The process is still ongoing in Round Harbour and in Snook's Arm, whereas it failed in Nippers Harbour, McCallum, and Gaultois[4] (see Table 4.1 and Figure 4.1).

**Table 4.1** (cont.)

| | Vote | Status (Reason) | Additional notes |
|---|---|---|---|
| **Gaultois** | N/A | Not relocated (insufficient interests) | |
| **Grand Bruit** | 2009- Yes: 85%<br>2015- Yes: 97% | Relocated July 2010 | |
| **Little Bay Islands** | 2015- Yes: 89.47%<br>2019- Yes: 100% | Relocated December 2019 | |
| **McCallum** | Initial community interests vote at 74% | Not relocated (insufficient interests) | |
| **Nippers Harbour** | N/A | Not relocated (did not pass CBA) | Requests for alteration to CBA policy to reduce allowance to $100,000. A further vote revealed that such measure only got 73% support locally. |
| **Round Harbour** | Yes: 100% | Waiting (approved since 2010, waiting for government approval) | |
| **Snook's Arm** | Yes: 100% | Waiting<br>(approved since 2015, waiting for government approval) | |
| **William's Harbour** | Yes: 96% | Relocated 2017 | |

While studies of resettlement globally have examined their drivers, their voluntary and involuntary dimensions, and their outcomes, they have paid less attention to the democratic resettlement decision-making process *within* communities themselves.[5] This gap needs addressing, particularly as community-driven resettlement projects become more common in democratic contexts.[6]

In this chapter, we ask: What can a migration-decision approach reveal about the community-driven resettlement process in Newfoundland and Labrador since 2009? How have communities approached and navigated the CRP procedures? Drawing from 1,100 pages of documents obtained by access to information requests as well as policy documents, media reports, and fieldwork (including interviews and participant observation) on Little

**Figure 4.1.** Newfoundland and Labrador communities that applied for relocation under 2009 and 2013 Community Relocation Policies. Map by Charles Conway.

Bay Islands, a Newfoundland community that has debated its closure for the last six years, this chapter shows that those who opt to stay are far from being passive pawns in the resettlement game. Two facets of the CRP decision-making process highlight the agency of the "stayers": (1) negotiating voting rights; and (2) voting for (or against) community relocation. A third characteristic — the slow nature of NL's CRPs — simultaneously curtails residents' agency, making alternatives to relocation increasingly non-viable. We conclude by drawing parallels with other ongoing programs of resettlement around the world.

## MOBILITY AND IMMOBILITY IN RURAL PLACES: RESETTLEMENT AND THE MIGRATION DECISION

Globally, population movements have always been a feature of social, economic, and political life throughout the world. Although mobility is widely seen as ubiquitous, studies have questioned whether it is as significant within contemporary societies as previously assumed. Hammar and Tamas, for example, point to official statistics that indicate that only a minority of the population in most countries move away from their home places or regions.[7] As such, they call for increased research on immobilities, particularly the reasons that lie behind people's decision *not* to migrate.

Rural places, in particular, are often depicted as "immobile." Indeed, dominant cultural constructions of rurality remain heavily laden with notions of stability, rootedness, attachment to place, and localism.[8] But underneath a "meta-narrative of stasis, tradition and localism, mobility constitutes an important shaper of [rural] place."[9] This mobility was historically the case via the mass out-migration of young people, and it has recently been the case through the flows of (working-class) tourists and (middle-class) holiday homeowners. Clearly, people have moved in and out of rural areas, and will continue to do so for the foreseeable future.

The migration decision represents a useful starting point for analyzing the community dynamics behind contemporary resettlement programs in democratic contexts. A multitude of individual, household, and contextual factors influence migration decisions, and the literature acknowledges the complex interlinkages of various forms of capital, attachments to communities at various scales, and mobility aspirations and desires.[10] As Zhang explains, the migration decision represents a pivotal dimension of any "approach which takes seriously the cultural agency of migrants; it is a conceptualization which marks a clear break with theories of migration as downward diffusions of structural power."[11]

Here, we place the migration decision at the forefront of our analysis of contemporary resettlement in Newfoundland and Labrador for four main reasons.

First, the migration decision is a useful frame for acknowledging that "staying" is also an active process. We find this acknowledgement particularly relevant for understanding communities in NL recently that have had failed resettlement votes. Migration studies have typically neglected the variegated "staying cultures" of rural areas in both Global North and South.[12] Scholars have equated rural "staying" with immobility — an inability to move, which has connotations of disempowerment, failure (i.e., "left behind"). As Stockdale and Haarsten note, this view of rural "staying" belies the agency of rural stayers and "devalues" the act of staying in rural areas.[13] Staying is not simply the "absence of movement," but rather should be understood as an "active," "complex," and "nuanced process" that reflects a specific series of decisions and negotiations made over the course of a lifetime, and in relation to past, present, and future migration desires.[14] From this perspective, as Coulter et al. argue, resettlement involves "relational practices" of both "mobility and immobility" that "link lives together and connect people to structural conditions through time and space."[15]

Second, in addition to framing staying as an active process, a migration-decision approach also encourages us to approach staying (and resistance to resettlement) with the same level of nuance as is afforded to "movers." It is important to differentiate among rural stayers who remain in place due to their attachments, those who aspire to migrate but remain in place even though they may have low levels of attachment (i.e., the "tied stayer"), and out-migrants who remain highly attached despite having left.[16] For Morse and Mudgett, a key characteristic of "contented stayers" is their interwoven attachments to both their communities and to the physical landscape.[17] As explained by Milbourne and Kitchen:

> Rural places provide important spatial mooring for residents, offering spaces of rest, community, cultural belonging, stability, home and connections with nature. Indeed, one of the main reasons why people remain in these types of rural locality in the face of the withdrawal of local services is their attachment to place.[18]

This development suggests that a focus on "stayers" (i.e., those who might contest resettlement schemes) may provide valuable insight on rural sustainability. For example, others have criticized the idea that place attachment and mobility are contradictory or mutually exclusive phenomena. Barcus and Brunn have shown that out-migration does not necessarily diminish attachment to place, whereas Gustafson suggests that, besides providing freedoms and new opportunities, mobility can be associated with loss and uprootedness, urging researchers to give more critical attention to the complex relations between mobility and fixity or, as he puts it, "roots and route."[19] Finally, a focus on "tied stayers" puts in stark relief the linkages between rural (im)mobilities and poverty. What are the financial costs of mobility in rural areas, and to what extent are these costs excluding those on low (and middle) incomes from rural places? After all:

> (im)mobility represents a significant dimension of rural deprivation, with the closure of local shops, the centralization of public and social services, and the retraction of public transport provision, trapping some groups within local space and forcing others to employ complex coping strategies to access facilities and services that have relocated to other places.[20]

Third, the concept of the decision provides an important counterpoint to popular narratives of abandoned "ghost villages of Newfoundland," which portray their remaining residents (i.e., "stayers") as passive victims of shifts in the province's resource economy.[21] "Haunting images of life inside Little Bay Islands," for example, have become part of Canada's (and the wider world's) social imaginary of Newfoundland.[22] These depictions of NL's "abandoned outports" inform how people understand the need for and the process of relocation. After all, societies "understand themselves through narratives," and it is therefore important to interrogate the narratives of abandonment that frame certain places as obsolete or becoming so. Herrmann, for example, emphasized the ways in which coastal Louisiana and Alaska are represented through visual media as "America's eroding edges," a narrative that informs how people understand their need for — and process of — relocation.[23] These communities are depicted in images of empty, blighted homes and through aerial views that underscore their powerlessness against nature. But such representations belie the agency of residents who are actively negotiating (for or against) their future relocation, and "naturalize" the community's decline, problematically "erasing the century or more of colonial, discriminatory policies that initially located these villages in vulnerable geographies and exacerbated socioeconomic vulnerabilities to ecological disasters."[24] Narratives of abandonment that frame certain places as obsolete or becoming so should therefore be questioned if not outright challenged.

Fourth, an emphasis on the greater context surrounding the migration decision allows us to examine the forms of pressures exercised on individuals' decision process, and questions how "voluntary" moving or staying really is. For Schmidt-Soltau and Brockington, the current understanding of "voluntary" resettlement is missing the needed emphasis on informed, prior, and free consent, along with the option *not* to relocate.[25] Their investigation of development-induced resettlement in Cameroon revealed how prevalent coercive pressures are, even in cases where people formally consented to, and were compensated for, relocation.[26] In contrast, Gebre's framework expands on the voluntary-involuntary dichotomy by introducing two additional categories of resettlement: compulsory-voluntary, where resettlement is deliberately induced by outside agencies or government, and induced-voluntary, where people embrace relocation out of desperation.[27] The latter draws parallels with Wilmsen and Wang's "coercion by deprivation," where people may "choose" to stay behind and not participate in resettlement programs, but are ultimately forced to relocate due to the long-term consequences of state-organized resettlement.[28]

## METHODOLOGY

To examine decision-making surrounding the CRPs, we adopted a multi-method framework, including media and policy document analysis, triangulated with participant observation and key informant interviews. Mixed data collection has the benefit of minimizing selection bias (*what* is covered) and description bias (*how* information is covered).[29]

We examined news articles covering the issue of population resettlement in Canada and NL from two national news agencies (the Canadian Broadcasting Corporation [CBC], Canada's national public broadcaster, and the *Globe and Mail*, one of Canada's leading daily newspapers) and two local newspapers (the *Western Star* based on NL's west coast and the *Telegram*, NL's major daily newspaper based in St. John's, the provincial capital). We also examined documents obtained via access to information and protection of privacy (ATIPP) requests in NL. The requests cover the period from 2009, when the CRP was first introduced, to December 2016. The final sample consists of 1,100 pages of documents and correspondence on behalf of communities that submitted expressions of interest in resettling to the provincial government, requested information on the cost and benefit analysis, or contacted government staff to express their opinion on resettlement.

A relatively new method for gathering qualitative data, ATIPP requests allow researchers to move beyond what is publicly available and access materials that government institutions may consider to be internal or even secret in nature.[30] We used these documents to gain a better understanding of the evolution of NL resettlement policies over time, including the relationship of resettlement to other issues like the centralization of the fisheries and service provision. These documents also allowed us to delve deeply into the themes of debates taking place *within* communities, and to explore the growing tensions existing between communities and government officials. Finally, in June of 2018, we conducted three days of fieldwork in Little Bay Islands, including participant observation, and two semi-structured interviews.

## THE 2009 AND 2013 CRPS

Resettlement in NL is closely intertwined with shifting resource geography. The first wave of resettlement (1954–77) was motivated by the impetus to modernize the province's economy, industrialize the province's fisheries, and centralize its rural population.[31] Informed by Francois Perroux's "growth pole" theory, centralization posited that "pushing" industry into clusters would generate "propulsive" regional change.[32] The resettlement or "centralization" of unemployed or underemployed fishing communities to growth centres, where there were more work opportunities and better educational and medical facilities, would thus help hit two birds with one stone.

Shifts in NL's fish economy in the early 1990s once again reignited debates about resettlement. The collapse of northern cod stocks shook NL's economy to its core, prompting a moratorium that put 35,000 fishers and plant workers out of work, inducing out-migration and decline across NL's coastal communities.[33] Following the moratorium, the NL fishery transitioned to shellfish, incentivized by new quotas. The rush to build new crab processing plants resulted in overcapacity and extreme competition for crab among companies, prompting a series of plant closures around the island, including in Little Bay Islands and in Gaultois. Chronic unemployment in the fisheries, along with an aging population, motivated rural communities to inquire about government assistance to relocate, whereas the strain of providing government services to a far-flung population simultaneously made the government more receptive to such community demands.[34]

The second wave of resettlement made sure not to repeat the same mistakes as the first, "top-heavy" phase, which had resulted in widespread public backlash in the media and academic circles.[35] All three instalments of the CRPs (2009, 2013, 2016) stipulated that the Department of Municipal Affairs could only distribute information about relocation "provided it receives clear indication that it is responding to a community-initiated, community-driven request for relocation assistance" via a petition from community residents or a written request from a municipality.[36] To qualify for resettlement under the initial CRP in 2009, communities were expected to pass four distinct stages: (1) an initial expression of interest demonstrating that at least 90 per cent of the permanent population is in favour of relocation; (2) a residency status determination conducted by the Department of Municipal Affairs confirming voter eligibility; (3) a costs and benefits analysis indicating clear savings for the government over a 20-year (then 10-year) period; and (4) a community vote confirming support from at least 90 per cent of the permanent population of the community considering resettlement. If the vote was positive, households would receive up to $100,000 to cover relocation costs. Four years later, the 2013 CRP nearly tripled the buyout available, bringing it to $270,000.

As Loo notes, the latest resettlement phase in NL was distinct from previous ones, reflecting the "new" and neo-liberalized "government game": "neo-resettlement comes in the wake of neo-liberalism."[37] Small government means that Ottawa and St. John's won't tell people where to go but are instead willing to let the market speak. Along similar lines, Kennedy notes that the current CRP model is a symptom of the oil boom, having emerged during the period of increased offshore oil revenue.[38] It views communities centred on renewable resources as unsustainable compared to "those on the Avalon Peninsula with oil-based economies."

While "movers" had some agency in the relocation process, notably in deciding where to relocate, so did the "stayers." In the following sections, we show that two facets of the CRP decision-making process — the negotiation of voting rights and the process of community voting — underscore the agency of the stayers. A third aspect — the slow nature of the resettlement process — captures the structural forces in play during resettlement talks that constrain residents' options.

## MOBILITY AND IMMOBILITY IN ACTION
### 1. Negotiating Voting Rights
Because relocation is ultimately decided by a community vote, this process needs to be examined in detail. The 2009 CRP restricted voting to permanent residents only, defined as those residing in the community for at least 183 days in each of the two

12-month periods immediately preceding the town's relocation request.[39] If the vote was positive, permanent residents would receive the full compensation package for the commercial and residential properties they were leaving behind. In contrast, seasonal residents were barred from voting on this issue and did not qualify for the full government buyout.

With such high stakes, deciding who had the right to vote became litigious. Since 2013, NL residents have filed 39 appeals in four separate relocation cases.[40] Given the size of most NL communities and the high threshold required for resettlement to proceed, a small adjustment to the number of eligible voters could have a major impact on the outcome. In the case of Little Bay Islands, a small fishing community off the northern coast of Newfoundland, the successful appeals of voting-aged permanent residents resulted in eight additional people able to cast their vote in the first resettlement vote in 2015.[41] Considering the close results of the vote, with 85 ballots in favour of resettlement and 10 against, the inclusion of a handful of votes may have been sufficient to sway the outcome.

Given the high stakes of the vote and the unpredictability of the outcome, residents quickly realized the importance of mobilizing support and getting a say in the matter. For that, they enlisted the help of journalists and government officials. Several Little Bay Islands residents expressed concerns that the vote was an "unfair process" because it included non-permanent residents who were absent from the community for nearly half a year.[42] Seasonal, non-permanent residents were equally irate for not having their voices heard and for being barred from financial compensation from the government for their seasonal residence, should resettlement proceed. Many wrote to government officials. As one letter to the Minister of Municipal Affairs from the Coalition to Save Little Bay Islands stated:

> We feel that if all homeowners/taxpayers do not have a say, they are being treated unfairly, as we are all taxpayers paying the same amount whether we live in the town full time or not as taxes are not adjusted for part time residents.[43]

Another Little Bay Islands resident addressed the Minister in a postcard, pleading: "This is my home. Please do not attempt to destroy it."[44] Seasonal residents of other communities considering resettlement shared similar concerns. A letter sent to the same Minister by seasonal residents in the southern shore community of McCallum stated:

> We have invested a great deal of money into our home and my question to you and your department Mr. O'Brien is why? Why should we have to lose everything that we have worked so hard over the years because the majority rules and we have no other choice but to leave?[45]

In response to these calls, a 2016 review of the CRP changed the definition of permanent residents to require year-round residency, with appropriate exemptions for work, schooling, and medical reasons. It is unclear, however, if this amendment will resolve the eligibility problems raised earlier by both permanent and temporary residents. Indeed, when asked about these changes, one part-time Little Bay Islands resident stated: "I'm not impressed. They [government officials] are just trying to separate one taxpayer from another."[46]

While some residents exerted their agency by filing an appeal to be granted the right to vote or wrote to their MHA to express their disagreement with the voting criteria for eligibility, others opted to vote with their feet by moving *into* communities after the relocation process was initiated, knowing full well they would not be able to vote. As one such person explained, "we basically stepped up our retirement because of all this resettlement stuff so that we could come back and be part of the community while it still existed as a community" (Interview, Little Bay Islands resident, 2018). This statement again reflects further nuance in migration decisions to stay or leave — indicating a household that migrated in order to stay, but yet not to be part of a formalized resettlement process.

## 2. Process of Community Voting

In most instances of voluntary migration, the decision to relocate is an individual or household one, though it is often the result of a long and intricate reflection on the respective pros and cons that will befall them should they move. In contrast, when relocation takes place at the community level — for example, when nearly every inhabitant of a community must agree to relocate for the resettlement scheme to go ahead — household decisions are compounded by many additional circumstances, notably, the need to decide the minimum threshold necessary for community relocation to take place.

Under the CRP, the threshold for resettlement was set at 90 per cent, significantly higher than the 50 per cent plus one vote usually required for a majority vote in democracies. Although meant to foster community-based decision-making, the high threshold for resettlement ultimately gave tremendous power to a handful of people (sometimes as few as one or two individuals) who steadfastly refused to relocate. A resident of George's Cove, a small community that failed to meet the threshold for resettlement, explained: "Quebec would have separated from Canada if they got 50-plus one per cent [*sic*]. If you have 70 or 80 per cent, they [the government] should let the people move who wants to move."[47] This criticism raises the question whether government-assisted resettlement may, in fact, be counterproductive, to the degree that it encourages holdouts among households with the means to relocate but who prefer to wait for the government buy-out package to do so. Were the financial incentives to disappear, such individuals would leave their community, thus allowing the government to stop ensuring services. While this question is valid, a newspaper interview with the town clerk from Little Bay Islands suggests that most people who had the means to relocate have already done so:

> I cannot believe that 10 people out of 95 are able to hold the other 85 of us hostage in this community, with the majority being seniors and the majority of them who worked in the fishery all their life and being seasonal workers, they don't have the income to back them up to move on their own.[48]

To avoid this "hostage" situation, the government had previously lowered the community consensus from 90 to 80 per cent.[49] But a lower threshold simultaneously means that resettlement may get the "go ahead" even if a larger proportion of the population is against it, resulting in criticisms that it forcefully uproots people who wish to remain in their communities. For this reason, the provincial government reinstated its 90 per cent threshold in 2009.

The results of the 2015 relocation vote in Little Bay Islands, with 89.47 per cent of the population in favour of resettlement, tested the strictness of government adherence to the threshold and highlighted the highly controversial nature of a few decimal points. A former mayor of Little Bay Islands cautioned: "It's not going to be a pleasant time in this community if the number is not there" (i.e., if the government did not round up the figure to the required 90 per cent).[50] After a lengthy review of the rules, the province re-affirmed that community relocation would only proceed if at least 90 per cent of all permanent residents in a town agreed.[51]

As expected, this decision was not received well in Little Bay Islands. When he found out the process of relocation for Little Bay Islands would not proceed any further, a resident indicated his "unbelief and utter disgust," claiming that after being part of this process for several years, residents of Little Bay Islands now feel as if they had been "kicked in the gut while we were down."[52] Another resident lamented: "My disappointment is not in the people of Little Bay Islands, my disappointment is in the government."[53] The residents of Little Bay Islands eventually mended their wounds and voted unanimously in favour of resettlement in February of 2019,[54] while the NL government recently approved $10 million to relocate the remaining 54 permanent residents.[55]

This threshold was adopted to ensure that no one would be forced to move against their will. But requiring such a high degree of consensus, where a handful of votes may suffice to prevent resettlement, has damaged the unity of small communities. Asked about the effect of resettlement talks in his town, a resident of McCallum explained: "There's a lot of animosity within the community and it's really hard to communicate with people . . . they've created a lot of broken families, friends and divided the community."[56] Part of the problem is that it is nearly impossible for people to vote truly anonymously in small communities, where everyone knows one another:

> No one knows who voted for or who voted against because that was never released by government, but of course you live in the town and it's a small place and you hear people say "Well I hope this don't go through" or "I hope it do go through", so you do have ideas of which way they voted. . . . Everyone has their suspicions.[57]

Alternatively, individuals who wanted to stay put often experienced coercive group pressures from the majority of the population. Here, employed permanent residents, often a small segment of the population in aging communities dependent on fishing, resented being driven from their homes by the unemployed or underemployed majority. As one employed resident of Little Bay Islands explained in his personal communication to the Minister of Municipal Affairs, not so subtle threats were made towards him and his family:

> We are being told by those wanting to leave, if we do not vote for the latest offer, this will not be a friendly neighbourhood. This program [resettlement] is already destroying our community and it will certainly destroy my life if I have to give up my job and move, but irreparable damage has already been done and for the safety and well-being of my family, I will have to go.[58]

In an effort to accommodate those wishing to stay put, the 2009 CRP initially ensured that the government would provide residual services (electricity, water, snow-clearing) to residents choosing to remain in a relocated community. This provision, however, was cut in the 2016 revisions of the CRP. Residents must now weigh their desire to stay in a community without drinking water or electricity, with saying goodbye to a place that has been their home for generations. One may wonder then about the impact of this subtle pressure on the people to move or do without amenities. The 31 permanent residents of Grand Bruit faced such a dilemma as they saw their school close, followed by the post office, and the end of ferry and power services in the summer of 2010.[59] With fewer and fewer services at their disposal, can we conclude reasonably that these individuals "chose" to relocate in the late summer of 2010? Was there truly an alternative for those who wished to stay? A clause in the CRP allows property owners who have received relocation assistance to retain title to their properties and access them as desired; however, they first need to obtain a permit to occupy properties in "vacated communities" as per the Evacuated Communities Act, 2016, and accessing and occupying properties in relocated communities is done so at the cost and risk of property owners.[60] Besides, emptied of its other residents, and with reports that resettled sites have sometimes been broken into, these deserted places are now nothing like the former homes that brought "spatial mooring" to people, connecting them to their communities and the physical landscape.[61]

## 3. Relocation in Slow Motion

The four distinct steps of the community relocation process can easily drag on for years, creating substantial uncertainty in those directly involved. In Little Bay Islands, from the time the community initially expressed interest in participating in the CRP in April 2013 to their actual relocation on 31 December 2019, after the second (unanimous) resettlement vote, over six years had elapsed.[62] During this waiting game, communities considering resettlement are frozen. Months and in some cases years of uncertainty drain small outport communities of their social vitality. Towns that are already struggling to prevent youth out-migration now face the seemingly insurmountable task of filling vacancies on the town council or maintaining a functioning fire department in the context of an aging population. Once these vital community services are lost, total abandonment is almost inevitable. Residents, fearing they will have to leave sooner or later, refuse to invest in the upkeep of either communal or private property, making it harder for them to sell their properties in the future were resettlement not to go ahead. In our interviews at Little Bay Islands, one resident noted that "it's almost like a self-fulfilling prophecy." He explained:

> you've stopped living today for the promise of something that may not come in the future, and if there's one sad thing about this whole thing it's that people have put their lives on hold for the promise of government money that may never arrive. (Interview, Little Bay Islands resident, 2018)

A series of letters written by Little Bay Islands residents to various government officials captured increasing frustrations at the length of the process and the nefarious impact it had on community morale and relations.[63] Little Bay Islands was not the only community in limbo. After a decisive 97 per cent vote in favour of resettlement in the spring of 2009, the community of Grand Bruit spent the summer wondering if the government would agree with its wishes. As the chair of the local service district explained:

> We've been on hold and everyone in the community has been worried about this all summer long. Some people have things they would want to do with their homes if they are going to be staying here for the next five years or more, but which can probably wait if they will only be using their homes as summer cottages.[64]

As the above indicates, residents' ability to decide their own fate was thus put to the test by the slow and uncertain nature of the resettlement process.

## CONCLUSION

The migration decision approach sheds a light on the agency of individuals in communities considering resettlement. Far from being a "done deal" inevitably resulting in out-migration and community closures, residents have fought for the right to stay put. Individuals deemed previously ineligible went to court to gain a say in the resettlement decision. Others contacted their MHA or various ministers to make a more personal plea. Still others decided to move into the communities considering resettlement while they remained "open" or hospitable. Attempts were made by individuals to cajole, sway, if not outright coerce, their fellow community members to vote against, or for, relocation. As this chapter shows, "no" votes should not be seen as embracing the status quo or passivity: they were often anything but.

And yet, decision-makers in democratic contexts also see their agency curtailed, notably by the very slow and time-consuming nature of the community-oriented resettlement process that inadvertently closes off some alternatives, making the "choice" of resettlement one in name only. If the government disrupts public services and stops ploughing the only road that connects a town to "the rest of the world," as done in Big Brook, or if it closes the school for lack of incoming pupils like it did in Grand Bruit in 2007, is there really a valid alternative for those wishing to avoid resettlement to remain in their hometown? Together with the case of Greenland, resettlement under CRPs provides an example of resettlement by default, or "passive resettlement" (see Christensen and Arnfjord, Chapter 5).

Newfoundland and Labrador's most recent experience with resettlement illustrates the prevalence of "contented stayers" (those who not only wish to stay but are willing to fight for their rights to do so) and "tied stayers" (those who are staying put in hopes that their community would soon qualify for a government buyout package), as well as "movers," including both *out-* and *in-*migrants. As suggested by Milbourne and Kitchen, the categories people fall under depend largely on their socio-economic means. Some people may be presented with the option to relocate and earn a living elsewhere or to stay put, but the most vulnerable and marginalized people (that is, the elderly and the unemployed) rarely are. It is this nuance that this chapter has aimed to elucidate.

Understanding the process by which democratic communities plan their own migration is increasingly urgent because of the substantial number of communities now facing relocation as a consequence of rising sea levels.[65] The imminent fear of losing one's place had previously been channelled into a powerful source of motivation and mobilization in Newfoundland and Labrador (see Withers, Chapter 3) and elsewhere, including in the Canadian Arctic (see Marshall, Chapter 7). While the places where people resettled from may still physically exist in Newfoundland and Labrador — which may not be the case much longer for future climate-induced refugees in the Canadian Arctic — the limited access people have to them and the deprivation of services and amenities mean that these places are hardly the "home" that they once were.

## NOTES

1   Parts of this chapter have been published in Isabelle Côté and Yolande Pottie-Sherman, "The Contentious Politics of Resettlement Programs: Evidence from Newfoundland and Labrador, Canada," *Canadian Journal of Political Science* 53, no. 1 (2020): 19–37. Reprinted with permission.

2   Government of Newfoundland and Labrador, *Community Relocation Policy* (Department of Municipal Affairs, Mar. 2013).

3   "Little Bay Islands Residents to Relocate by Dec. 31st," *CBC News*, 12 Sept. 2019, https://www.cbc.ca/news/canada/newfoundland- 4 labrador/little-bay-islands-relocation-agreement-1.5281048.

4   Regarding toponymy, in consultation with Dr. Philip Hiscock, we use local conventions around the use of apostrophes wherever possible. William's Harbour, for example, is said to be named after William Russell, hence we use the apostrophe, although the *Encyclopedia of Newfoundland and Labrador* spells it as "Williams Harbour." The etymology of other place names is less clear: Nippers Harbour may stem from the name Nippard or could refer to the presence of "nippers" (mosquitos). Snooks Arm is locally often spelled as "Snook's Arm," although other sources omit the

apostrophe. See Cyril F. Pool and Robert H. Cuff, eds., *Encyclopedia of Newfoundland and Labrador*, vols. 3–5 (St. John's: Harry Cuff Publications, 1994).

5    Samuel Bazzi, A. Gaduh, A.D. Rothenberg, and M. Wong, "Skill Transferability, Migration, and Development: Evidence from Population Resettlement in Indonesia," *American Economic Review* 106, no. 9 (2016): 2658–98; Michael M. Cernea, "The Risks and Reconstruction Model for Resettling Displaced Populations," *World Development* 25, no. 3 (1997): 1569–87; Isabelle Côté, "Horizontal Inequalities and Sons of the Soil Conflict in China," *Civil Wars* 17, no. 3 (2015): 357–78; Brooke McDonald, M. Webber, and D. Yuefang, "Involuntary Resettlement as an Opportunity for Development: The Case of Urban Resettlers of the Three Gorges Project, China," *Journal of Refugee Studies* 21, no. 1 (2008): 82–102; Brooke Wilmsen and M. Webber, "Mega Dams and Resistance: The Case of the Three Gorges Dam, China," in *Demanding Justice in the Global South*, eds. J. Nem Singh, L.B. Fontana, A. Uhlin, and J. Grugel (London: Palgrave Macmillan, 2017), 69–98.

6    L.C. Hamilton, K. Saito, P.A. Loring, R.B. Lammers, and H.P. Huntington, "Climigration? Population and Climate Change in Arctic Alaska," *Population and Environment* 38, no. 2 (2016): 115–33; J.K. Maldonado, C. Shearer, R. Bronen, K. Peterson, and H. Lazrus, "The Impact of Climate Change on Tribal Communities in the US: Displacement, Relocation, and Human Rights," *Climatic Change* 120, no. 3 (2013): 601–14.

7    T. Hammar and K. Tamas, "Why Do People Go or Stay?" in *International Migration, Immobility and Development: Multidisciplinary Perspectives*, eds. T. Hammar, G. Brochmann, K. Tamas, T. Faist (New York: Berg, 1997), 1–19.

8    P.J. Cloke, P. Milbourne, and R. Widdowfield, "The Complex Mobilities of Homeless People in Rural England," *Geoforum* 34 (2003): 21–35.

9    Paul Milbourne and Lawrence Kitchen, "Rural Mobilities: Connecting Movement and Fixity in Rural Places," *Journal of Rural Studies* 34 (2014): 328.

10    Jørgen Carling and Francis Collins, "Aspiration, Desire and Drivers
      of Migration," *Journal of Ethnic and Migration Studies* 44, no. 6
      (2018); Derek McCormack and Tim Schwanen, "Guest Editorial:
      The Space—Times of Decision Making," *Environment and Planning
      A* 43, no. 12 (2011): 2801–18; Vickie Zhang, "Im/mobilising the
      Migration Decision," *Environment and Planning D: Society and
      Space* 36, no. 2 (2018): 199–216; Francis L. Collins, "Desire as a
      Theory for Migration Studies: Temporality, Assemblage and
      Becoming in the Narratives of Migrants," *Journal of Ethnic and
      Migration Studies* 44, no. 6 (2018): 964–80; Anna Hjälm, "The
      'Stayers': Dynamics of Lifelong Sedentary Behaviour in an Urban
      Context," *Population, Space and Place* 20, no. 6 (2014): 569–80;
      Charyl E. Morse and Jill Mudgett, "Happy to Be Home: Place-Based
      Attachments, Family Ties, and Mobility among Rural Stayers,"
      *Professional Geographer* 70, no. 2 (2018): 261–69; Clara H. Mulder
      and Gunnar Malmberg, "Local Ties and Family Migration,"
      *Environment and Planning A* 46, no. 9 (2014): 2195–2211.

11    Zhang, "Im/mobilising the Migration Decision," 202.

12    Aileen Stockdale and Tialda Haartsen, "Editorial Introduction:
      Putting Rural Stayers in the Spotlight," *Population, Space and Place*
      24, no. 4, e2124 (2018).

13    As noted by Stockdale and Haarsten, "Editorial Introduction."

14    Hjälm, "The 'Stayers'," 577; Aileen Stockdale, Nicky Theunissen,
      and Tialda Haartsen, "Staying in a State of Flux: A Life Course
      Perspective on the Diverse Staying Processes of Rural Young
      Adults," *Population, Space and Place* 24, no. 1, e2139 (2018): 1.

15    R. Coulter, M.V. Ham, and A.M. Findlay, "Re-thinking Residential
      Mobility: Linking Lives through Time and Space," *Progress in
      Human Geography* 40, no. 3 (2016): 367.

16    Holly R. Barcus and Stanley D. Brunn, "Place Elasticity: Exploring a
      New Conceptualization of Mobility and Place Attachment in Rural
      America," *Geografiska Annaler: Series B, Human Geography* 92, no. 4
      (2010): 281–95; Morse and Mudgett, "Happy to Be Home."

17    Morse and Mudgett, "Happy to Be Home."

18    Milbourne and Kitchen, "Rural Mobilities," 335.

19  Barcus and Brunn, "Place Elasticity"; Per Gustafson, "Roots and
    Routes: Exploring the Relationship between Place Attachment and
    Mobility," *Environment and Behavior* 33, no. 5 (2001): 667–68.
20  Milbourne and Kitchen,"Rural Mobilities," 328.
21  Luke Spencer, "The Ghost Villages of Newfoundland," *Atlas
    Obscura*, 26 July 2017.
22  Tristin Hopper, "Haunting Images of Life inside Little Bay Islands,
    a Depopulated Newfoundland Town," *National Post*, 1 Feb. 2018.
23  Victoria Herrmann, "America's First Climate Change Refugees:
    Victimization, Distancing, and Disempowerment in Journalistic
    Storytelling," *Energy Research & Social Science* 31 (2017): 205–14.
24  Ibid., 211.
25  Kai Schmidt-Soltau and Dan Brockington, "Protected Areas and
    Resettlement: What Scope for Voluntary Relocation?" *World
    Development* 35, no. 12 (2007): 2194.
26  Ibid., 2184.
27  Y.D. Gebre,"Contextual Dimension of Migration Behaviors: The
    Ethiopian Resettlement in Light of Conceptual Constructs," *Journal
    of Refugee Studies* 15, no. 3 (2002): 270.
28  Brooke Wilmsen and Mark Wang, "Voluntary and Involuntary
    Resettlement in China: A False Dichotomy?" *Development in
    Practice* 25, no. 5 (2015): 617.
29  Liza M. Mügge, "Bridging the Qualitative-Quantitative Divide in
    Comparative Migration Studies: Newspaper Data and Political
    Ethnography in Mixed Method Research," *Comparative Migration
    Studies* 4, no. 1 (2016): 17.
30  Sarah Turnbull, "Using Access to Information Requests to Gather
    Qualitative Data," University of Oxford, Faculty of Law, 6 Apr. 2015,
    https://www.law.ox.ac.uk/centres–institutes/centre-criminology/
    blog/2015/04/using-access-information-requests-gather.
31  Miriam Wright, *A Fishery for Modern Times: The State and the
    Industrialization of the Newfoundland Fishery, 1934–1968* (Toronto:
    Oxford University Press, 2001), 148.
32  Benjamin Higgins, *Regional Development Theories and Their
    Application* (New York: Routledge, 1997), 91.

33   Charles Mather, "From Cod to Shellfish and Back Again? The New Resource Geography and Newfoundland's Fish Economy," *Applied Geography* 45 (2013): 402–09.

34   "Resettlement Offer Appealing to Tiny N.L. Communities, Say Leaders," *CBC News*, 29 Mar. 2013.

35   George Withers, "Reconstituting Rural Communities and Economies: The Newfoundland Household Resettlement Program, 1965–1970," PhD diss., Memorial University of Newfoundland, 2016.

36   Government of Newfoundland and Labrador, *Community Relocation Policy.*

37   Tina Loo, "'The Government Game:' Resettlement Then and Now," *Canadian History and Policy, Active History,* 16 June 2013, http://activehistory.ca/2013/06/the-government-game-resettlement-then-and-now/.

38   John C. Kennedy, *Encounters: An Anthropological History of Southeastern Labrador* (Montreal and Kingston: McGill-Queen's University Press, 2015).

39   Access to Information and Protection of Privacy Act (ATIPP), request addressed to Department of Municipal Affairs, Government of Newfoundland and Labrador: "All documentation and calculations related to the Cost Benefit Analysis for the community relocation of Snooks Arm, McCallum, Round Harbour, Williams Harbour, Nippers Harbour, AND Grand Bruit," 12 Dec. 2016, 28.

40   Ibid., 1, 62.

41   ATIPP, request addressed to Department of Municipal Affairs, Government of Newfoundland and Labrador: "Any and all communications to and from the office of the Minister of Municipal Affairs relating to the closure or resettlement of any community within Newfoundland and Labrador for the period January 1, 2010 to the present (April 10, 2013)," 30 May 2013, 10.

42   Garrett Barry, "N.L. Government Holds Line on 90% Threshold for Resettlement: Changes Coming to Relocation Policy in Newfoundland and Labrador," *CBC News*, 29 Nov. 2016.

43   ATIPP, 30 May 2013, 183–84.

44   For example, ibid., 176–77.

45  ATIPP, 30 May 2013, 318–20.

46  Julia Cook, "Resident of Little Bay Islands 'Not Impressed' by Changes to Relocation Policy," *CBC News*, 1 Dec. 2016.

47  C. Hurley, "Everybody in George's Cove Wants to Resettle: A Survey," *The Western Star*, 24 May 2013.

48  "Q&A: One Resident's Thoughts on a Failed Bid to Resettle Newfoundland Community," *The Telegram*, 27 Jan. 2016.

49  B. Walsh, "Exodus from Joey's Outports: Voyage to a Finer Life?" *The Globe and Mail*, 30 Nov. 1968.

50  "Fate of Little Bay Islands Unknown after Close Resettlement Vote," *CBC News*, 12 Nov. 2015.

51  Barry, "N.L. Government Holds Line."

52  ATIPP, 12 Dec. 2016, 57–58.

53  Cook, "Resident of Little Bay Islands 'Not Impressed'."

54  "Little Bay Islands Votes Unanimously to Resettle," *CBC News*, 14 Feb. 2019, https://www.cbc.ca/news/canada/newfoundland-labrador/littlebay-islands-unanimous-resettlement-vote-1.5019053; "Little Bay Islands Residents to Relocate by Dec. 31st," *CBC News*, 12 Sept. 2019.

55  Leigh Anne Power, "Little Bay Islands Gets $10M to Cover Resettlement Tab," *CBC News*, 19 Apr. 2019.

56  L. Howells, "Resettlement Policy Needs Reform: McCallum Resident," *CBC News*, 8 June 2015.

57  "Q&A: One Resident's Thoughts," *The Telegram*.

58  ATIPP, 30 May 2013, 174.

59  B. Thomas, "Resettlement: Last Residents Leave Grand Bruit," *The Telegram*, 15 July 2010.

60  Government of Newfoundland and Labrador, "Evacuated Communities Act" (2016); Government of Newfoundland and Labrador, "Community Relocation Policy, FAQ" (2019).

61  See, for example, Glen Whiffen, "Newfoundland and Labrador's Forced Resettlement a Historic Injustice, Brothers say," *The Telegram*, 15 Dec. 2017, https://www.thetelegram.com/news/local/newfoundland-and-labradors-forced-resettlement-a-historic-injustice-brothers-say-170787/.

62 ATIPP, request addressed to Department of Municipal Affairs, Government of Newfoundland and Labrador, "All documentation and calculations related to the Cost Benefit Analysis for the community relocation of Little Bay Islands and the final report," 29 Feb. 2016.

63 For example, ATIPP, 12 Dec. 2016, 65, 67.

64 G. Kean, "Decision Time: Residents Offered up to $100,000 to Relocate," *The Western Star*, 24 Sept. 2009.

65 For example, Hamilton et al., "Climigration?"

# PART II:

RESETTLEMENT IN GREENLAND,
IRELAND, AND CANADA'S ARCTIC

# CHAPTER 5

## Resettlement, Urbanization, and Rural–Urban Homelessness Geographies in Greenland

JULIA CHRISTENSEN *and* STEVEN ARNFJORD

### INTRODUCTION

On a June 2018 evening in Nuuk, Greenland, with the Arctic summer sun still gleaming, we stood on Steven's balcony overlooking downtown Nuuk. "One, two, three, four . . . ," we counted the construction cranes scattered across the skyline. "Five, six, seven, eight . . . nine!" From the vantage point of Steven's townhouse we were able to count two hands' worth of cranes, busily assembling new residential high rises and government buildings across the Nuuk skyline. The total number of cranes we counted that evening was only a fraction of those we saw in Nuuk over the course of that summer. A local newspaper ran the headline "Bygge-Boom" (building boom) across its front page, an image that it then featured in poster promotions all summer long. In a participatory photography workshop we held as a part of our ongoing research on housing and homelessness in Nuuk, the topic of rapid development in the city was frequently discussed. Nothing was the same, and yet so much was: the rural–urban disparities driving the most recent wave of urban development were a familiar reflection of resettlement policies that have framed settlement geographies in Greenland since the earliest days of Danish colonization. What we see today in the city, and what we wish to explore in this chapter, is the mutual process of (re)settlement[1] and urbanization that has, through various programs and over various decades, come to characterize Greenlandic social, cultural, economic, and political landscapes, and that frames the geographies of housing insecurity and homelessness that we explore in our work.

During the 1950s and 1960s the Danish state, together with a Greenlandic council, actively pursued the centralization of previously nomadic Greenlanders (Kalaallit/Inuit).[2] Though (re)settlement policies were enacted to promote Greenlandic participation in the wage economy and facilitate administration by the colonial state, there were profound social and spatial implications as well. Among the key tools to promote settlement were the expansion of a public health program and improved social welfare services, including education, public housing, and income support. The intention was to bring Greenlanders into the administration and culture of the Danish state — including language and culturally-rooted practices of home, health, family, and social organization. The Greenlandic language and traditional culture were undermined through policies like "Danification" (*Danisering*), and select "promising" youth were removed to boarding schools in Denmark. These practices disrupted and dislocated Greenlandic homes, health, family, and community — the effects of which are ongoing today in what scholars articulate as the intergenerational effects of colonialism, namely, negative effects on mental and physical health, family and community relations, sense of place, and cultural identity.

Significantly, Christensen and Hansen and Andersen have suggested that these uneven geographies of social welfare institutions have a critical presence in Arctic homeless pathways, and Greenland is no exception.[3] Those at particular risk of homelessness include low-income northerners who face compounding life challenges, framed in large part by chronic housing need, poor mental health (including trauma), developmental disabilities, addictions, and breakdowns in intimate, family, and community relationships, risk factors that are indelibly tied to the socio-cultural and material legacies of colonialism and modernization in the Arctic.[4] The absence of key health and social supports in villages (*bygder* in Danish and *nunaqarfik*[5] in Kalaallit) and their concentration in urban centres is an important outcome of resettlement that directly affects the (im)mobility of Greenlanders experiencing housing insecurity and homelessness.

Today, Nuuk, with a population of about 18,000, is a city undergoing incredible expansion, building up and out at a pace that is almost impossible to track. The fervent push behind this rapid development, however, is not only to meet the needs of people who currently call the city home, but also the thousands of Greenlanders that the municipality of Sermersooq (which includes Nuuk) and the Greenlandic government plan to resettle in the coming years. Twenty minutes from central Nuuk, a new Sermersooq subdivision — Siorarsiorfik — will be the largest urban development project ever in Greenland, designed to address significant population growth and persistent housing need in the municipality, as well as draw young Greenlanders living abroad back to the country's capital. Two new primary schools, one secondary school, and a 20,000 square metre retail area are also planned. In addition, a large indoor stadium and art museum —

both to be designed by the famous Danish architect Bjarke Ingels — are also proposed. A large tunnel will be constructed to link the new neighbourhood to Nuuk Centre.

As we explore in this chapter, this latest urban expansion plan is part of a very long historical trajectory of (re)settlement and urbanization in Greenland. This trajectory has been a core element in Danish colonial policy in Greenland, and has thus rendered urban and colonial forms and processes largely inextricable. Yet the current push towards an urban Greenland is not being led from outside by Danish settlement policy, but rather by a single Greenlandic municipality. In contemporary Greenland, an ever-sharpening urban focus has become central to the self-rule government, and in this way resettlement and urbanization have become key strategies towards self-determination, decolonization, and, ultimately, total independence from the Danish state. These urban aspirations have been achieved, we suggest here, by both passive and overt urbanization strategies aimed over the years at rendering village life economically unsustainable.

Greenland is the world's largest island, covering an expanse of more than two million square kilometres and stretching from Cape Farewell in the south to Oodaq Island in the high North. Approximately 80 per cent of the land surface is covered by an ice sheet. Greenland's 56,000 inhabitants are settled in 17 towns and some 60 smaller settlements primarily along the west and east coast, which since 2018 have been administratively organized into five municipal regions (see Figure 5.1). Notably, there is no national road system, and therefore transportation between settlements is achieved primarily by helicopter, small airplane, boat, dogsled, and snowmobile. Not surprisingly, transportation is expensive, which further limits mobility between communities.

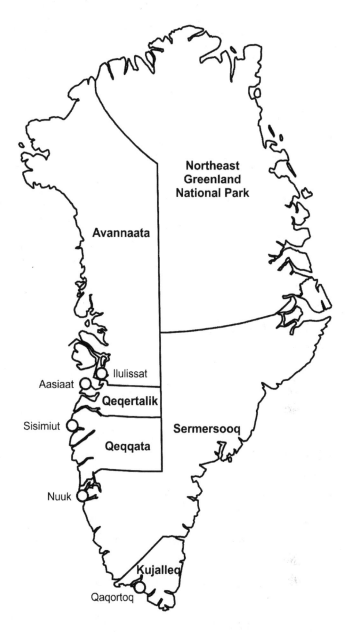

**Figure 5.1.** Greenland's main regions. Map by Jonathan Carter.

About 90 per cent of Greenland's population is ethnically Green-landic (Kalaallit/Inuit) and the remainder is mainly Danish.[6] While Greenlandic is the country's official language, Danish is also widely spoken.[7] However, Hansen et al. note significant dis-parities in Danish literacy levels between villages and urban communities in Greenland.[8] Today, Greenland is self-governed (hereafter referred to as Self Rule). While Greenland is still in-cluded within the Danish Realm, the country has autonomy over its central governmental activities, including social policy, educa-tion, health, economy, and housing. Greenland has universal health care and is considered a welfare society following the Scan-dinavian model, meaning that taxpayers pay close to half their income in taxes in exchange for a wide spectrum of publicly administered services.

The population is highly urbanized, with well over 30 per cent of Greenlanders living in the capital city, Nuuk, and over 85 per cent living in the four largest settlements combined. Thus, towns and cities play a significant role in the lives of Greenland-ers.[9] While Greenland's towns and cities are not large in popula-tion relative to urban centres in Europe or elsewhere in the world, its largest settlements constitute important administrative, politi-cal, economic, educational, and social centres. "The definition of a town in Greenland," according to Sejersen, "is thus not only re-lated to its size, but moreover to its importance as a centre."[10] The trend towards urbanization in Greenland is only growing, with urban populations rising while the number of rural dwellers is on the decline.[11] This is due in part to the fact that Greenlandic towns have been singled out as drivers of the kind of social change sought after by the Self Rule government.[12] At a referendum in 2008, roughly 75 per cent of the Greenlandic population voted yes to a law giving more self-rule to Greenland, which was later approved by the Danish parliament for implementation in 2009. This move necessitated an aggressive and clearly defined approach to self-determination and independence. At the same time, to finance greater independence from Denmark, the Self Rule government has largely looked to industrialization to lessen its dependency on the annual block grant from Denmark.[13] Speculation around the potential for industrial development has been heightened as a result of possible outcomes surrounding climate change, which suggest easier access to Greenland's resources and placing the country in a strategic position globally vis-à-vis oil and gas development as well as the shipping industry.[14]

Yet, while the Self Rule government plods ahead with its Sermersooq expansion plans in Nuuk, we are interested in what continued rural–urban migration, urbanization, and resettlement mean for Greenlanders experiencing housing insecurity and forms of homelessness. We also seek to explore how the concept of welfare colonialism can be used to interpret the Danish colonial focus on resettlement in order to facilitate the extension of social welfare programs into Greenlandic lives, how social welfare here was intended as a main driver in cultural assimilation and "Danification," and ultimately how the emerging rural–urban welfare geography underlies homeless (im)mobilities in Greenland. Much of the literature on Arctic rural–urban migration has identified this phenomenon as motivated by the pursuit of educational and employment opportunities. Yet in our work on housing insecurity and homelessness in Alaska, the Canadian North, and Greenland, we see a second stream occurring among those who are marginalized from educational and employment opportunities and reliant on institutionalized health and social services.

This has had a particular impact in recent years on Greenlandic youth, who are increasingly represented among those living without secure housing in Nuuk.[15] Finally, we argue that in Greenland's pursuit of modernization and independence through urbanization, without adequate social policy responses to chronic housing need and increasing visible homelessness in Nuuk, a significant number of Greenlandic citizens continue to be marginalized through resettlement. Though the policies and political powers have shifted over the years, and Greenland is now self-governed, the Self Rule government today has done very little to improve or plan for the housing and social welfare needs of socially marginalized Greenlanders.

This chapter emerges from our larger study aimed at understanding the social dimensions of homelessness in Nuuk, Greenland, which began in 2015.[16] We begin with a brief overview of the history of colonialism, resettlement, and urbanization in the Greenlandic context, with a particular focus on the capital city of Nuuk. We also introduce the concept of welfare colonialism and its role in shaping these geographies. The colonial experience in Greenland has been facilitated through the social welfare state, a process that involved significant manipulation of the ways in which Indigenous people organized themselves spatially and socially while simultaneously implicating them in the affairs, desires, and decision-making of state powers in Denmark and then the emerging Greenlandic elite. Thus, the processes of urbanization cannot be disentangled from the larger context of welfare colonialism and its effects on the health and social geographies of the Greenlandic people. Finally, we conclude with a discussion of key themes from our research in Nuuk to illustrate how welfare colonialism and passive and overt urbanization policies intertwine with the absence of social policy on housing and homelessness to exacerbate homelessness in the capital city.

## COLONIALISM, RESETTLEMENT, AND URBANIZATION IN GREENLAND

Greenland was first colonized by Denmark in 1721. Historically, Greenlandic people lived largely nomadic lives, moving across the physical and spiritual bounds of their territories according to the seasons and the availability of the animal and plant resources upon which their lives depended.[17] At the beginning of the colonial period, trade was based primarily on whaling, but by the closing of the eighteenth century the Royal Greenlandic Trade Company (a state company formed in 1776) had established a large number of small trading posts along the west coast.[18] The Company offered basic provisions to Greenlandic hunters in exchange for skins and furs. The Danish state favoured this decentralized settlement pattern at the time, believing it supported a high level of self-sufficiency and facilitated trade in products of the hunt, while still encouraging traditional subsistence lifestyles.[19] Of course, this was a naive way of thinking, as Greenlanders were increasingly implicated in Danish trade, religion, and social life, not to mention the marriages, families, and friendships that resulted from relationships between Greenlanders and Danes.

However, the decentralized settlement pattern was a thorn in the side of the Christian missionaries, who felt it was prohibitive to religious education and cultural assimilation.[20] Thus, the mission encouraged Greenlandic concentration at the trading posts where missionaries were already present.[21] These conflicting settlement strategies enmeshed Greenlandic people into complicated relationships with both the church and the state as they came to depend on the mission and trade for help and support. Many of the emerging colonial towns constituted centres for larger regions and were indeed attractive for many Greenlanders due to the trade goods, job opportunities, welfare system, and social security compared to the conditions in the smaller communities and trading posts.[22] This structure of colonial establishments ("colonies"), villages, and outposts stayed unchanged until the years following World War II.

Similar to experiences in Alaska and the Canadian North, the period around and following World War II brought about unprecedented transformation for Greenland. During the war, Greenland was entirely cut off from Denmark, and relationships with the US as well as Canada were established. After the war Denmark signed a new constitution that changed Greenland's status as a colony of Denmark to that of a province, and gave Danish citizenship to all Greenlanders. As Stenbaek explains, this shift in relationship led many Danes to believe that Greenlanders (or "northern Danes") and Greenland should be remade into a northern Denmark — a social, spatial, and indeed cultural reflection of the state of Denmark.[23] As such, "a pseudo-blueprint of Danish society — its institutions, its architecture, its educational system, etc. — should be impressed on Greenland."[24] A shift in ideology thus occurred during and following the war as the Danish state saw the economic, administrative, and geopolitical advantages of centralization and of the assimilation of Arctic peoples into Danish cultural practices and modes of social organization. World War II became "the threshold between the old and the new" in Greenland.[25]

The most aggressive resettlement and modernization period occurred from the 1950s to 1970s, under consecutive reform schemes launched in 1950 (G50) and 1964 (G60).[26] These two parliamentary reports — the Report from the Commission for Greenland, published in 1950 and later referred to as G50, and the Report from the Greenland Committee of 1960, published in 1964 and referred to as G60 — were authorized by the Danish government to review the possibilities for development in Greenland. Danish and Greenlandic politicians believed the industrialization of fish production to be an efficient way to improve Greenlandic standards of living. To improve the level of welfare, education, living standards, and the labour market, movement to a handful of chosen towns along the west coast was encouraged by the Danish authorities. Though families were initially invited to relocate through promises of new housing and better economic prospects, many communities were closed down outright, or investments were withheld to encourage a concentration of the population in centres of industrial development, where modern educational, social, and health establishments could be centralized.[27]

Under G60, economic development in Greenland was concentrated in the coastal towns. Between 1952 and 1963, approximately 3,000 households, which included families and extended families, were moved from smaller coastal settlements of roughly 100–200 inhabitants each to fast-growing towns as part of this modernization process. Substantial investments were channelled into infrastructure, housing, production facilities, and education as well as health institutions.[28] Towns became centres of construction work on a previously unknown scale, resulting in abrupt changes to their physical layout, with the building of factories and concrete apartment buildings, as well as roads and other infrastructure. As Sejersen writes, "the construction and running of these fast-growing towns . . . were primarily in the hands of Danes

and, increasingly, the majority of Greenlanders felt like bystand-
ers in the development of their own homeland."[29]

Although improvements to Greenlandic social welfare were
the stated objective, this rapid resettlement had the effect of alien-
ating people from their culture and livelihoods, imposing living
conditions that people were not used to and not culturally prepared for, and led to new social problems.[30] Housing needs were
calculated as the total required for renewal, migration, and population increase.[31] The new apartment units built in the coastal
towns were very small, and were designed primarily for small or
nuclear families, a practice that continues today, despite the fact
that many Greenlandic families lived (and continue to live) in
multi-generational settings. Promises of housing and employment, including bloc housing projects in Nuuk, were central to
these resettlement strategies. One of the infamous symbols of this
period, these high-density apartment buildings, lined in rows in
the centre of Nuuk's downtown, were built to house the hundreds
of families who were resettled from outlying settlements. The new
housing and development plans emphasized high-density housing programs in regional centres alongside the expansion of social
welfare services, which included the implementation of public
health programs, education, and income support.[32] These housing
projects were modern (by the standards of that era) apartment
blocks with sanitation, electricity, and central heating, and larger
indoor spaces were part of a broader modernization project in
Greenland from 1950 to 1980.[33] The apartments were designed for
families engaged in modern employment, and were established
by Danish-organized political committees with little appreciation
for the needs and wants of traditional Greenlandic society. For example, the housing was not suitable for traditional subsistence

activities like butchering a seal, although they did have such modern facilities as sanitation, running water, and electricity. Meanwhile, massive resettlement actually resulted in limitations for the employment and housing opportunities promised by the state, as migration increased competition for the limited supply of both.[34]

These towns were created by direct intervention from the Danish state, planned and partly executed in Danish-led political forums, and finally erected in Greenland by a workforce that, to a large degree, came from Denmark.[35] These workers came to build houses for families from closed-down villages who were moving into towns in Greenland, but these settlements were not really created with the needs of their inhabitants in mind. Instead, they were intended as solutions to the administrative and economic problems of the Danish state.[36] At this time, Greenland experienced what has been described as the period of its most direct colonial oppression, despite the fact that it was no longer legally considered a colony of Denmark, as the welfare system was introduced and Danish intervention was at its highest.[37] Not surprisingly, Greenlanders started to perceive the urbanization process as a colonial project even though the colonial status of Greenland had been formally abolished. The town became the symbolic, as well as concrete, manifestation of Western cultural and political dominance and the arena for assimilation of Greenlanders into a Danish way of thinking and behaving. A similar sense of disempowerment over decisions that have such bearing on daily life can be seen in experiences of relocation and resettlement in Newfoundland and Labrador (see Côté and Pottie-Sherman, Chapter 4).

Critics of G50 and G60 argued that the Greenlandic population was denied a choice in the matter of Greenlandic development, and that the success of the resettlement and centralization policy was ensured through the denial of any possibility for development in the small settlements.[38] As Deth Petersen writes:

> schools and stores were closed down, breadwinners moved away, and the remaining people had to seriously consider whether they had a future in a community whose economic and social organization was partly destroyed by the resettlement process. Those in an economically weak position, such as widows, lost an important source of their livelihood, because donations of meat and other kinds of reciprocal help, depending on the surplus production of the good hunter, had been reduced.[39]

In the 1970s, when the political movement of young Greenlanders pushed for more self-determination as well as societal and cultural processes based on Greenlandic values — the so-called Greenlandization (*Grønlandisering*) — the key words were: decentralization, participation, and co-operative ownership.[40] When Home Rule was consequently introduced in 1979, a financial and political focus was therefore put on a decentralized settlement structure, with an emphasis on small places to compensate for years of negligence by the Danish state.[41] However, the timing of this return to small settlement life was ill-fated: during the 1980s, a shift in sea temperature made expansion of the shrimp fishing industry possible, which then refocused the attention of government away from small settlements and towards the shrimp-based economy in the coastal towns.[42] This, along with efforts to manage the mounting challenges of an aging housing stock and, at the same time, to bolster increased independence from Denmark, led to renewed resettlement and urbanization efforts.

## CONTEMPORARY RESETTLEMENT AND URBAN-IZATION: PASSIVE AND OVERT CENTRALIZATION

Though the 1950s to 1970s brought about significant and un-precedented change to Greenlandic settlement patterns, a prior-itization of the urban and an encouragement of rural–urban resettlement persist today. Centralization now continues through both passive and overt policies meant to disincentivize rural life and encourage urbanization. The geography of settlement in Greenland from its beginning was built around the interests of the Danish state, not around economic sustainability. Though the social welfare state has allowed for the persistence of small villages, the lack of sustainable local wage economies has meant that when services and investment are pulled back, it becomes financially difficult for local residents to stay.[43] This kind of tactic has been employed time and again in Greenland in an effort to encourage migration to Greenland's largest centres. The promo-tion of an uneven geography of key health and social welfare ser-vices on the part of the Danish government, and now the Self Rule government is, we argue, a passive form of resettlement policy that acts as a continuation of early Danish colonial policy in significant ways. Similarly, Ervin postulated that federal policy in Canada promoted the incipient urbanization of Arctic and sub-Arctic regions, encouraging the concentration of northern people into settlements built on southern models, where north-ern Indigenous people experienced minority group status and resulting marginality.[44]

The social welfare state and its uneven spatialization have been central to resettlement efforts in Greenland. Attending to the socio-spatial consequences of this geography is central to un-derstanding the contemporary geographies of housing insecurity and homelessness. Three conceptual bodies work to explain the role of entanglements of resettlement, social welfare, and institutional geographies, and their effects on marginalized Greenlanders. The first is the concept of welfare colonialism.[45] Danish colonial attitudes in the mid-twentieth century established a relationship between Indigenous people and the state that can be understood as welfare colonialism, a concept first articulated by Paine to describe the uneven political and economic landscape for Indigenous peoples in the Canadian North.[46] Since then, the term has been taken up to describe more widely the policies and practices through which liberal democratic (settler) governments both recognize the citizenship of Indigenous peoples vis-à-vis access to welfare benefits, and at the same time effectively deny their citizenship by nurturing their dependency on the state.[47] Through the workings of welfare colonialism, an unequal relationship of dependency is established, through which social welfare programs are then rationalized and used to equalize the material conditions of Indigenous peoples while preserving and upholding the dominant, state-driven ideological framework. Of course, the workings of social welfare colonialism have been enacted in different ways across colonial contexts, and are also uneven in their effects within and between Indigenous communities.

Second, those whose lives have been most significantly altered by way of these relations have experienced, and continue to experience, these dynamics of dependency in particular ways. One such way is through institutionalization, which is in effect the management of the social and health outcomes of colonialism, and the direct result of culturally and contextually inappropriate social welfare programs that fail to effectively address the actual roots of the problems they seek to remedy.[48]

Third, service dependency gives a geography to institutional-ization in the sense that it serves to explain the socio-spatial consequences of institutional change and unevenness, namely that of the rural–urban migration of Greenlanders most vulnerable to homelessness. The concept of service dependency speaks specifically to the relationships of poverty, health and social support needs, and mobility. In the past, academic interest in service dependency has focused on the phenomenon of "service-dependent population ghettos" in North American inner cities, which are spatial concentrations of welfare populations and the facilities designed to assist them. Here, visible homelessness is a direct consequence of the failures of the deinstitutionalization process.[49]

However, while the service dependency literature is focused on large urban centres in southern Canada and the US, where there is considerable diversity between neighbourhoods, the concept offers potential for understanding homelessness and urbanization in the Arctic. Urban centres like Nuuk, or Iqaluit and Yellowknife in the Canadian North, do not have similar neighbourhood diversity, but they instead act as areas of concentrated services for people already in the communities, as well as for those from smaller, outlying settlement communities. In this way, service dependency facilitates an examination of the social and institutional factors that contribute to rural–urban migration among those at risk of homelessness, as well as the rising visibility of homelessness in Arctic urban centres.

Extension of the social welfare state to Greenland following World War II was a key strategy in what was effectively an ongoing Danish colonial interest in Greenland. The centralization of key health and social services in Greenlandic towns and cities produced an uneven institutional geography across Greenland, one that is particularly important to the lives of marginalized Greenlanders who are at highest risk of housing insecurity and forms of homelessness. Under the Self Rule government in Greenland today, urbanization is facilitated through deliberate policies. The most important change in this direction is probably that the 18 Greenlandic municipalities were merged into five large municipalities in 2018, and as a consequence most of the city administration and associated jobs have been gathered in the five municipal centres. Not only has there been a significant centralization of a number of public functions where most publicly or semi-publicly owned corporate offices and administrations gradually have been gathered in Nuuk, but this in turn has had a significant impact on the centralization of post-secondary education, public housing, and health and social services. Parallel to the centralization of municipalities has been the ongoing centralization of health facilities since 2011.[50] The 16 former health districts were amalgamated into five health regions. This centralization was justified by economic advantages and administrative arguments that it would improve the quality of health care.

While important social welfare functions have been concentrated in the core centres of these five municipalities, the implementation of a simultaneous "real costs" policy has also played a key role in encouraging rural–urban movement. While Hendriksen argued that the social welfare state previously served to facilitate small settlement dwelling due to subsidy programs that supported village/settlement life, particularly the uniform price system, policy change in 2005 resulted in a partial reform (*huslejere reform*) of this system.[51] The uniform price system subsidized electricity, heating, and water for the smaller communities, but since 2005 this has been gradually clawed back to create prices in the smaller communities that reflect "real costs" — a reform geared to benefit the economic dynamics in the towns and to promote a transfer of populations from local communities to the more competitive towns.[52] As a result, the smaller communities increasingly find themselves stigmatized and isolated due to changes in the transportation structure and the pricing system. A similar sense of rural stigmatization is found in the Newfoundland case illustrated by Côté and Pottie-Sherman in Chapter 4, where public discourse pits urban Newfoundlanders against those living in small, isolated island settlements reliant on subsidized ferry services.

Framing the landscape of housing insecurity and homelessness in Greenland are the country's historical and contemporary dimensions of resettlement and rural-to-urban mobility. Though the resettlement plans of the mid-twentieth century were enacted to promote Greenlandic participation in the wage economy and facilitate administration by the colonial state, they also had profound social and spatial implications.[53] Centralization policies put into motion a distinct rural–urban geography in Greenland, a geography that frames the emergence of visible forms of homelessness in Greenlandic urban centres. The shifting spatial dynamics of the Greenlandic social welfare state have particular consequences for those who are without adequate education or who depend on health and social services. The very institutions that are central in the lives of Greenlanders living with housing need or homelessness are precisely those that are increasingly centralized in urban Greenland: public housing, emergency shelters (including those related to family violence), the child welfare system, and the spectrum of health services. It is this relationship between historical and contemporary resettlement and homeless geographies that we want to examine here.

## HOUSING AND HOMELESSNESS IN GREENLAND

Homelessness as a Greenlandic social phenomenon is, with few exceptions, presented as predominantly urban and largely Nuuk-centred.[54] A municipal count in 2017 cites an estimate of approximately 878 people living homeless in Greenland as a whole.[55] The absence of a standardized definition of homelessness in Greenland makes it difficult to assess who is homeless and to draw meaningful comparisons between village/settlement and urban communities, or to assess the scale and scope of homelessness within Greenland as a whole. In Nuuk, the conservative estimate of people living under a more permanent state of homelessness is 100–200.[56] Our research, however, has uncovered anecdotal evidence from NGO-based support providers that the number of homeless individuals in Nuuk alone affects upward of 300 people.[57] Moreover, we have found four main experiences of homelessness: (1) men over 30 years of age who struggle with substance abuse and do not have housing; (2) youth with family, social, or economic problems who migrate from small settlements to larger centres in hope of new opportunities; (3) women who either are single or no longer have custody of their children, and who have often been victims of domestic violence; and (4) men and women over 55 who have been evicted from their housing after failure to pay rent.[58] It is predominantly the second and third groups whose experiences of homelessness are framed by the kinds of passive and overt resettlement policy we describe in this chapter.

Recent efforts on the part of the Self Rule government to promote resettlement to urban centres have included a steady decline in funding for housing in smaller settlements and the redirection of those funds towards public housing in the larger urban centres, mainly Nuuk.[59] Public housing in the Greenlandic context, however, does not necessarily mean it is housing for low-income Greenlanders. In Greenland, housing is viewed as a matter of public responsibility and consists mainly of public housing. Thus, the bulk of rental housing in Nuuk, and in Greenland as a whole, is public. Rental housing in Greenland, in other words, is largely administered in one of two ways: through public housing or through public-sector employment. To access public housing, which is administered by Greenland's public housing authority, INI (*Inatsisartut Inissiaatileqatigiifik*), one can add one's name to the housing list starting at age 18. These waiting lists, however, can be incredibly long. In Nuuk, for example, it can take up to 15 years to get an apartment on one's own. Meanwhile, certain jobs within the public sector (i.e., teacher, nurse, university professor) come with apartment assignments. As long as one maintains the post, one gets to keep the assigned rental apartment. Alternatives to the public housing waiting list include (1) getting an education in order to find a job with an assigned apartment or (2) purchasing a private house or apartment, which tend to be both expensive and in short supply. Thus, the Greenlandic housing landscape can be highly problematic for those Greenlanders who do not have adequate education or employment. As several scholars have found, in Greenland there is a distinct village/settlement–urban disparity to Danish literacy, education levels, and employment outcomes, leaving those who migrate from small settlements to the larger centres at a significant disadvantage in the employment and housing markets.[60]

However, the factors contributing to homelessness in Greenland are not only a matter of unemployment, material poverty, or housing insecurity; rather, these factors tightly intersect with trauma and other psychological issues, such as addiction, domestic violence, and other forms of abuse.[61] Hansen and Andersen have documented the existence of vast social issues connected to homelessness in Greenland, such as abuse, problematic upbringing, poor social resources, unemployment, and so on.[62] In addition, a critical linkage exists between the housing situation in Greenland, characterized in particular by chronic housing need, and the emergence of homelessness. For example, as noted above, the housing stock in Greenland consists mainly of public housing, and some of this housing is in poor condition or located in communities where employment, educational, and cultural opportunities are in decline. Yet, alongside the geography of worsening housing need is the continued process of centralization in Greenland.

While the literature on Greenlandic homelessness, though sparse, touches on the dynamics of social marginalization, very little explicitly conceptualizes homelessness in Greenland within its specific geographical, cultural, or social context. For example, research suggests that village/settlement-to-urban and Greenland-to-Denmark migration is a significant factor in Greenland homeless geographies, but the dynamics of rural-to-urban mobility and its role in Greenlandic homelessness have not been well explored.[63] Rasmussen surveyed a representative 1,550 people on the motivations behind their village/settlement-to-urban move.[64] Top responses included education and employment, living conditions, social network, leisure opportunities, and access to public services.[65] Furthermore, the majority of Greenlanders engaging in this migration were young people between the ages of 15 and 25, which reflects a similar observation by Hansen and Andersen that youth at risk of homelessness were likely to engage in such a move.[66]

With the lack of investment in economic and educational opportunities in many of the small settlements, young people in
these communities are forced to seek these opportunities in regional urban centres or beyond. Hansen and Andersen's study, as
well as ours, reveals a growing trend of youth migration to the
cities, particularly Nuuk, and yet young people are doing so without housing.

Meanwhile, the challenges of maintaining an adequate public
housing stock in Nuuk and other regional centres have led to the
adoption of more punitive housing policies. For example, Hansen
and Andersen also indicate an increase in evictions from public
housing between 2005 and 2013, which were due largely to increasing enforcement of rent and housing rules in light of diminishing housing stock.[67]

Uneven rural–urban geographies, intergenerational impacts
of colonialism, and social welfare dependency have been observed
in the context of homelessness in Greenland, and many of these
themes are directly related to critical social issues visible within
Greenlandic welfare society today, including a rise in the number
of children facing social problems and violence against women.[68]
Underneath these immense challenges is the escalation in
homelessness. In fact, housing insecurity has been identified as a
critical element in violence against women in Greenland.[69] Yet
curiously, homelessness is not a prioritized social political issue
in Greenland.

Our interviews with women experiencing homelessness in
Nuuk also indicate a gendered dimension to rural–urban resettlement and housing insecurity. In particular, we have found that
homeless women are an especially neglected group in the spectrum of Greenlandic social policies and services.[70] Raadet for

Socialt Udsatte (The Authority for the Socially Marginalized) has previously declared that women constitute one of the most vulnerable groups of people living with homelessness in the country.[71] Yet Nuuk does not have specific strategies aimed at securing a safe shelter for women in marginalized situations, despite approximately 750 reports of domestic disturbances in the city annually.[72] Moreover, there is nothing in place for women moving to the city to escape intimate partner violence in their home communities, a narrative that presented itself frequently in our interviews with women experiencing homelessness as well as with frontline support providers. Chronic housing need has been shown to exacerbate intimate partner violence in northern communities in Canada, where similar efforts to leave violent homes connect to women's homelessness in northern urban centres.[73] Though there is support for mothers with young children and elderly women, very little exists for single women or women living in or leaving violent relationships.[74]

One further step or strategy is for people to leave the country entirely to seek opportunities elsewhere within the Kingdom of Denmark (which includes the Faroe Islands). This typically means travelling to Denmark, where Greenlanders hold citizenship and where more than 14,000 Greenlanders currently reside.[75] Yet this kind of move does not always mean a brighter future. Recently, the Danish Council of Social Marginalization released a follow-up to a previous report on Greenlandic women living homeless in Denmark.[76] The report describes problematic conditions for these women, such as language barriers, issues with access to education and employment, and disempowered social networks. Thus far, there has been little joint effort between Greenland and Denmark to offer public help to or safeguard for the homeless

Greenlandic women in Denmark, leaving them in the care of local Danish NGOs.[77]

Several signs suggest that homelessness in Nuuk is set to increase over the coming years. Employment and educational opportunities, as well as cultural activities, are increasingly concentrated
in the capital city. The municipality of Sermersooq, which includes
Nuuk, is allocating more land for housing, but not for the low-
income groups. A principle in Greenland's democratic welfare society is that the people affected by political decisions are given a
chance to voice their concerns through public forums. However, in
recent years there has been a shift in the political climate towards
the kinds of neo-liberal, market-oriented policies seen in Alaska
and increasingly in the Canadian North, and decision-making
about housing policy is evolving within the political environment
with no public hearings. Despite the fact that Greenland does have
a small organization of homeless people, homeless people are rarely
included in development of policy, such as the policy that governs
the daily operations of the public shelter in Nuuk.[78]

## RESETTLEMENT, URBANIZATION, AND HOMELESSNESS

Several themes emerge to illustrate the ways in which resettlement and urbanization policies, over time and through both Danish colonial and Greenland Self Rule administrations, have laid
the foundation for visible homelessness in Nuuk. First, in stark
contrast to policy attention towards the encouragement of rural–
urban movement stands the total absence of social policy on
homelessness. There is currently no anti-homelessness social policy in existence at the municipal or national level in Greenland.

The limitations of the ideological belief in housing as a public responsibility are revealed in the absence of social policy directed specifically towards the Greenlandic homeless population. At the same time, we observe the entrenching of significant class divides within Greenland through housing policy: public housing is largely accessible through education or employment, and as a result, class divides are reinforced through housing policy (or the lack of housing policy) as often only those with employment or student status have access to housing. Meanwhile, a multitude of push and pull factors, many of them caused or exacerbated by the centralization policies of the Danish and then the Greenlandic state, encourage the movement of Greenlanders to urban centres. The lack of a social policy response to homelessness in Nuuk results in a holding pattern for those who find themselves without suitable, secure shelter. A very limited number of beds in a municipal shelter are the only option provided by the state, with no emphasis on transitional or supportive housing and associated programs.

Second, the lack of engagement by the public sector has been enabled in some sense by the active engagement of the non-profit sector in programs and services for the housing insecure and homeless.[79] In fact, these new forms of urban community and caring organizations are a positive outcome of the trends towards an increasingly urban Greenland. Local NGOs collaborate with one another to provide services to people living homeless in Nuuk, and they also express a common agenda to empower homeless people and provide forums and networks for people within the environment to voice their concerns. NoINI, Kofoeds Skole, the local chapter of the Red Cross, and Frelsens Hæri (Salvation Army) are filling the gaps in public-sector support, and what is particularly interesting and problematic here is that much of the funding is provided through foreign sources, local fundraising, or a very, very few short-term pockets of funding from the municipal government. If the headquarters for these organizations determined different priorities and refocused their funds elsewhere, the consequences would be disastrous for Nuuk and Greenland as a whole. Significantly, there is very little funding and policy direction from the national government. This is a big concern because housing and other social supports are delivered by municipalities, and with little to no co-ordination or follow-up between municipalities there is a need for more leadership from the Self Rule government. With little federal involvement, the onus falls on the municipalities and does not reflect the national geography of homelessness. Some initial research has been conducted on the developing individual and collective actions of Nuuk NGOs, although it is still at an early stage.[80]

Third, the village/settlement–urban migration patterns of people living without secure housing in Nuuk are bound up in key institutional geographies. In particular, we have heard stories from youth who have been released from boarding homes without housing in Nuuk, men and women who have been sent to Nuuk for psychiatric care and then released without housing, men and women sent to Nuuk for hospital care and then released without housing, men going to the jail but then released, again without housing, and finally women who have migrated to Nuuk to escape violence at home, only to encounter tremendous difficulty in accessing housing once in Nuuk. All told, these geographies reflect the reframing of the intergenerational social and health effects of rapid socio-cultural change and ongoing colonial frameworks as sites for institutional intervention.

Fourth, homelessness as a Greenlandic social policy issue is, with few exceptions, presented as a predominantly urban, and largely Nuuk-centred, phenomenon. Another related factor is the subtle administrative process of prioritizing public housing in the larger urban cities, mainly Nuuk. Therefore, the urban focus is not limited to the facilitation of the wage economy, but also to the administration of health and social services. That homelessness is seen as a distinctly urban issue becomes self-fulfilling or re-enforcing. In order to understand, and ameliorate, visible forms of homelessness in Nuuk, we must expand our focus outside urban bounds to fully attend to the significance of rural–urban dynamics. Moreover, Nuuk is enmeshed in rural–urban, Greenland–Denmark dynamics that extend beyond northern bounds, particularly along historical or contemporary colonial-administrative relations.

## CONCLUSION

On flights out of Nuuk that summer in 2018, there was an in-flight Air Greenland magazine in the seat pocket. Inside was a glossy display of images promoting Nuuk as the cornerstone of urban Greenland — filled with coverage of the emerging new Greenlandic cuisine food scene and modern Greenlandic fashion — side by side with a feature-length article on what resource development could mean for the Greenlandic economy. Though the Self Rule government's plans for urban growth differ from the historical objectives of Danish-sanctioned resettlement, both administrations have used resettlement as a means to promote human territoriality. For contemporary Greenland, urbanization is instrumental in promoting greater independence and autonomy from Denmark, as it cuts down on social welfare administration costs and facilitates the concentration and accumulation of economic resources. Yet in examining the historical and contemporary dimensions of resettlement in Greenland, we find ourselves questioning the agency of socio-economically marginalized Greenlanders in contemporary patterns of rural–urban migration, given the forms of passive and overt incentivization that the Danish and Greenlandic states have imposed over time to encourage centralization. While Greenlanders were excluded from the political decision-making and settlement planning of the Danish colonial state, today's self-governed Greenland is itself exclusionary towards those Greenlanders who have been unable, for various reasons, to fully participate in and benefit from contemporary Greenland society.

Indeed, as Pottie-Sherman, Côté, and LeDrew suggest in Chapter 1, the true costs — economic, political, socio-cultural — of resettlement projects have been largely underestimated, or rather under-appreciated. In particular, we are troubled by the contemporary ways in which the social welfare state has been spatialized unevenly, resulting in a manipulation of vulnerabilities entrenched through welfare colonial forms. These vulnerabilities are particularly significant among those Greenlanders experiencing homelessness, and they are woven throughout the narratives of homelessness shared with us in our research. In this way, the ongoing legacies of (re)settlement are evident, as the intergenerational effects of early resettlement policy underlie the health and social support needs of those Greenlanders experiencing housing insecurity and homelessness in Nuuk today. Loo, in Chapter 2, also explores the contemporary legacies of historical, state-sponsored relocation programs, deftly illustrating how the "will to improve" through resettlement eventually conspired with neo-liberal aspirations more firmly rooted in reducing administrative costs, regardless of the broader social costs. At the same time, resettlement and urbanization are representative of the welfare colonial process as Denmark sought to transform Greenland into a northern image of itself, much in the same way that Withers, in Chapter 3, describes resettlement as symbolic of broader cultural disruptions in Newfoundland.

Yet this is not merely a story of Danish colonial policy. Rather, as we have illustrated in this chapter, present-day urban policy is being crafted and implemented by the Greenlandic Self Rule government. Moreover, this government has been slow to develop a social policy response to housing insecurity and homelessness. This suggests that the dynamics of welfare colonialism, and how passive and overt forms of centralization manipulate service-dependent and housing-insecure Greenlanders, have been entrenched in a trajectory that spans Danish and Greenlandic administrations. It also suggests that many of the spatial and structural inequities imposed by Danish colonial policy and planning in Greenland are tremendously difficult to dismantle. Thus, as Nuuk continues to expand at a fervent pace, and an urban Greenland is promoted to local and international audiences, there is an urgent need for social policy that directly addresses the homelessness in Greenland at a national scale that recognizes the historical geographies underlying what is commonly understood to be a contemporary phenomenon. In fact, housing insecurity and homelessness in Greenland today cannot be extricated from the broader, historical, welfare colonial context. State efforts to encourage resettlement to Nuuk must include comprehensive and robust efforts to ensure the inclusion of all Greenlanders in its urban self-image.

## NOTES

1   We use the term "(re)settlement" with brackets to highlight the
often simultaneous colonial processes of settlement and resettlement in the Greenlandic context. The Danish state implemented
extensive settlement programs in the early colonial period, followed
by historical and contemporary resettlement programs under both
Danish colonial and Greenlandic Self Rule governments.

2   Jens Dahl, "Identity, Urbanization and Political Demography in
Greenland," *Acta Borealia* 27, no. 2 (2010): 125–40; Frank Sejersen,
"Urbanization, Landscape Appropriation and Climate Change in
Greenland," *Acta Borealia* 27, no. 2 (2010): 167–88.

3   Julia Christensen, "Homeless in a Homeland: Housing (in)Security
and Homelessness in Inuvik and Yellowknife, Northwest Territories, Canada" (PhD diss., McGill University, 2011); K.E. Hansen
and H.T. Andersen, *Hjemløshedi Grønland [Homelessness in
Greenland]* (Aalborg, Denmark: Statens Byggeforskningsinstitut,
University of Aalborg, 2013).

4   Peter Bjerregaard and Tine Curtis, "Cultural Change and Mental
Health in Greenland: The Association of Childhood Conditions,
Language, and Urbanization with Mental Health and Suicidal
Thoughts among the Inuit of Greenland," *Social Science & Medicine*
54, no. 1 (2002): 33–48.

5   *Nuna* = land, *qarfik* = place of

6   CIA (Central Intelligence Agency). *The World Factbook: Greenland,
2017.*

7   Ibid.

8   Klaus Georg Hansen, Søren Bitsch, and Lyudmila Zalkind,
*Urbanization and the Role of Housing in the Present Development
Process in the Arctic. Nordregion Report 2013:3* (Stockholm: Nordregio,
2013).

9   Sejersen, "Urbanization, Landscape Appropriation."

10  Ibid., 167.

11  Hansen et al., *Urbanization and the Role of Housing.*

12  Sejersen, "Urbanization, Landscape Appropriation."

13  Mark Nuttall, "Self-rule in Greenland — Towards the World's First

Independent Inuit State," *Indigenous Affairs* 8, nos. 3–4 (2008): 64–70.

14  J.N. Larsen, "Climate Change, Natural Resource Dependency, and Supply Shocks: The Case of Greenland," in *The Political Economy of Northern Regional Development*, ed. G. Winther (Copenhagen: Northern Council of Ministers, 2010), 205–18.

15  Julia Christensen, Steven Arnfjord, Sally Carraher, and Travis Hedwig, "Homelessness Across Alaska, the Canadian North and Greenland: A Review of the Literature on a Developing Social Phenomenon in the Circumpolar North," *Arctic* 70, no. 4 (2017): 349–64.

16  Homelessness in Greenland includes hidden and visible homeless-ness, ranging from couch surfing to sleeping rough. The latter often involves sleeping in the heated stairwells or utility rooms of apartment buildings. In this chapter, we consider the full spectrum of homelessness.

17  Sejersen, "Urbanization, Landscape Appropriation."

18  J. Viemose, *Dansk kolonipolitik i Grønland* (København: Demos, 1977).

19  Nils Ørvik, *Sikkerhets-politikken, 1920–1939; fra forhistorien til 9. april 1940*, vol. 2 (JG Tanum, 1960), 68.

20  Sejersen, "Urbanization, Landscape Appropriation"; Bo Wagner Sørensen, "Nuuk," *Tidsskriftet Antropologi* 48 (2005).

21  Sejersen, "Urbanization, Landscape Appropriation."

22  O. Marquardt, "Socio-økonomiske tilstande i Vestgrønland på Rinks tid: Befolknings-koncentration i kolonibyer og dannelse af loakle 'Brædtmarkeder'," *Grønlandsk kultur og samfundsforskning* 92 (1992): 147–82.

23  Marianne Stenbaek, "Forty Years of Cultural Change among the Inuit in Alaska, Canada and Greenland: Some Reflections," *Arctic* (1987): 300–09.

24  Ibid., 301.

25  Ibid.

26  These development schemes also included the controversial fødestedskriterie, which "made Greenlanders so angry that it

became a catalyst for political and cultural change because of its inherent discrimination." Ibid.

27  Ibid.

28  Jes Barsøe Adolphsen and Tom Greiffenberg, *The Planned Development of Greenland 1950–1979* (Institut for Samfundsudviklingog-Planlægning, Aalborg Universitet, 1998).

29  Sejersen, "Urbanization, Landscape Appropriation," 171.

30  Guldborg Chemnitz, "Udviklingen Som En Grønlænder Ser Den," in *Grønland i Udvikling*, eds. G. Chemnitz and V. Goldschmidt (Fremad, 1961); Marie-Louise Deth Petersen, "The Impact of Public Planning on Ethnic Culture: Aspects of Danish Resettlement Policies in Greenland after World War II," *Arctic Anthropology* (1986): 271–80; Steven Arnfjord, "50 år med socialadministration og socialfaglighed– del 1," *Tidsskriftet Grønland* 65, no. 2 (2017).

31  Deth Petersen, "The Impact of Public Planning on Ethnic Culture."

32  T. Rosing Olsen, *I skyggen af kajakkerne: Grønlands politiske historie 1939–79 [In the Shadow of Kayaks: Greenland's Political History 1939–79]* (Nuuk, Greenland: Atuagkat, 2005).

33  Ibid.

34  Deth Petersen, "The Impact of Public Planning on Ethnic Culture."

35  Helge Kleivan, "Dominansog kontrol i moderniseringen af Grønland," in *Grønlandifokus, ed.* Jan Hjarnø (Copenhagen: Nationalmuseet, 1969), 141–66; Robert Paine, "The Path to Welfare Colonialism," in *The White Arctic. Anthropological Essays on Tutelage and Ethnicity*, ed. Robert Paine (St. John's: ISER Books, 1977), 7–28.

36  Susanne Dybbroe, "Is the Arctic Really Urbanising?" *Études/Inuit/Studies* 32, no. 1 (2008): 13–32.

37  Paine, "The Path to Welfare Colonialism"; Axel Kjaer Sørensen, *Danmark-Grønlandi det 20. Århundrede-en historisk oversight* (Copenhagen: Nyt Nordisk Forlag Arnold Busck, 1983).

38  Deth Petersen, "The Impact of Public Planning on Ethnic Culture."

39  Ibid., 271.

40  Jens Dahl, "Greenland: Political Structure of Self-government," *Arctic Anthropology* (1986): 315–24.

41  Jens Dahl, *Saqqaq: An Inuit Hunting Community in the Modern World* (Toronto: University of Toronto Press, 2000).

42  Larsen, "Climate Change, Natural Resource Dependency, and Supply Shocks."

43  See K. Hendriksen, "Grønlands bygder: Økonomi og udviklings-dynamik" ["Greenland's settlements: Economy and development dynamics"] (PhD thesis, Aalborg Universitet and Danmarks Tekniske Universitet, 2013).

44  Alexander M. Ervin, "Conflicting Styles of Life in a Northern Canadian Town," *Arctic* (1969): 90–105.

45  Paine, "The Path to Welfare Colonialism."

46  Ibid.

47  William Tyler, "Postmodernity and the Aboriginal Condition: The Cultural Dilemmas of Contemporary Policy," *Australian and New Zealand Journal of Sociology* 29, no. 3 (1993): 322–42.

48  See Julia Christensen, "Indigenous Housing and Health in the Canadian North: Revisiting Cultural Safety," *Health & Place* 40 (2016): 83–90; Julia Christensen, *No Home in a Homeland: Indigenous Peoples and Homelessness in the Canadian North* (Vancouver: University of British Columbia Press, 2017).

49  Michael J. Dear and Jennifer R. Wolch, *Landscapes of Despair: From Deinstitutionalization to Homelessness* (Princeton, N.J.: Princeton University Press, 2014).

50  See Hendriksen, *Grønlands bygder*.

51  Ibid.

52  Gorm Winther, ed., *The Political Economy of Northern Regional Development*, vol. 1 (Copenhagen: Nordic Council of Ministers, 2010).

53  See Dahl, "Identity, Urbanization and Political Demography"; Anthony J. Dzik, "Settlement Closure or Persistence: A Comparison of Kangeq and Kapisillit, Greenland," *Journal of Settlements and Spatial Planning* 7, no. 2 (2016): 99; Sejersen, "Urbanization, Landscape Appropriation."

54  Media reports on homelessness in Greenland first appeared in the 1990s; however, they remained largely focused on Nuuk. See P.

Kleist, *Hjemløsbeder om hjælp [The homeless ask for help]* (Nuuk, Greenland: Atuagagdliutit, 1997); Steven Arnfjord and Julia Christensen, "Understanding the Social Dynamics of Homelessness in Nuuk, Greenland," *Northern Notes* 45 (2016): 4–5.

55 S. Petersen, "Der er 878 hjemløseilandet," *Sermitsiaq. Ag,* 27 Nov. 2017, http://sermitsiaq.ag/node/201653; T.M. Veirum, "Nye tal: 878 borgere lever somhjemløse," *Kalaallit Nunataa Radioa,* 27 Nov. 2017, https://knr.gl/da/nyheder/878-borgere-lever-som-hjeml%C3%B8se.

56 Departementet for Familie og Sundhed, *Hjemløsi Grønland: Et skøn over samtligekommunershjemløse [Homelessness in Greenland: An estimate of homelessness by municipality]* (Nuuk, Greenland: Departementet for Familie og Sundhed, 2008); Hansen and Andersen, *Hjemløshedi Grønland.*

57 Arnfjord and Christensen, "Understanding the Social Dynamics of Homelessness."

58 Ibid.

59 See Hendriksen, "Grønlands bygder."

60 Hansen and Andersen, *Hjemløshed i Grønland*; Hendriksen, "Grønlands bygder"; Rasmus Ole Rasmussen, *Mobilitet i Grønland: Sammenfatning af hovedpunkter fra analysen af mobiliteten i Grønland [Mobility in Greenland: Summary of main points from an analysis of mobility in Greenland]* (Nuuk, Greenland: Mobilitetsstyregruppen, 2010).

61 Departementet for Familie og Sundhed, *Hjemløs i Grønland.*

62 Hansen and Andersen, *Hjemløshed i Grønland.*

63 See ibid.

64 Rasmus Ole Rasmussen, "Why the Other Half Leave: Gender Aspects of Northern Sparsely Populated Areas," in *Demography at the Edge: Remote Human Populations in Developed Nations,* eds. D. Carson, R.O. Rasmussen, P. Ensign, L. Huskey, and A. Taylor (Farnham, UK: Ashgate, 2011), 237–54.

65 Ibid.

66 Rasmussen, *Mobilitet i Grønland;* Hansen and Andersen, *Hjemløshed i Grønland.*

67 Hansen and Andersen, *Hjemløshed i Grønland.*

68 Ibid.; Skatte og Velfærdskommissionensbetænkning, *Voresvelstan-dogvelfærd — kræver handling nu [Our prosperity and our wellbeing require action now]* (Nuuk, Greenland: Grønlands Selvstyre, 2011); C.P. Pedersen and P. Bjerregaard, *Det sværeungdomsliv — unge-strivseli Grønland 2011: Enundersøgelse om de ældstefolkeskoleelever [The difficult life of youth — the wellbeing of youth in Greenland 2011: A survey of the oldest high school students]* (Copenhagen: Statens Institut for Folkesundhed, 2012); J. Fievé and P. Hansen, *Flerekvin-dersøgerhjælp [More women are seeking help]* (Nuuk, Greenland: KNR, 2016); M. Poppel, "Citizenship of Indigenous Greenlanders in a European Nation State: The Inclusionary Practices of Iverneq," in *Reconfiguring Citizenship: Social Exclusion and Diversity within Inclusive Citizenship Practices*, eds. M. Moose-Mitha and L. Domi-nelli (London: Routledge, 2016), 127–36; Raadet for Socialt Udsatte, *Udsatte grønland skekvinderi København — Enundersøgelseafkvin-derneslivssituation, problemer, ressourcerogbehov [Marginalized Greenlandic women in Copenhagen – a survey of women's life situations, problems, resources and needs]* (Copenhagen: Raadet for Socialt Udsatte, 2016).

69 M. Poppel, "Kvinderogvelfærdi Grønland [Women and Welfare in Greenland]," in *Kvinderogvelfærdi Vestnorden*, ed. G.L. Rafnsdóttir (Copenhagen, Denmark: Nordisk Ministerraad, 2010), 39–68.

70 Steven Arnfjord and Julia Christensen "De søgertrygheden' — Kvin-derramtafhjemløshedi Nuuk," *Psyke & Logos* 38, no. 1 (2017): 51–71.

71 Raadet for Socialt Udsatte, *Udsatte grønlandske kvinder i København.*

72 Grønlands Politi, *Aarsstatistik 2016 [Annual statistics 2016]* (Nuuk, Greenland: Grønlands Politi, 2016).

73 See Julia Christensen, "'They Want a Different Life': Rural Northern Settlement Dynamics and Pathways to Homelessness in Yellowknife and Inuvik, Northwest Territories," *Canadian Geographer* 56, no. 4 (2012): 419–38; Christensen, "Indigenous Housing and Health."

74 Poppel, "Citizenship of Indigenous Greenlanders."

75 S. Baviskar, *Grønlænd erei Danmark: Enregisterbaseretkortlægning*

*[Greenlanders in Denmark: A census-based mapping]* (Copenhagen: SFI, 2015).

76   Raadet for Socialt Udsatte, *Udsatte grønlandske kvinder i København.*

77   Steven Arnfjord, *Sociale udfordringer hos et mindretal af grønlandske kvinder i DK skal håndteres i (Rigs)fælleskab [Social challenges concerning a minority of Greenlandic women in Denmark need to be handled within the Realm]* (København: Socialpolitisk Forening, 2016).

78   See B. Rørdam, "Mange hjemløsei Grønland [Many homeless in Greenland]," *Hus Forbi* 20, no.1 (2016): 5–6.

79   See Barry and Côté, Chapter 6, for a parallel discussion of non-profit roles in housing provision and resettlement.

80   Steven Arnfjord, "Social udsathed og tuberkulosei Nuuk [Social marginalization and tuberculosis in Nuuk]," *Tikiusaaq* 2, no. 23 (2015): 20–24; Steven Arnfjord, "Hjemløshedi Grønland — og social politiske perspektiver," *Grønland* 67, no. 2 (2019): 71–81.

# CHAPTER 6

## Non-State Actors and Resettlement in Reverse: The Case of Rural Resettlement Ireland

HANNAH BARRY *and* ISABELLE CÔTÉ

### INTRODUCTION

In 1991, the Republic of Ireland experienced a decline in population for the first time in over 30 years as a host of socio-economic problems gave rise to meagre opportunities for employment.[1] This was particularly prevalent in rural areas where industries such as agriculture had traditionally prevailed. Consequently, rural communities experienced a decline in economic and political importance.[2] Meanwhile, the rise in information technology and telecommunication transformed urban centres such as Dublin into hotspots for economic and financial development. Between 1986 and 1991, approximately 23,000 people,[3] mostly young graduates and professional families, resettled from their rural homes to urban centres contributing to rapid urbanization, a social housing shortage, and rising rates of poverty and unemployment.[4]

In the face of such demographic and economic challenges, the Irish government's response remained surprisingly piecemeal.[5] The lack of a coherent state-led strategy for both rural revitalization and urban sustainability opened the door for non-state actors and civil society organizations to develop their own social and spatial policy initiatives. It was out of these circumstances that in 1991, Jim Connolly, a sculptor who had resettled his own family from Limerick city to rural Kilbaha in County Clare, founded Rural Resettlement Ireland (RRI), a free, non-profit, non-partisan program that sought to help urban families resettle into vacant rural homes.[6] Acting almost entirely independent from the state — though receiving limited amounts of government funding — the scheme offered a multi-dimensional solution to both Ireland's urban housing crisis and its problem with rural population decline.

This chapter assesses the opportunities and limitations inherent to resettlement schemes spearheaded by non-state actors, using RRI as a case study. In contrast to the resettlement programs covered in this edited volume that are both funded and organized by state actors — whether provincial, like Newfoundland and Labrador, or national, like Greenland — this chapter asks how effective non-state actors are in devising and implementing resettlement programs meant to redistribute population away from its metropolitan areas and into the countryside. Furthermore, from a theoretical perspective, this study underlines the dilemma of government assistance for resettlement programs. What obligations does a government have in responding to uneven population growth and distribution? How much, if any, is the "right" amount of state involvement in resettlement programs? How can state and non-state actors work together to achieve a common goal, while maintaining separate spheres of influence?

We start by putting Irish population trends in context, presenting a brief overview of the important economic and social transformations that have affected Ireland and other Western countries, before examining the role of counter-urbanization and rural resettlement programs in regenerating rural and urban areas. After summarizing our methodological approach, including our media analysis, we then provide an in-depth assessment of the Irish resettlement experience. We show that the very opportunities and limitations the program generated are intrinsically tied to the limited involvement of the Irish state, for better or for worse. We conclude with an analysis of the lessons learned from the Irish experience and explore whether such a bottom-up approach to resettlement might work elsewhere.

## RURAL DEPOPULATION, URBAN DEGENERATION, AND RESETTLEMENT

Rural depopulation is neither new nor unique to Ireland. It has been endemic since the 1850s in most of Europe and North America.[7] Driven by the out-migration of the "bright and young" following the restructuring of regional labour markets,[8] rural depopulation was a key player in restructuring rural areas into a more "post-productivist" role, as rural economies transitioned from agricultural production to an increasingly consumptive role.[9] Rural out-migration also had a multitude of non-economic impacts, including the aging of the local population and a decline in rural services and facilities, as well as affecting landscape abandonment.[10]

How, then, to regenerate and repopulate declining areas? Most of the literature has focused on measures geared towards regenerating distressed *urban* areas: e.g., the clearance and reconstruction of city slums, improving the provision of social services, or using property development as a catalyst for economic and population growth.[11] But these strategies are ill-advised to regenerate declining *rural* areas, owing to their relative abundance of rural housing left vacant by out-migrants, the ongoing cuts in rural services, and property developers' limited interests for rural areas in general. Instead, the solution appeared to be the very factor that put rural depopulation into motion: convincing people to come back to the land. As Bracey stated 60 years ago, "mobility and migration hold the key to the future of the countryside."[12] Young people are in a particularly important position as far as the future of remote rural areas is concerned, for without the renewal of their population from within, these areas cannot remain viable nor can they maintain their economic functions in the long-term.[13] The need to reverse rural out-migration is even more acute today, as recent economic programs promote endogenous, bottom-up development requiring the presence of local human capital and migration processes may either remove or introduce human capital.[14]

While various aspects of rural population growth and rural in-migration have been studied, including "back-to-the-land" movements,[15] return migration,[16] and lateral rural migration,[17] much has been framed in terms of counter-urbanization processes. First identified in the US by Berry (1976),[18] counter-urbanization, i.e., "population movements into the less densely populated areas of a country at the expense of its main cities,"[19] is now a feature of many countries. Claiming that the term was too broad to cover its depth of meaning, Mitchell[20] proposed three forms of counter-urbanization based on their respective motivation: (1) ex-urbanization (where people retain their jobs in urban areas but choose to live in "bucolic" rural communities); (2) displaced urbanization (where a move to the countryside is motivated by the need for new employment, lower costs of living, and/or available housing); and

(3) anti-urbanization (where anti-urban motivations push residents to escape crime, taxes, congestion, and pollution prevalent in urban areas). Counter-urbanization is thus expected to impact both rural and urban areas for rural in-migrants hail from metropolitan areas, thereby easing demographic pressures on already scarce urban social housing, services, and jobs as they relocate.

It would be a mistake, however, to view rural migration in isolation, as if occurring in a vacuum. Few individuals and households are truly free to move and choose a place of residence without the influence of control factors, such as housing availability and financial means. Local zoning policies or bylaws may give precedence to certain groups while marginalizing others. Likewise, state policies play a key role in affecting the decision-making process of individual migrant households. Examining state intervention and the impact on rural mobility flows in Northern Ireland,[21] Stockdale found that the relaxation of rural planning policies did not automatically permit a rural population revival, though the removal/reduction of these barriers gave way to greater freedom of residential choice. State intervention, she concludes, was seen as a catalyst for a rural population revival.

Besides affecting housing policies and rural planning control, another tool at the state's disposal is population resettlement schemes, i.e., the mass relocation of people. While some of these resettlement programs had a clear economic rationale, many were also devised to redistribute the population away from the country's overcrowded "core" and into its more rural "peripheries," solving some of the country's urban overcrowding problems. China's "Poverty Alleviation Resettlement"[22] and Indonesia's transmigration program[23] are two such examples. Other resettlement programs had more "pro-rural" objectives in mind, for example, to counter rural depopulation and spur rural revitalization in China,[24] Sweden,[25] and Ireland.[26] Given the difficulties in competing with the deep pockets of the state, the literature on resettlement programs initiated, organized, or funded by non-state, not-for-profit actors is, to our knowledge, almost non-existent.

While some studies have highlighted the positive impacts of migration to rural areas, including employment creation, prospects for increased rural expenditure, maintenance of local services, and changes in the composition of rural communities,[27] the dominant narratives of recent population changes — even those focusing on internal rather than international migrants — have been much narrower and more negative, honing in on its detrimental impacts to the host communities, e.g., incomers' "taking over" the running of community activities, rising property prices, "Nimby-ism,"[28] and loss of a distinctive community identity. For Milbourne,[29] the movement of outside groups into rural places, for example, the in-movement of socially disadvantaged and culturally marginalized groups in rural contexts, such as homeless people and travellers, are particularly likely to generate tensions, conflicts, and problems given how these types of mobility are culturally constructed as "out of place" in rural spaces. For him, the movements of disadvantaged people across rural and urban spaces are complex, and may include short-distance moves up the rural settlement hierarchy to places that offer improved employment, housing, and welfare service opportunities, as well as movements of low-income groups into rural places.[30]

What the above discussion puts in stark relief is that incoming rural populations are far from homogeneous, ranging from middle-aged gentrifiers[31] to the urban poor.[32] This level of diversity is perhaps unexpected given how, after all, resettled people or in-

ternal migrants are all citizens of the same country and often be-
long to the same ethnic, religious, and linguistic groups. Yet, it
has been shown that internal migrants' various precarity levels
and access to political and economic resources affect local responses to in-migration.[33] For Lumb,[34] local responses are a matter of the following four factors: (1) the size of the migrant
group(s); (2) how long ago the move was; (3) migrants' previous
links to the host community; and (4) the degree of homogeneity
within the migrant group and in relation to the host population.

Rural population changes are complicated, to say the least. To
use the words of Paul Milbourne, they are composed of "journeys
of necessity and choice; economic and lifestyle-based movements;
hyper and im-mobilities"; conflicts and complementarities; and
uneven power relations and processes of marginalization.[35] Now
that we have better contextualized the economic and social contexts behind contemporary rural and urban population changes,
we turn our attention to our Irish case study.


## METHODOLOGY

In pursuing our research on rural resettlement in Ireland, we adopted a multi-pronged methodological framework, which includes a media analysis,[36] review of policy documents and census
data collection, key informant interviews, and field visits to primary
sites of analysis, including Dublin and County Limerick.

Newspapers are important data sources because they provide
an information record of human activity and enable historical and
comparative analysis.[37] We used news stories as a record of public
debate on resettlement, allowing us to make inferences about the
impacts and limitations of the non-state program.[38] We analyzed

197 newspaper articles covering the issue of population resettlement in Ireland from four national and regional newspapers that best represent the regional and national information landscapes: *Irish Examiner, Irish Independent, West Limerick Leader,* and *Irish Times.* The media analysis covers the period from 1990, when the first mention of RRI — the first program of its kind in the country — was made, to December 2016. Table 6.1 summarizes the frequency of relevant articles in the sample by newspaper and years of coverage.

**Table 6.1.** Media analysis of Irish newspapers.

| Irish Newspapers | Years Covered | Number of Articles |
|---|---|---|
| *Irish Examiner* | 1991–2004 | 40 |
| *Independent* | 1991–2007 | 41 |
| *West Limerick Leader* | 1993–2000 | 9 |
| *Irish Times* | 1990–2015 | 107 |
| **Total** | | **197** |

After compiling the articles, we developed and applied a coding scheme that categorized excerpts according to three objective-driven research frames: Government, Economic and Social Development, and Contentious Politics. The Government frame was used to code excerpts referring to the role that the Irish government played in the planning and execution of resettlement processes, the Economic and Social Development frame includes all references to the economic rationale for rural resettlement, whereas the Contentious Politics frame includes all excerpts that associated resettlement with violent and non-violent resistance. Figure 6.1 shows the distribution of codes as they appeared over each year of the sample.

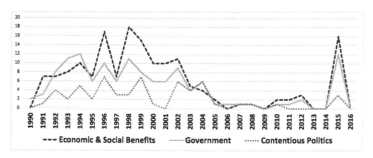

**Figure 6.1.** Media analysis coding distribution.

Finally, in April of 2017, we conducted fieldwork in Dublin and County Limerick in Ireland, which involved three in-depth key informant interviews with local experts on population resettlement in Ireland, including an interview with the founder and chairman of RRI, Jim Connolly. These interviews explored the history of and rationale for the RRI project and for rural resettlement projects in general. Internal documents and reports related to RRI and rural resettlement were also collected during this fieldwork.

## CASE STUDY: RURAL RESETTLEMENT IRELAND
### Overview

The contemporary Irish experience with resettlement is the result of a single grassroots organization, RRI, which was conceived in late 1990 in response to the socio-economic environment of the country at that time. A brief discussion of prior trends in migration and industry is therefore necessary before analyzing RRI's goals and repercussions.

The 1960s and early 1970s were characterized by an Irish economic boom fuelled by an increase in exports.[39] Ireland's entrance into the European Economic Community (EEC) in 1973 led to further job creation, modern skills development, and the diversification of industry. For the first time in over two centuries the small Western European state reported net in-migration instead of out-migration, a strong indication that Ireland's economy was, in fact, expanding.[40] However, soon after, the country experienced a significant financial crash due to the global oil crisis of 1973, which caused the unemployment rate to rise to 18.5 per cent.[41] Two decades later, Ireland was still a poor country by Western European standards, with high poverty and unemployment, inflation, and low growth. Things took an unexpected turn for the better from the mid-1990s to 2008, when the Irish economy expanded at an average rate of 5–9 per cent, thanks to foreign direct investment. This era, commonly known as the "Celtic Tiger,"[42] lasted until 2008, when the global financial crisis nearly brought Ireland's economy to a halt.

The seemingly rapid socio-economic transformations of the 1990s gave way to policy reforms that had a lasting impact on both urban and rural life.[43] Traditionally, the agricultural sector had always been one of Ireland's leading industries — particularly in the rural West.[44] Prior to the 1960s, the majority of the population resided in peripheral areas, where they primarily lived off the land. However, due to the effects of globalization and the rise in information technology and telecommunications, the service sector of urban centres grew in importance.[45] As shown in Table 6.2, such broad economic changes profoundly affected population distribution in Ireland. By 1991, 57 per cent of the population resided in urban hubs.[46] Dublin City and the surrounding counties of Kildare, Wicklow, and Meath all experienced a rapid surge in population growth due to their proximity to employment opportunities,

**Table 6.2.** Population change across Ireland's 26 counties, 1971–1991.

| Province | County | Percentage Change in Population (%) | | | |
|---|---|---|---|---|---|
| | | 1971-1979 | 1979-1981 | 1981-1986 | 1986-1991 |
| Leinster | Co. Carlow | + 7.9 | + 7.6 | + 2.9 | - 0.1 |
| | Co. Dublin | + 9.4 | + 5.0 | + 1.8 | + 0.4 |
| | Co. Kildare | + 20.6 | + 18.8 | + 11.6 | + 5.5 |
| | Co. Kilkenny | + 7.6 | + 6.1 | + 3.4 | + 0.6 |
| | Co. Laoighis | + 6.3 | + 6.3 | + 4.1 | - 1.8 |
| | Co. Longford | + 5.5 | + 2.9 | + 1.1 | - 3.8 |
| | Co. Louth | + 8.9 | + 7.0 | + 3.7 | - 1.2 |
| | Co. Meath | + 16.0 | + 13.5 | + 8.9 | + 1.4 |
| | Co. Offaly | + 6.5 | + 4.3 | + 2.6 | - 2.2 |
| | Co. Westmeath | + 7.2 | + 7.0 | + 3.0 | - 2.4 |
| | Co. Wexford | + 7.1 | + 7.0 | + 3.5 | - 0.5 |
| | Co. Wicklow | + 15.9 | + 10.7 | + 8.1 | + 2.9 |
| Munster | Co. Clare | + 8.1 | + 8.0 | + 4.3 | - 0.5 |
| | Co. Cork | + 7.5 | + 4.1 | + 2.6 | - 0.6 |
| | Co. Kerry | + 4.2 | + 5.1 | + 1.1 | - 1.8 |
| | Co. Limerick | + 7.4 | + 6.9 | + 1.8 | - 1.6 |
| | Co. Tipperary | +10.1 | + 5.6 | + 2.0 | - 5.6 |
| | Co. Waterford | + 7.9 | + 3.8 | + 2.9 | + 0.5 |
| Connacht | Co. Galway | + 7.6 | + 6.3 | + 3.8 | + 1.0 |
| | Co. Leitrim | - 1.1 | - 2.1 | - 2.1 | - 6.4 |
| | Co. Mayo | + 2.5 | + 1.6 | + 0.4 | - 3.9 |
| | Co. Roscommon | + 0.8 | + 1.6 | + 0.1 | - 4.9 |
| | Co. Sligo | + 5.3 | + 4.0 | + 1.0 | - 2.3 |
| Ulster (part of) | Co. Cavan | + 1.3 | + 0.6 | + 0.2 | - 2.2 |
| | Co. Donegal | + 7.7 | + 6.6 | + 3.6 | - 1.2 |
| | Co. Monaghan | + 5.5 | + 4.1 | + 2.3 | - 2.1 |

whereas nearly all rural counties experienced widespread and consistent population decline.

The mass exodus of rural migrants into Dublin and surrounding counties caused a regional crisis within Dublin's inner city. A rapidly growing population gave rise to increasing unemployment. By 1992, approximately 300,000 people in Ireland were unemployed, more than 100,000 of whom lived in Dublin.[47] The rapid population growth also put added pressure on the city's already scarce social housing. More than 50 per cent of Dublin's population resided in some form of public housing, while 30,000 families waited upward of two years for minimal accommodations.[48] Due to financial constraints posed by an overwhelming demand for housing, some young families in economically precarious situations were rendered homeless.[49] The housing problem only widened the gap between Dublin's social classes, and members of the lowest tier experienced greater degrees of marginalization.[50]

As the population of rural communities continued to move east, thousands of homes across the western seaboard became vacant,[51] while the provision of public services declined further. The closure of local schools and post offices and the loss of teaching posts indicated that life in certain communities would soon be extremely limited, if not completely unsustainable.[52] The deterioration of rural life represented something more than simply a generational change in industry and population; it also signified an end to the traditional rural ways of Irish life, the loss of people's habitat and of its voice.

It was in these trying demographic and economic times that RRI was implemented. In 1990, after talking on the radio about the growing problems of rural depopulation and urban poverty in Ireland, Jim Connolly suggested that "craftworker" families from urban centres should receive support to create a life in rural Ireland.[53] Hundreds of people answered his call, and despite having no institutional or governmental assistance, Connolly single-handedly relocated seven families that year, mostly in County Clare where he resided.[54] In 1991, thanks to fundraising efforts, charitable trusts, national grants, and volunteers, RRI was set up as a formal organization.[55] Except for a short stint as a government-sponsored housing pilot project[56] in the early 2000s the program operated almost entirely outside of the government's oversight.[57] Its main objective was to strengthen the future prospects of rural communities; the improvement of migrating families' quality of life was largely a pleasant, though secondary benefit. In order to accomplish that, RRI set out to do four things; (1) purchase empty rural houses; (2) renovate those needing repairs; (3) match urban families with suitable rural units and assist them in making their move through lease or purchase; and (4) facilitate a smooth transition so that families had the resources to succeed, particularly in their ability to become financially independent.[58]

Both host communities and migrants were expected to be active participants in the overall resettlement process.[59] Families interested in availing themselves of RRI's services were required initially to fill out a questionnaire (see Figure 6.2), which allowed the program to gauge interest and comprehensively understand their needs. Ninety-seven per cent of applicants to the RRI program were Dubliners; most of whom were unemployed and receiving social welfare.[60] If deemed suitable for the program's requirements, families were then placed on a wait list. Applicants were asked to check back with the program every two weeks or so, as those who were most enthusiastic and committed to the organization's mission were prioritized for resettlement.[61] During this

## Family Questionnaire

Rural Resettlement Ireland, Kilbaha, Kilrush, Co. Clare
Telephone No: 065-9058034/ 0818 300 444
Fax No: 065-9058243

You are requested to fill in this form on an entirely voluntary basis. This information is required only for the purpose of assisting you to resettle in rural Ireland. NOTE: Should you not wish to answer any particular question, your decision will be respected. Most of the information requested was probably stated in your first contact with us, but it will greatly facilitate our filing system if you could repeat it on this form.

**IMPORTANT:** If you do not return this form either fully or partially completed, it will be assumed that you are no longer interested in moving.

**YOUR DETAILS:**

First Name/s:

Surname/s

Home address:

Telephone No.:

Marital Status: □ Married  □ Cohabiting
□ Single  □ Separated

Adult Ages:

No. of Children (Moving):

Children's Ages:

**OCCUPATION DETAILS:**

Employed:  □ Yes  □ No

Trade / Profession:

Skills, Interests:

If you are receiving support from "Social Services" you should discuss any proposed move with them before making a final decision.

Do you give Social Services permission to discuss your case with RRI personnel?
□ Yes  □ No

**CURRENT RESIDENCE DETAILS:**

Property Status: □ Home Owner
□ Renting

Residence Type: □ Local Authority
□ Private

No. of Years at Present Address:

**PREFERRED RESIDENCE DETAILS:**

Min No. of Bedrooms:

I Would Prefer a House in: *(State County in Order of Preference)*
1)

2)

3)

4) □ Anywhere

I Would Prefer a House in: *(please select on option)*
□ A Town  □ A Villiage  □ The Country

Preferred House Model:
□ Rent  □ Purchase

If Rent, Maximum Rent Affordable:

If Purchase, Maxium Price Affordable:

I Could Buy a Site and Build: □ Yes  □ No

Car Owner: □ Yes  □ No

Special Requirements: (e.g., Special Schools, Location)

Referral to a house is based on a preliminary inspection by our Feild Officer. Families may commission an engineer's report at their own expense if they wish; with the agreement of the house owner.

The provision of a lease is the responsibility of the owner.

Rental agreements are a private matter between landlord and tenant. RRI is neither legally or financially involved. I understand that house owners, or RRI may request confirmation from my present landlord that my rent is paid up to date. The final decision to accept a house for rent is up to myself.

Signed:

Date:

**Figure 6.2.** Family questionnaire used by Rural Resettlement Ireland.

time, RRI's role was more that of a facilitator or middle man between urban families who wished to be resettled and rural landlords who were hoping to sell or rent their properties, though its
role did evolve somewhat over the years as the scheme matured
and new needs arose with its rising demand.

RRI's innovative, grassroots approach to rural depopulation
attracted significant international attention. In 1997, the *Irish Examiner* reported that "Senior Brussels officials" had met with Jim
Connolly to discuss the nature of RRI as a grassroots project, as
the EU was allegedly interested in developing a similar scheme to
revive rural areas across the continent.[62] Domestically, several initiatives were designed to investigate the synergy between RRI,
resettlement, and other socio-economic initiatives. In 1999, the
Irish Department of Tourism, Sports and Recreation commis-
sioned a one-year Pilot Scheme for Rural Resettlement to devise
a national strategy for rural regeneration, as well as develop and
manage a mechanism to enhance understanding of the challenges
linked to rural resettlement, particularly with regard to employment, training, and vocational integration. Years later, in 2015, as
Dublin's housing crisis worsened and 490 families — including
over 1,000 children — were considered homeless in Dublin,
Connolly initiated talks with Dublin City Council to see whether
rural resettlement could be a mutually beneficial arrangement to
both parties.[63]

The closure of RRI in 2017, five years after its already limited
government funding was permanently cut by the Irish state,
brought an end to these conversations. In its 27 years of operation,
RRI managed to resettle more than 800 families, including 700
children,[64] across 22 rural Irish counties, moving on average 50
families a year.[65] Figure 6.3 shows the geographical spread of

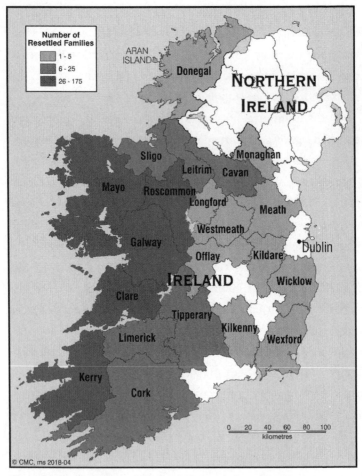

**Figure 6.3.** Irish counties where families resettled as of 2006.

RRI's operations in Ireland. Counties in dark grey are those where most families resettled as of 2006, with County Clare leading the pack with 175 resettled families, followed by County Mayo (95), County Kerry (91), County Roscommon (73), and County Galway (66); however, 11 out of the 22 counties where RRI operated had less than 5 families resettled.

We will now assess the opportunities generated by RRI for local communities, resettled families, and the Irish state, before exploring the main impediments that brought the program's downfall.

## Opportunities
### 1. Local Communities
Given its mandate, host rural communities stood to benefit the most from RRI. By prioritizing families with children for resettlement, RRI made it clear that it sought to maintain the provision of public services, "saving" as many rural schools and teaching posts as possible. Counties that were slated to imminently lose schools or teachers were quickly matched with families whose children helped to boost student enrolment.[66] As of 1999, 50 teaching positions had been saved as a direct result of rural resettlement, while several other schools had marginally avoided closure.[67] Many host communities acknowledged the beneficial role migrants played in preventing further decline in other rural services and facilities. A 2002 survey indicated that 56 per cent of local populations directly credited migrants with keeping local schools, shops, and post offices open in their small communities.[68] The arrival of new families also brought in a modest influx of labour and skills to small communities. Even when resettled families relied on social welfare, the rural economy benefited because they purchased items locally, increasing — if modestly — local purchasing power.[69]

Simultaneously, the relocation process allowed for 162 vacant social housing properties to be returned over the years to local authorities in Dublin.[70] These homes were vacated by migrants who had previously relied on social welfare and were subsequently made available for other urban dwellers in need. By 2000, 10 million Euros worth of property had been handed back to Dublin County Council as a result of the out-migration of people from the capital city to rural Ireland.[71] This, in turn, lessened wait times for other families on social housing lists and helped to decrease urban congestion.

RRI did not merely provide a temporary Band-Aid solution to rural decline and depopulation. A survey conducted after 10 years of operation is testament to its efforts in halting rural depopulation. While the number of resettled families may have been small in absolute terms — often only one or two households per rural locality — nearly 80 per cent of the families that remained in contact with RRI successfully integrated into their new communities and opted to remain in rural Ireland in the long-term.[72] The remaining 20 per cent did not solely account for families who chose to return to urban living, but also for resettled families who are still believed to reside in rural areas, yet simply lost formal contact with the organization. Allowing for this variance, RRI's scheme resulted in significantly *more than 80 per cent* of its families having stayed in rural homes.

## 2. Resettled Families

RRI's operations also provided substantial socio-economic benefits to resettled families, notably the provision of affordable housing, new economic opportunities, and favourable environmental amenities.

At its onset, RRI played the role of a middle man between urban families who wished to be resettled and rural landlords who were hoping to rent their property. After finding families a suitable unit, RRI facilitated their move and provided pre- and post-settlement support.[73] Most of these homes needed repairs but they could be acquired at prices that were comparatively on par with rental rates in Dublin. However, rural homes were much more spacious and the overall cost of living in the countryside was cheaper.[74] Therefore, making the move from Dublin's public housing units to rural family homes was, in most cases, more economical.[75] As the scheme progressed, however, it became apparent that renting rural properties was only a "stop-gap measure" in avoiding urban poverty and homelessness.[76] Instead, facilitating homeownership for resettled peoples became a goal of RRI. In 1996 the organization formed several public–private partnerships that sought to aid applicants in permanently acquiring their own homes.[77] By 2000, a third of resettled families had achieved just that through shared mortgage and national subsidy schemes.[78] Homeownership meant that families had permanently settled in their new county towns and were less likely to pack up and go back to the city, therefore slowing down trends in rural decline that had led to the creation of RRI in the first place.

Migrants also reaped substantial economic benefits from their participation in RRI. Indeed, part of Connolly's scheme aimed to permanently get families off the "dole" by encouraging them to develop their own skills and means of sustainable employment.[79] The process of rural relocation gave unemployed families a second chance to create a more prosperous life for themselves away from the city, where job markets were chronically flooded. As Shane O'Sullivan suggests, the restructuring of rural areas in the face of globalization created a host of new economic opportunities for families residing there, particularly within sectors pertaining to tourism and the arts. By 1998, more than half of the families who had resettled through RRI had at least one member engaged in full- or part-time work;[80] this took the form of new rural woodworkers, painters, weavers, writers, musicians, pub-owners, landscapers, and the like.[81] Despite the lack of formal employment opportunities in rural areas, many resettled migrants were eventually able to support themselves financially.[82]

Finally, our media analysis revealed that resettled families had relocated to rural areas in hopes of benefiting from lower stress level and more favourable environmental amenities associated with rural areas.[83] For many, Dublin was no longer considered safe due to the rise in urban poverty and crime. When interviewed by *The Irish Times* in 1991, a recently resettled couple explained why they chose to partake in RRI and move to the Irish countryside:

> We ended up putting bars on our windows after two attempts were made to break into our home. I saw what was happening to the kids on the estate and I didn't want our children to grow up like that. I wanted to give them something better than what they had.[84]

As another newly resettled man claimed: "If I had stayed in Dublin, I'd be on pills from worrying. Down here [in County Clare] you can live with your worries. I'd never go back to Dublin, no way."[85] Others found joy cultivating the land around them in their new home and developed more sustainable ways of living. One family recalls the first season they entered a local bog to collect their own "turf" as a source of fuel.[86]

> We had never been in a bog in our lives, but we saved our own turf and it'll see us through the winter. We footed it

and stacked it and had a great time doing it. Every day when the weather was good we'd have a picnic out there on the bog. That's something that we would never have been able to do in Dublin.[87]

Rural living, therefore, provided a certain lifestyle that could not be replicated within crowded and polluted city streets. Resettled Dubliners found solace in working together to create a simple life through several back-to-the-land practices,[88] and many families took advantage of their abundant land to provide for themselves through sustainable means of living.[89]

Thus, participation in RRI appealed to families with both anti-urban motives (e.g., regional differences in house prices) and pro-rural motivations (e.g., the more clement immediate residential environment). As such, it draws parallels from two of the three forms of counter-urbanization devised by Mitchell:[90] displaced urbanization driven by greater housing affordability, and anti-urbanization driven by a desire for a more sustainable, worry-free lifestyle.

## 3. *Irish State*

Besides the positive impacts for and from local communities and resettled families, the Irish state may have also benefited financially from RRI in the long term. As the section above shows, many resettled people indicated experiencing less stress and greater peace of mind, which was expected to lower the needs for health services. To quote a resettled man:

I never walked in Dublin but here I walk for miles without knowing how far I've gone. When we decided to leave, all my friends and relatives were saying I was a raving lunatic to be moving to the country. Well, all I know is that I haven't been to see a doctor once since we came down here.[91]

This, in turn, could have been translated into a decline, albeit modest, in state expenditure on public health services and the psychiatric system in the long term. The closure of RRI's head office in late 2017 put an end to any future health dividends the RRI could have had for the Irish state.

## Limitations

As the above discussion highlights, Connolly's rural resettlement scheme provided substantial benefits to rural and urban communities, the resettled families themselves, and, to a certain degree, the Irish state. Given this track record, RRI was praised by some rural supporters as a "resounding success."[92] It had also received verbal support over the years from political parties across the Irish *Dail* (Parliament), including from the Labor Party,[93] Fine Gael — a Christian democratic political party currently in power in Ireland[94] — and independent representatives.[95] And yet, RRI was forced to gradually wind down after funding was cut by the government in 2012, resulting in the organization's final closure in late 2017. What challenges and limitations brought RRI to a halt?

### 1. Chronic Lack of Financial and Institutional Resources

Over the years, RRI received financial assistance from several sources, including government grants, annual governmental budget allocations, and private donations from individuals and other institutions. After its first year of operations in 1991, the Irish government allocated £10,000 to the program; however, this figure paled in comparison to the estimated £40,000 it needed to get by.[96] The years 1992–93 were wrought with financial difficulties for the resettlement scheme, and Connolly considered terminating its service. However, in a last-ditch effort to keep the program up and running, he set up a charitable branch in New York that appealed to the Irish diaspora there for financial support.[97] This was somewhat successful in gaining just enough money to supplement its annual funds. In 1993, based on a steep increase in demand, RRI requested a resettlement grant of £1 million from the government, but was instead allocated £40,000.[98] According to Jim Connolly, the largest amount RRI received from the national treasury was 135,000 Euros a year, a sum deemed barely sufficient to keep the office open and employ five staff members.[99]

The mismatch between the funds required and those secured was the cause of much tension between RRI and government actors. Despite receiving continuous verbal support from all sides of the Irish *Dail*, Connolly questioned where the government's money really was; on several occasions he challenged the nation's priorities and accused state-level actors of favouring urban, over rural, development,[100] a critique that was particularly applicable during the "Celtic Tigers" years, when planning conducted under the Department of the Environment was considered "absolutely antirural."[101] Another point of contention lay in Connolly's frustration that the state did not adequately "value" the work that had been completed by RRI, which ultimately benefited Dublin County and the country as a whole.[102] Needless to say, RRI is not the first non-profit civil society organization that feels unappreciated — and under-funded — by the state. According to public administration researcher Chris McInerney, at the heart of the problem is the lack of a clear rural development strategy in Ireland:

For the state and civil society groups to work together, their imperatives must coalesce; if not, then it becomes a potential for confrontation or a struggle to get your perspectives heard. This was partly the case here. The imperative of rural resettlement as pursued by RRI didn't necessarily "match" the imperatives of the various departments responsible for rural development over the years. As a result, they've always struggled to gain traction. So they got a certain amount of funding, because there was a certain degree of support for it, but there wasn't really any longer-term commitment. But even then, it didn't fit, because there was no clear rural development strategy.[103]

In the absence of a strong institutional infrastructure around rural development at the state level, RRI was doomed to remain a fairly marginal — if not marginalized — program, led by one outspoken individual. Given its chronic lack of resources, RRI's energy was constantly spent asking for money and new donors in an effort to stay afloat. Its modest means restricted its ability to relocate more people, to find more houses, and to renovate the ones it did.[104] By 1998, 315 families had been successfully resettled, but the waiting list for rural housing amounted to nearly 4,000 applicants.[105] The declining level of government aid over the years severely affected RRI's ability to provide applicants the level of support they needed for their relocation. As explained by Connolly, one of the greatest obstacles to moving to a rural area was in families giving up a tenancy with no guarantee of a new tenancy or social supports, such as rent allowance, in the county to which they planned to move. "In the past, we had help from Government departments, and we could give people letters saying they would get rent allowance. But RRI was told in 2012 that there would be no more money,"[106] thus drying up the main source of revenue for the charitable organization after 27 years of rural resettlement in Ireland.

## 2. Group Tensions and Contentious Politics

The tensions, conflict, and problems associated with the resettlement of "outsiders" into rural places also affected the successful operations of RRI. In the early years, from 1991 to 1995, there was not a single media report of contention between locals/migrants. This is not to say that locals did not have reservations about migrants settling in. Negative stereotypes towards migrants — or "blow-ins" in this case — are not new and are often prevalent in communities, worldwide, that have large migrant populations.[107] Informally, some rural residents feared that Dubliners would bring with them undesirable behaviour often associated with inner-city life, including crime, gang violence, and drugs. In other cases, locals questioned whether they would be able to maintain their unique "cultural fabric" in the face of large urban influxes,[108] whereas others were concerned that rural areas would lose their "ruralness" or that newcomers may contaminate Ireland's pristine countryside.[109]

As shown in Figure 6.1, the period of 1996–98 saw an increasing (and overwhelmingly negative) portrayal of RRI in the local and national newspapers. It started when Senator Mary Kelly accused RRI of not properly vetting its applicants[110] — a critique typically made against international migrants. She claimed that criminals and drug dealers were taking advantage of the resettlement scheme to set up rural drug "networks" in less-populated counties.[111] Though unfounded, these claims had a devastating effect on the program's reputation. Communities began to question the legitimacy of their own migrant families and reports of contention quickly spiralled.[112]

The case of Kilmovee was the first and allegedly most extreme in terms of resistance to migrant populations. After Kelly's remarks, the small community in County Mayo fought back against foreign settlement of any kind, saying "We don't want drug pushers and undesirables bringing down the tone of our community."[113] Residents of Kilmovee wrote a letter to local county councillors with 100 signatures, expressing their concerns over the fact that most migrants were recipients of social welfare.[114] In light of such public outcry, RRI responded by stating that no community would ever be forced to host resettled people — even if it meant doing away with possible economic windfall — as it did not want to resettle anyone where they were not explicitly made to feel welcome.[115]

This type of othering discourse, also known as Nimby-ism, continued for several years, eventually morphing into the basis for nativist homebuilding legislation.[116] By 1998, Counties Kerry, Galway, and Clare — three of the counties where RRI had been the most active — had placed a ban on the purchase of land or homes by "non-indigenous" peoples seeking resettlement. In other words, these counties would only allow their own local diaspora to return and settle in back home.[117] Though highly contentious, these planning policies proved effective in keeping resettled Dubliners out. Despite many complaints, Connolly was unable to bring an end to the ban as county councils have the ultimate right to prioritize locals over non-locals in regards to the selling of land and property. However, it was to their own social and economic loss, as it was estimated that these regions lost out on €750,000 in redistributed income and regional investment.[118]

The notion that migrants brought crime with them was, for the most part, groundless. RRI did not resettle applicants with known criminal connections and, in fact, families often explicitly stated that they wished to participate in RRI to escape criminal activities prevalent in urban centres. And yet, several isolated incidents helped cement the perception that resettled populations were dangerous. The first came in 1997 when a young, resettled couple was violently murdered in their new County Roscommon home.[119] The couple, originally from Dublin, had moved to the quiet town of Carane in 1993 with their four children. On 16 August 1997 the wife's sister and her boyfriend came to visit the family for a weekend. Within hours of their arrival the couple was stabbed to death and the sister was severely injured by the boyfriend, who was later arrested and convicted of murder.[120] The town of Carane, with a population of 60 people, was shocked by what had happened. Never before had anyone there witnessed even "the smallest assault" — such a violent crime was considered "horrific."[121] Despite pleas made by a local resident to keep supporting rural areas, many people's perceptions of RRI had been permanently tainted.[122]

Matters were made worse in 1998 when a serial rapist was discovered to have been living with his family, who had resettled a year earlier from Dublin to the town of Ballybunion, County Kerry.[123] The family had been living in a housing estate, where approximately 80 children also resided, when their nephew was released from a maximum-security state prison.[124] The man was known to have served 10 years of a 12-year sentence for violently raping two women and previously having stabbed a neighbour.[125] His presence had not been made known to RRI, nor was it supposed to have been, as the organization had not been in contact with the family since they had resettled. However, residents in Ballybunion were terrified to learn that a criminal had been living within their midst and publicly blamed RRI for its negligence. When asked about the incident, one resident said, "I no longer felt safe"; another, "I think now the Rural Resettlement scheme has lost respect in this area."[126]

What became increasingly obvious for the local population was that RRI was not aiding the resettlement of middle-class or well-off people; after all, these people had the means to move on their own if they wanted to. Instead, the organization was bringing in people who were unemployed and didn't have access to housing in Dublin; in other words, RRI was moving people from a state of reliance on welfare in an urban context to a state of reliance in a rural context. Resettled households' economic precarity was a point of contention raised by several local newspapers. Commentators took offence with the fact that welfare recipients were allowed to move and live wherever they wished within Ireland, without any obligation to be near centres of economic opportunities.[127] For them, Irish citizens who were receiving aid from the state should have been denied benefits upon relocating to a community with no viable job market. Seen as such, unemployed people were thus condemned to a life of poverty and immobility, thereby fuelling increasingly widespread narratives aimed at "disciplining the poor."

Even though the local population accepted that stopping population decline was essential for the future of the Irish countryside, the word on the street was that RRI was bringing in the "wrong kind of people" — i.e., poor, homeless, and other socially disadvantaged groups often afflicted by negative stigmas of crime and violence.[128] Instead of bringing new people in, local people would have preferred to implement policies that *maintained* the existing population as it was, preventing the younger generations from leaving. The introduction of nativist planning policies, where county councils explicitly favoured land bids made by local people or returned migrants, did just that. As Lisa Moran, an Irish sociologist, found in her research, local people often indicated that their children should be allowed to build in a given area because they had "relational sustainability," that is, they had the "right" to inhabit the countryside going forward, whereas people who had just moved in did not.[129] Being able to claim physical or relational ties to a piece of land, even if such claims were tenuous or had been interrupted after years of residency elsewhere, was considered reason enough to be granted preferential access to rural assets.

Yet, a number of factors prevented host communities' negative feelings towards migrants and isolated violent events from being transformed into widespread anti-resettlement discourse and violence in Ireland. First and foremost, the Irish resettlement process needs to be initiated by two sets of actors: the very individuals interested in resettling in the countryside, and rural people contacting RRI and making housing available to resettled families. As such, — and unlike resettlement programs in Newfoundland and Labrador and in Greenland — it gives agency to migrants *and* host communities, transforming both groups into key agents of relocation and giving them all a stake in the successful, conflict-free relocation of urban families. The presence of what can best be described as two-way consent and agency and the near-complete absence of government interference in the process made resettlement almost violence-free — though not tension-free — in Ireland. It also provided a degree of flexibility often absent from larger, state-led resettlement programs. For instance, RRI did not go against the wishes of the county councils that implemented nativist homebuilding legislation, and simply reoriented its efforts to other communities that welcomed immigrants. Another important factor mitigating the risks of conflict between migrants and host communities was the comparatively modest scale of such programs, reducing the "demographic threat" posed by resettled families to the host regions. Host communities experienced small-scale population growth over the years; in fact, half the counties where RRI operated had less than five families resettled overall (see Figure 6.3), so migrant integration was neither sudden nor overwhelming. Finally, a key factor facilitating the (comparatively) smooth integration of resettled populations into Irish host communities was their shared ethnic, linguistic, and religious roots. In Ireland, both resettled families and host communities were almost exclusively English-speaking and of Irish descent.[130] This contrasts, for instance, with the highly contentious situation in Xinjiang, China, where the resettled Han Chinese migrants are ethnically distinct from and economically dominant compared to the native and marginalized Uyghur minority.[131] To sum up, while resettled families in Ireland may have moved fairly recently and lacked prior personal connections or "relational sustainability" with the rural host communities, their small numbers and ethnic/linguistic similarities with the host population — two factors identified by Lumb[132] as facilitating in-migration — played in their favour.

## CONCLUSION

Despite the prevalence of rural-to-urban migration trends around the world, the Irish case is revelatory in terms of its innovative approach to facilitating counter-urbanization by having a non-profit organization run by non-state actors in charge. The program was successful in part thanks to its small, voluntary, bottom-up approach that gave it the flexibility required when tensions emerged, and which its non-state credentials facilitated. But not being the product of government-led intervention meant not having access to the deep pockets of the state and lacking institutional infrastructure. Despite its proven record, the program could not continue its operation once its limited state funding was cut, eventually resulting in the close of its headquarters in late 2017.

Ironically, just as RRI's last staff member received a final redundancy payment, the Irish Prime Minister, Leo Varadkar, declared that a voluntary rural resettlement scheme could be "part of the solution" to alleviate the housing crisis in Ireland. "It's eminently logical that parts of the country where there's been rural depopulation, where there are properties available, where there are places in schools, where there are services available, I can certainly see a place for a rural resettlement scheme,"[133] he explained. Whether RRI will be brought into this conversation, however, remains to be seen.

The Irish experience with resettlement underscores that even non-state resettlement programs rely, to a certain degree, on government assistance, without which resettlement schemes may be forced to close. State involvement varied significantly over the duration of RRI, from a few thousand pounds with limited strings attached in the early 1990s, to the development of public–private partnerships worth millions of Euros in the late 1990s. Availability of state funding and whether RRI's goals dovetailed with the mandate of the political party in power affected state involvement in resettlement affairs. Perhaps there is more complexity here, and instead of asking *whether* the state is involved, one should ask about the *degree* of state control and oversight over the resettlement schemes.

The Irish experience with resettlement also highlights the agency of ordinary people like Jim Connolly, which echoes a point made earlier by Withers in his investigation in Chapter 3 of the 1965–70 Fisheries Household Relocation Program in Newfoundland and Labrador. It also shows that non-government actors can be brought into the process of developing appropriate rural development policy. However, for successful co-operation to develop between government and non-government actors on resettlement issues, grassroots initiatives must be given consistent and sufficient amounts of financial support from state institutions. The few instances where resettlement practices were challenged by the local population occurred when resettled families were marginally associated with criminal events. If such a scheme were to be pursued again in the future, increasing applicant screening processes may reduce the likelihood of contentious events caused by stereotypes associating urban migrants with drugs and crime. However, sophisticated means of screening thousands of applicants requires designated staff, resources, and funding, all of which RRI sorely lacked.

Given the operational methods that RRI developed and the relative success it was able to achieve, the scheme holds potential to be replicated in other similar contexts of rural depopulation and/or urban housing crisis, especially in places where welfare recipients are not bound to live in a given area and may relocate as they wish. However, local and national socio-economic contexts must be considered, as periods of economic volatility may affect the need for resettlement services. For example, Ireland's scheme was largely influenced by the presence of the mid-1990s "Celtic Tiger," which exacerbated the state's already volatile housing crisis. Had the 1990s been economically stagnant, rather than experiencing such financial highs and lows, Dublin's urban housing crisis may not have occurred and the need for counter-urbanization may not have been as great.

Going forward, the insights gained from the Irish case could potentially be applied to current schemes meant to facilitate the relocation and integration of foreign migrants worldwide. Indeed, the Irish case has shown that locals often welcome in-migrants when they help maintain the provision of public services and contribute to the local economy.[134] However, as these new resettlement schemes typically involve ethnically distinct refugee populations rather than a population of similar ethnic and linguistic background, as was the case in Ireland, such projects may pose significantly larger social challenges. Having the means to mitigate, and therefore limit, contention during resettlement will once again require specific resources, consistent political support, and adequate amounts of reliable funding. It remains to be seen, on a case by case basis, whether these conditions can be met.

**NOTES**

1   Central Statistics Office, *Ireland Census 1991, Volume 1: Population Classified by Area* (Dublin: Stationary Office and Central Statistics Office, June 1993), 7.

2   James G. Eustace, "Tallaught New Town," *The Irish Times*, 2 Mar. 1990; "New Life for City Towns?" *Limerick Leader*, 10 Apr. 1993;

Tom Sheil, "State Rapped on Poor Rural Policy," *Irish Independent*, 27 Mar. 1995.

3    Central Statistics Office, *Ireland Census 1991, Volume 1: Population Classified by Area*, 10.

4    Michael Finlan, "Swapping the City Smoke for the Clean Open Spaces," *The Irish Times*, 10 Apr. 1991; Michael Finlan, "Jobless Dubs Look to West for Integrity," *The Irish Times*, 4 Oct. 1991; John Waters, "A Rock on Which FF Could Perish," *The Irish Times*, 3 Mar. 1992.

5    Several campaigns and programs have been created over the years to address these issues, including the "Look West" campaign, the Western Development Partnership, the Western Development Commission, the Irish National Spatial Strategy, and the Rural Renewal Scheme (RRS), but few if any of these were ever thoroughly implemented, and without an all-encompassing rural development strategy, they lacked overall cohesion.

6    Ann Mooney, "Launch," *Irish Examiner*, 21 June 1991; Finlan, "Swapping the City Smoke for the Clean Open Spaces"; James Downey, "'Move West' Scheme Now Has Waiting List of 500," *Irish Independent*, 23 Aug. 1991.

7    Trevor Nuttall, *Methods to Stop Rural Depopulation and to Involve Citizens in the Development of These Regions* (Strasbourg: Council of Europe, 1980).

8    Aileen Stockdale, "Contemporary and 'Messy' Rural In-migration Processes: Comparing Counterurban and Lateral Rural Migration," *Population, Space and Place* 6, no. 22 (2015): 355.

9    Terry Marsden et al., *Rural Restructuring: Global Processes and Their Responses* (London: David Fulton Publishers, 1990).

10    DETR, *Our Countryside: The Future — A Fair Deal for Rural England* (London: Department of the Environment, Transport and the Regions, 2000).

11    Menelaos Gkartzois and Mark Scott, "Countering Counter-Urbanisation: Spatial Planning Challenges in a Dispersed City-Region, the Greater Dublin Area," *Town Planning Review* 81, no. 1 (2010).

12    H.E. Bracey, *English Rural Life: Village Activities, Organizations and Institutions* (London: Routledge and Kegan Paul, 1959), 232.

13   Toivo Muilu and Jarmo Rusanen, "Rural Young People in Regional Development — The Case of Finland in 1970–2000," *Journal of Rural Studies* 19, no. 3 (2003).

14   Stockdale, "Contemporary and 'Messy' Rural In-migration Processes."

15   Keith Halfacree, "Going 'Back-to-the-Land' Again: Extending the Scope of Counterurbanization," *Espaces, Populations, Sociétés* 1, no. 2 (2001).

16   Caitríona Ní Laoire, "The 'Green Green Grass of Home'? Return Migration to Rural Ireland," *Journal of Rural Studies* 23, no. 3 (2007).

17   Stockdale, "Contemporary and 'Messy' Rural In-migration Processes," 355.

18   Brian Berry, *Urbanization and Counterurbanization* (Beverly Hills, CA: Sage, 1976).

19   Halfacree, "Going 'Back-to-the-Land' Again," 161.

20   Clare Mitchell, "Making Sense of Counterurbanization," *Journal of Rural Studies* 20 (2004): 23–24.

21   Aileen Stockdale, "State Intervention and the Impact on Rural Mobility Flows in Northern Ireland," *Journal of Rural Studies* 8, no. 4 (1992): 419.

22   Longyi Xue, Mark Y. Wang, and Tao Xue, "'Voluntary' Poverty Alleviation Resettlement in China," *Development and Change* 44, no. 5 (2013): 1159–80.

23   Riwanto Tirtosudarmo, "Demography and Security: Transmigration Policy in Indonesia," in *Demography and National Security*, eds. Myron Weiner and Sharon Stanton Russel (New York: Berghahn Books, 2001).

24   Kevin Lo, Longyi Xue, and Mark Wang, "Spatial Restructuring through Poverty Alleviation Resettlement in Rural China," *Journal of Rural Studies* 47 (2016): 496–505.

25   Yuheng Li, Hans Westlund, Xiaoyu Zheng, and Yansui Lui, "Bottom-up Initiatives and Revival in the Face of Rural Decline: Case Studies from China and Sweden," *Journal of Rural Studies* 47 (2016): 506–13.

26 Halfacree, "Going 'Back-to-the-Land' Again."

27 Aileen Stockdale, Allan Findlay, and David Short, "The Repopulation of Rural Scotland: Opportunity and Threat," *Journal of Rural Studies* 16 (2000).

28 NIMBY: "Not-in-My-Back-Yard".

29 Paul Milbourne, "Re-Populating Rural Studies: Migrations, Movements and Mobilities," *Journal of Rural Studies* 23 (2007): 385.

30 Ibid., 383.

31 Martin Phillips, "Investigations of the British Rural Middle Classes — Part 2: Fragmentation, Identity, Morality and Contestation," *Journal of Rural Studies* 14, no. 4 (1998).

32 Janet M. Fitchen, "Spatial Redistribution of Poverty through Migration of Poor People to Depressed Rural Communities," *Rural Sociology* 60, no. 2 (1995).

33 Isabelle Côté, "Horizontal Inequalities and Sons of the Soil Conflict in China," *Civil Wars* 17, no. 3 (2015).

34 R. Lumb, "Migration in the Highlands and Islands of Scotland," *Institute for the Study of Sparsely Populated Areas, University of Aberdeen* 1, no. 3 (1980).

35 Milbourne, "Re-Populating Rural Studies," 385–86.

36 The media analysis was part of a larger project led by Côté and Pottie-Sherman that examined media reports of resettlement programs in Canada and Ireland.

37 Jennifer Earl et al., "The Use of Newspaper Data in the Study of Collective Action," *Annual Review of Sociology* 30 (2004).

38 Liza M. Mügge, "Bridging the Qualitative-Quantitative Divide in Comparative Migration Studies: Newspaper Data and Political Ethnography in Mixed Method Research," *Comparative Migration Studies* 4, no. 1 (2016): 17.

39 Piaras Mac Einri, "Some Recent Demographic Developments in Ireland," *Études Irlandaises* 22, no. 1 (1997); Mary E. Cawley, "Population Change in the Republic of Ireland 1981–1986," *The Royal Geographical Society (with the Institute of British Geographers)* 22, no. 1 (1990).

40 Mac Einri, "Some Recent Demographic Developments in Ireland."

41  Trutz Haase, "Divided City: The Changing Face of Dublin's Inner City," *Dublin Inner City Partnership* (2009); Cawley, "Population Change."

42  Lizette Alvarez, "Suddenly Rich, Poor Old Ireland Seems Bewildered," *New York Times*, 2 Feb. 2005, https://www.nytimes.com/2005/02/02/world/europe/suddenly-rich-poor-old-ireland-seems-bewildered.html.

43  Haase, "Divided City"; Shane John Herbert O'Sullivan, "Rural Restructuring and Rural In-Migration Patterns in Ireland" (doctoral diss., Mary Immaculate College, University of Limerick, 2013), https://dspace.mic.ul.ie/handle/10395/1989.

44  O'Sullivan, "Rural Restructuring and Rural In-Migration Patterns in Ireland."

45  Ibid.; Cawley, "Population Change."

46  Central Statistics Office, *Ireland Census 1991*; Haase, "Divided City."

47  Waters, "A Rock on Which FF Could Perish."

48  Haase, "Divided City."

49  Padraig Yeates, "Homeless Increase Causes Money Problems for Simon," *The Irish Times*, 17 Oct. 1994; Jimmy Walsh, "Tax Relief 'Boosting Home Prices'," *The Irish Times*, 6 Feb. 1998.

50  Haase, "Divided City."

51  Downey, "'Move West' Scheme Now Has Waiting List of 500."

52  Michael Finlan, "Trading Places," *The Irish Times*, 31 Aug. 1991; "New Life for City Towns?" *Limerick Leader*, 10 Apr. 1993; Gordan Deegan, "Resettlement Group Seeks to Stem the Flight from Land to Cities," *Irish Examiner*, 1999.

53  Interview with Jim Connolly, 21 Apr. 2017.

54  Finlan, "Swapping the City Smoke for the Clean Open Spaces"; Jane Katherine Rosegrant, "Rural Resettlement Ireland: An Example of Assisted Counterstream Migration, Its Impact on Participants and Communities," (doctoral diss., University of Edinburgh, School of Earth, Environmental and Geographical Sciences, 2002), 70, http://hdl.handle.net/1842/14328.

55  Mooney, "Launch."

56  Launched in 2001 by the Departtment of Housing and Urban

Renewal, the Rental Subsidy Scheme sought to fund RRI's acquisition of rural land and housing units for the purpose of resettlement, under the assumption that all other logistical responsibilities associated with property rental would be assumed by the organization. The program was limited to applicants within Dublin City who were willing to give up their local authority housing units for rural homes in the County of Clare, Leitrim, Limerick, Mayo, or Offaly. It remains unclear exactly how long the pilot scheme lasted or how much money was received on its behalf; however, newspaper articles indicate that funding was still present in 2004.

57 Geraldine Collins, "Families Leave City for New Life in the Country," *Irish Independent*, 1997.

58 Mooney, "Launch."

59 Ibid.; Rosegrant, "Rural Resettlement Ireland."

60 Michael Finlan, "Resettlement Scheme Returns Life to Rural Communities," *The Irish Times*, 26 Oct. 1992.

61 Rosegrant, "Rural Resettlement Ireland," 76.

62 "EU Studies Rural Resettlement Here," *Irish Examiner*, 1997.

63 Claire McCormack, "Homeless Urban Families Could Rescue Rural Ireland," *The Independent*, 19 July 2015, http://www.independent.ie/irish-news/homeless-urban-families-could-rescue-rural-ireland-31387064.html.

64 Connolly interview, 21 Apr. 2017.

65 Jane Suiter, "Shared Home Ownership Schemes Still Too Dear to Help Many Low-Income Households," *The Irish Times*, 18 June 1998.

66 "Rural Schools Fear Staff Shortage — Survey," *The Irish Times*, 29 Dec. 1997.

67 Deegan, "Resettlement Group Seeks to Stem the Flight from Land to Cities."

68 Rosegrant, "Rural Resettlement Ireland," 244.

69 "New Life for City Towns?" *Limerick Leader*, 10 Apr. 1993.

70 Judy Murphy, "Back to the Roots," *Irish Examiner*, 16 Mar. 1998.

71 Ibid.

72  Jerome Reilly, "Farming Out the City's Housing Problem," *Irish Independent*, 1999; Eibhir Mulqueen, "Country and Western," *The Irish Times*, 19 Jan. 2001.

73  Mooney, "Launch"; Steve Dodd, "Into the West," *Irish Independent*, 1993.

74  Finlan, "Trading Places"; Tommy Brown, "Back to Land Group Fails in Cash Bid," *Irish Independent*, 1993; Olivia Kelly, "How a Family Went from Ballyfermot to Ballyshrule, with Plenty of Baggage," *The Irish Times*, 17 Oct. 2000.

75  Waters, "A Rock on Which FF Could Perish."

76  "Moves to Resettle Urban Families in Rural Areas," *Cork Examiner*, 5 Feb. 1993; "New Life for City Towns?" *Limerick Leader*, 10 Apr. 1993.

77  "Bank of Ireland Provides Mortgages for Unemployed," *The Irish Times*, 23 Feb. 1996; Trish O'Dea, "Limerick City Tenants May Not be Entitled to Rural Move," *Limerick Leader*, 9 Nov. 1996; Aine De Paor, "Pioneer Family Malone Head Out West," *Irish Independent*, 1996.

78  Anita Guidera, "'Dream' Homes to Rent," *Irish Independent*, 2000.

79  Mooney, "Launch"; Michael Finlan, "How to Make the Transition to Country Life," *The Irish Times*, 1 Nov. 1994.

80  Murphy, "Back to the Roots."

81  Finlan, "How to Make the Transition to Country Life"; "New Life for City Towns?" *Limerick Leader*, 10 Apr. 1993.

82  Suiter, "Shared Home Ownership Schemes."

83  Finlan, "Swapping the City Smoke for the Clean Open Spaces"; Waters, "A Rock on Which FF Could Perish."

84  Finlan, "Swapping the City Smoke for the Clean Open Spaces."

85  Ibid.

86  Finlan, "Resettlement Scheme Returns Life to Rural Communities."

87  Ibid.

88  Brown, "Back to Land Group Fails in Cash Bid."

89  Finlan, "Resettlement Scheme Returns Life to Rural Communities"; "A New Country Life," *Irish Independent*, 8 Jan. 1992; "Moves to Resettle Urban Families in Rural Areas," *Cork Examiner*, 5 Feb. 1993; Kelly, "How a Family Went from Ballyfermot to Ballyshrule."

90  Mitchell, "Making Sense of Counterurbanization."

91  Finlan, "Resettlement Scheme Returns Life to Rural Communities."

92  Michael Finlan, "Cable Car Plan Could End Inishbiggle's Isolation," *The Irish Times*, 8 Apr. 1996.

93  McCormack, "Homeless Urban Families Could Rescue Rural Ireland."

94  Deborah McAleese, "Leo Varadkar Sees a Place for Rural Resettlement Scheme to Ease Ireland's Housing Crisis," *The Independent*, 31 Dec. 2017.

95  Seanad Debates, "Commencement Matters: Rural Resettlement Scheme," 31 May 2017, https://www.kildarestreet.com/sendebates/?id=2017-05-31a.37.

96  Tom Sheil, "Cash Threat to Rural Housing," *Irish Independent*, 9 Jan. 1992.

97  "US Aid," *Irish Examiner*, 28 Dec. 1993.

98  Ray Ryan, "Grants to Stem Rural Rot Sought," *Irish Examiner*, 1993; Tom Browne, "Urban Renewal Scheme Queried," *Limerick Leader*, 19 June 1993.

99  Connolly interview, 21 Apr. 2017.

100  Browne, "Urban Renewal Scheme Queried"; John Waters, "A Working Model for Rural and Urban Reconstruction," *The Irish Times*, 9 Nov. 1993.

101  Connolly interview, 21 Apr. 2017.

102  "Cash Crisis for RRI," *Irish Examiner*, 6 Aug. 1992.

103  Interview with Chris McInerney, 25 Apr. 2017.

104  Roger Garland, "The Trouble with Tourism," *The Irish Times*, 26 Aug. 1998.

105  Suiter, "Shared Home Ownership Schemes."

106  Tom O'Brien, "Closed-Down Rural Housing Body May Resume Activity," *The Irish Times*, 1 Jan. 2018, https://www.irishtimes.com/news/ireland/irish-news/closed-down-rural-housing-body-may-resume-activity-1.3342454.

107  Yolande Pottie-Sherman and Rima Wilkes, "Does Size Really Matter? On the Relationship between Immigrant Group Size and Anti-Immigrant Prejudice," *International Migration Review* 51, no. 1 (2017).

108 McInerney interview, 25 Apr. 2017.

109 Peter Leonard, "Villagers Don't Want Dublin 'Drug Pushers and Undesirables' Settling in Their Nice Community," *Irish Examiner*, 18 Mar. 1996.

110 Trish O'Dea, "Kelly Remarks on Pushers Anger Rural Resettlement," *Limerick Leader*, 1996.

111 Ibid.

112 Ibid.; "Stop the Intolerance," *Irish Examiner*, 13 Mar. 1996.

113 Leonard, "Villagers Don't Want Dublin 'Drug Pushers and Undesirables'."

114 Ibid.

115 Finlan, "Cable Car Plan Could End Inishbiggle's Isolation."

116 "Stop the Intolerance," *Irish Examiner*, 13 Mar. 1996; Gordan Deegan, "Council Rethinks Ban on Outsiders Building Homes," *Irish Independent*, 1 Nov. 1999; Gordan Deegan, "Clare Wanted to Impose No-go Building Zones for Blow-ins," *Irish Examiner*, 1999; Deegan, "Resettlement Group Seeks to Stem the Flight from Land to Cities"; Declan Varley, "Councillor Wants Locals Housed First," *Irish Examiner*, 1998.

117 Deegan, "Council Rethinks Ban on Outsiders Building Homes"; Deegan, "Clare Wanted to Impose No-go Building Zones for Blow-ins"; Deegan, "Resettlement Group Seeks to Stem the Flight from Land to Cities"; Varley, "Councillor Wants Locals Housed First."

118 Gordan Deegan, "Rural Activist Protests Building Ban," *Irish Independent*, 2002.

119 Uinsionn Mac Dubhghaill, "Dead Couple Had Moved to Country to Escape the Bustle of Dublin," *The Irish Times*, 18 Aug. 1997; Uinsionn Mac Dubhghaill, "Support Urged for Rural Life Despite Killings," *The Irish Times*, 19 Aug. 1997.

120 Mac Dubhghaill, "Dead Couple Had Moved to Country to Escape the Bustle of Dublin"; Mac Dubhghaill, "Support Urged for Rural Life Despite Killings"; Rita O'Reilly, "Couple Knifed to Death as Children Slept, Trial Told," *Irish Independent*, 7 Oct. 1998.

121 Mac Dubhghaill, "Support Urged for Rural Life Despite Killings";

Sheila McArdle, "Poignant Removal of Murder Victims," *Irish Examiner*, 1997.

122 Mac Dubhghaill, "Support Urged for Rural Life Despite Killings."

123 *Irish Examiner*, 9 Apr. 1999; John O'Mahony, "Locals Want Sex Attacker Removed from Their Town," *Irish Examiner*, 1999.

124 Dick Hogan, "Estate Relieved at Departure of Convicted Rapist," *The Irish Times*, 17 Apr. 1999.

125 O'Mahony, "Locals Want Sex Attacker Removed"; Hogan, "Estate Relieved at Departure of Convicted Rapist."

126 Hogan, "Estate Relieved at Departure of Convicted Rapist"; "Resettlement Scheme Jolted by Incident in Ballybunion Housing Estate," *The Irish Times*, 20 Apr. 1999.

127 Geraldine Kennedy, "McCreevy Denies Threat to Cut Off 'Good Life' Welfare Payments," *The Irish Times*, 5 Mar. 1992; Waters, "A Rock on Which FF Could Perish."

128 For a similar conclusion regarding Scotland, see Charles Jedrej and Mark Nuttall, *White Settlers: The Impact of Rural Repopulation in Scotland* (London: Routledge, 1996).

129 Interview with Lisa Moran, 9 May 2017

130 Interview with Jim Connolly, 21 Apr. 2017; Rosegrant, "Rural Resettlement Ireland," 186.

131 Côté, "Horizontal Inequalities and Sons of the Soil Conflict in China."

132 Lumb, "Migration in the Highlands and Islands of Scotland."

133 McAleese, "Leo Varadkar Sees a Place for Rural Resettlement Scheme."

134 "New Life for City Towns?" *Limerick Leader*, 10 Apr. 1993; Deegan, "Resettlement Group Seeks to Stem the Flight from Land to Cities."

# CHAPTER 7

## Climate Resettlement in Canada's Arctic

NICOLE MARSHALL

### INTRODUCTION

Nearly 634 million people — one-tenth of the global population
— live in coastal areas, just a few metres above existing sea levels.[1]
Three-quarters of these people live in flood-prone, densely populated river deltas or in low-lying small island states where flooding
is not only anticipated, but expected to permanently alter the geography of the region.[2] As sea levels continue to rise due to climate
change, 136 of the world's largest cities are likely to face annual
flood losses of up to US$1 trillion by 2050.[3] From 2001 to 2010,
the global economic loss related to hydro/meteorological events
was US$660 billion, which marked a 54 per cent increase com-
pared to 1991–2000.[4] The next decade is currently on track to see
this cost nearly double. The world over, the conditions of climate
change are initiating significant economic and resettlement concerns for a growing number of people: individuals, population
segments like the residents of Isle de Jean Charles in Louisiana,
United States, and possibly even entire island states like Tuvalu,
Kiribati, and the Maldives.[5] Still, and in part *because* of the increasing clarity of these issues, some of the more nuanced challenges

associated with climate migration are just beginning to emerge, many of which reflect the themes of this volume: the legacies of resource extraction and colonialism on threatened populations, the role of expert knowledge and its interplay with local and Indigenous knowledges, and the place for agency in the ongoing cycles of de-territorialization and re-territorialization associated with re-settlement, particularly that associated with government-initiated efforts. In the case of climate-induced displacement, each of these intersections is further complicated by the fact that, though imminent, this area of study largely addresses potential future resettlement rather than ongoing relocation.

Focusing on the legacies of colonialism, dispossession, agency, and the legitimacy of state and non-state actors, this chapter explores these themes for potential climate migrants in Canada's Indigenous Arctic communities. Particularly, it raises ethical questions about the legitimacy of distinguishing domestic climate migrants from their sovereign counterparts, and explores some of the potential impacts of this distinction on Indigenous claims for restitution. Indeed, as this chapter will suggest, the particular circumstances of many domestic, non-sovereign, populations present unique challenges in articulating and receiving due recognition for their struggles in climate justice, especially as these relate to resettlement. Taking Canada as an example, this chapter illustrates how a history of settler colonialism collapses Indigenous claims for climate justice into citizenship claims against the state that do not support international recognition of their ethical status as climate migrants. This process, I will suggest, has the effect of ethically minimizing the perceived legitimacy of Indigenous claims for "loss" vis-à-vis their territorially sovereign counterparts (small island states) experiencing similar practical challenges and near-identical ethical claims for recognition. In other words, I will suggest that the key difference between small island state (potential) climate migrants and Canada's (potential) Inuit climate migrants is their political status as a state versus that of domestic citizens.

Thus, the chapter will argue that Indigenous populations in Canada face additional obstacles as (potential) climate migrants in comparison to their sovereign counterparts because of the unique historical burdens they face under the legacy of settler colonialism — where they are viewed as a domestic, non-sovereign population — and *not* because of a differentiated ethical condition. Moreover, I will argue that this distinction matters because it challenges many of the traditional ways academics and policy-makers conceptualize the ethical burdens associated with climate change resettlement: along political grounds and in terms of state-based rights. The chapter offers three points of argument: first, how climate migrants might be understood from an ethical perspective; second, how a history of settler colonialism affects how we should expect climate resettlement to play out in Canada; and third, how this history undermines the political execution of climate justice for Inuit in the context of resettlement.

## CONCEPTUALIZING ETHICALLY ENTITLED CLIMATE MIGRANTS

Who are ethically entitled climate migrants? In many ways, the distinction between the various motivations to migrate (economic, environmental, or other) is most difficult to make in the context of climate migration: we know people migrate, and we know that environmental conditions like rising sea levels, soil erosion, permafrost melt, or extreme weather conditions can deeply impact decisions over when and why to migrate. Still, it remains difficult to distinguish the extent to which these decisions are influenced by economic, personal, or other factors: did the small-scale farmer move because of persistent drought, or because persistent drought made her livelihood economically unsustainable?[6] While it is likely safe to assume that more than one element will impact decisions to migrate, it is important to remember that these decisions also emerge against a backdrop framed by international law, which shapes both how climate migrants see themselves as well as their international recognition (or its lack) as a "vulnerable" population. For example, one of the landmark documents in international law that defines vulnerable migration is the 1951 United Nations Convention Relating to the Status of Refugees.[7] Notably, this Convention does not acknowledge environmental factors as capable of triggering protected status because environmental hardship does not meet the standard of "persecution," which is understood as either being carried out, or not protected against, by the state.[8] In other words, it is exclusively framed as a dysfunctional political, citizen–state relationship and not as an ethical breach. Beyond the Refugee Convention, much of international law and domestic policy relating to vulnerable migration generally follows an ethic that understands migration as more vulnerable, and thus ethically "legitimate" the more "necessary" it is: if one's life is at risk by staying, it is generally recognized that s/he has a legitimate right to leave, including an ethical right to enter another state.[9] Outside of this point, migration is typically understood as some degree of "optional" and largely left to the discretion of potential receiving states. Here, weighing the migrant's potential benefit to receiving state's goals is ethically considered to be a valid factor in the potential receiving state's decision-making process.[10]

Outside of political threat to life, or perceived (often, economic) value to the receiving state, clear migration paradigms begin to break down.[11] In the context of this chapter, I have environmental motivations in mind where, to date, no domestic immigration policy officially acknowledges environmental migration as triggering protected status. In this, it is not yet a commonly recognized migration rationale in the way that economic or forced migration is. Even where the environment is recognized as a legitimate migration motivator, it is often framed as a stay of deportation and not a reason to permanently resettle across state borders.[12] The same principles also tend to frame domestic recognition of environmental resettlement, where resettlement is either expected to be temporary (for example, Hurricane Katrina survivors in the United States)[13] or politically less significant than cross-border forced migration because it does not sever citizenship status for the affected population (see, for example, the resettlement of Isle de Jean Charles, Louisiana, or the inward retreat of the Tulele Peisa on the Carteret Islands).[14] In this way, the breaking of cultural histories and ties to the land are not (legally) recognized as a political loss in the same way that loss of citizenship might be for a "sinking" state.[15] Neither is the loss of "place" (associated with the loss of cultural or historical ties to the land)[16] captured in the legal rationale that captures loss of "property" as something that can be replaced or monetized.[17] I will say more about this later, but for now it is sufficient to note that while there is a clear emerging discussion about the ways in which climate change impacts resettlement, the international community of states — both in terms of domestic and cross-border relocation — is still struggling to clearly frame climate migration as a recognized, normalized re-settlement process.

Challenging traditional understandings of loss as exclusively material, some academics have sought to capture the ethical question underlying this debate through the loss of autonomy: to what extent did the climate migrant *choose* to move, and to what extent was she *forced* to relocate. Scholars like Diane Bates and Craig Johnson use this rationale to distinguish environmental migrants from "normalized" migrants who receive protection under the current international regime.[18] For example, Johnson argues that the application of the capabilities approach to the experience of environmental migrants better captures the question of choice, which is often overlooked in debates about how we should understand rights.[19] The capabilities approach broadly centres two ethical claims: first, that the freedom to achieve well-being is of primary moral importance; second, that the freedom to achieve well-being should be understood in terms of people's capabilities (i.e., their real opportunities to *do* and *be* what they value).[20]

Following the work of Martha Nussbaum and Amartya Sen, Johnson argues that decisions about where to live, and how to live, should be allowed to be made in relation to one's own preferences about individual values and personal well-being.[21] In other words, you should be able to make decisions about where and how to live based on your own chosen set of values. Further, he suggests that in order to decide the fundamental questions about life, livelihood, and well-being effectively, one must be free from poverty, intolerance, persecution, and other forms of human deprivation.[22] You cannot be considered "free to choose" your career if you are deeply constrained by poverty and have had to take multiple minimum-wage jobs to survive. In this, the capabilities approach offers a framework for understanding effective, ethical, and sufficient compensation for loss because of its expanded understanding of the potential for loss.[23] Pushing Johnson's application of the capabilities approach a bit further, this framework allows for an understanding of loss that is not reduced to a list of things that can be monetized (like property), nor to loss of pseudo-material legal rights (like citizenship), but is instead capable of understanding loss in terms of authenticity: the loss of being oneself, on one's own terms. Thus, I would argue that under the capabilities approach, we can understand an ethically entitled climate migrant as someone who suffers a loss sufficient to diminish or sever her ability to be herself. Here, the loss of culture and ties to place (rather than property or territory) would be recognized as legitimate losses *equal to* the loss of material property, similarly deserving restoration.

In the context of climate change, where human suffering is linked to the actions of others (in terms of anthropogenic greenhouse gas emissions, etc.), the capabilities approach gains traction because of the general acceptance that any necessary migration resulting from climate change should be considered a direct violation of normative human rights.[24] For communities where forced climate migration severs political autonomy, culture, or sovereign land claims, it has further been argued that these ethical losses should be elevated to the status of a violation of political human rights, similar to those of refugees.[25] For many, this logic is clear in the case of small island states like Tuvalu or Kiribati, where the entire island nation is expected to be submerged by rising sea levels sometime this century.[26] In these cases, a clear physical loss of territory/property, as well as a clear loss of autonomy, would accompany the loss of sovereign status. These losses, however, are more complicated to see in cases where the loss of land and autonomy do not follow the standard formula set out by Westphalian sovereignty: territory + political authority = sovereignty. In the Canadian context, these nuances become stark when we consider the expected resettlement of coastal Inuit communities in the Arctic.

## CLIMATE RESETTLEMENT UNDER A LEGACY OF SETTLER COLONIALISM

Overall, we are seeing (and anticipating) the impact of climate change on settlement in Canada in four primary ways, all of which parallel the global experience: coastal invasion, prairie drought, extreme weather, and ice melt.[27] That said, Canada's climate has been disproportionately affected by climate change. For example, between 1950 and 2010, both the rate of warming (1.5°C)[28] and the rate of permafrost melt and coastal invasion nearly doubled the global average in Arctic regions.[29] The Inuit, in part because they live in small, remote northern communities, are especially sensitive to these changes in climate, where food security is increasingly threatened as hunters experience restricted access to traditional travel routes and hunting grounds on both land and ice due to climate change.[30] Moreover, coastal erosion, flooding, and permafrost thaw related to sea-level rise and generally warming temperatures increasingly threaten the viability of Arctic housing developments, damage heritage sites, and affect infrastructure ranging from municipal buildings, sewage systems, and local roadways to the seasonal ice roads used to transport food and other basic necessities to remote communities.[31] While large-scale resettlement efforts have yet to begin, concerns over their impending reality are beginning to take centre stage, especially within Indigenous communities.

In their work on mapping climate change through Indigenous knowledge, Huntington and Fox summarize some of the concerns raised during a First Nations Council discussion in the Yukon:

> In the northern Yukon, freezing rains in November have meant that animals cannot eat. Birds that usually migrate south in August and September are now being seen in October and November. In some areas, thawing permafrost has caused the ground to drop and in some cases has made the area smell foul. In more southerly communities, rings around the moon are no longer seen, although they are still visible in the northernmost community. There are increased sightings of new types of insect and an increase in cougar (*Puma concolor*) and mule deer (*Odocoileus hemionus*). People used to be able to predict when it would get colder by looking at tree leaves. It is difficult to do that now. Lakes and streams are drying up, or are becoming choked with weeds, making the water undrinkable. Many animals are changing their distribution and behavior. Bears used to go into their dens in October and November, but are now out until December. One bear was spotted in winter sleeping under a tree but above ground, rather than in a den, which was regarded as an exceptional and unprecedented sighting.[32]

Accounts from this meeting further express Elders' fears about these changes, where one Elder explained that he "had never expected to see the day when people would worry about water, but now [he] hears about that all the time."³³ Indeed, for communities living in the Arctic, it is widely expected that the impacts of climate change will progress to the point where the possibility for sustainable living will collapse, necessitating resettlement towards the southern provinces and economic centres.³⁴

Here, the capabilities approach brings questions of agency to the forefront: who decides when and where migration will take place? How will these decisions be made, and will cultural relationships with the land be considered in the process? Since "[c]ulture is inextricably linked to the [land] with knowledge of seasonal rhythms, weather predictions, animal migration routes, in addition to the quantity and quality of sea ice," the anticipated resettlement of Inuit communities would mean more than a loss of property; it could mean a loss of being Inuit on their own terms.³⁵ Yet, federal and territorial governmental responses have been relatively silent on these issues, or — where they have spoken — have framed resettlement as an issue of development, suggesting that Indigenous northerners may have to resettle in southern Canada to better integrate into the Canadian economy.³⁶

Ethically, the use of a development frame raises significant concerns over the lack of recognition it gives to Canada's Indigenous peoples and their own knowledge, experiences, and adaptability.³⁷ The ethical challenge presented by this framework gap becomes even more concerning when one compares the decision-making process that will apply to Indigenous climate resettlement vis-à-vis their sovereign small island state counterparts. Here, Indigenous peoples facing forced climate resettlement are ethically disadvantaged as a direct result of the way in which we conceptually distinguish political agency for sovereign and non-sovereign (citizen) groups: as citizens, any forced resettlement is fundamentally conceived of as the responsibility of the government, thus limiting the agency of affected populations to the intellectual and legal bounds of government authority. Under the capabilities approach, Inuit relocation would also mark a further severing of culture and tradition — of the ability to be oneself, to make one's own decisions — by moving people away from their historic lands and ways of being, while simultaneously reaffirming state control over a colonized people in terms of resettlement management.[38] In contrast, Indigenous peoples who hold sovereign authority (autonomy), like those on the small island states of Tuvalu and Kiribati, either do not face this challenge or face it in a way that maintains their political voice. By this, I mean that should resettlement be necessitated, political space would be carved out for them in the decision-making process outlined by their governmental structure (not that they would be able to avoid resettlement).

Here, I suggest the primary conceptual hurdle that differentiates these otherwise similar groups is how the international community has traditionally understood sovereignty: singularly. Under the international imaginary, there is one sovereign (i.e., ultimate) political authority per piece of territory, and "sovereignty" captures the nexus between power, authority, and land as "owned" territory.[39] In Canada, however, this singular idea of sovereignty is challenged by the settler-colonialism paradigm. Under settler colonialism, two sovereign autonomies are bound under one political authority. Here, sovereignty breaks down the traditional relationship of political authority, people, and land in that it reifies the sense of sovereign authority over the ownership of land. In this, "sovereignty" can be dislodged from the homeland (Britain, in this case), so that it can travel with a settler population. It becomes their own, detached from the notion of territory.[40] As Lauren Benton describes, since "subjects could be located anywhere, and the tie between sovereign and subject was defined as a legal relationship . . . authority was not bound territorially."[41] In this, sovereignty is created, or recreated, by the settler population, and then applied to territory (in Canada, through land-use projects, the application of deeds for real estate, and, most significantly, control over Indigenous populations through the restriction of access to settler lands).[42]

Scholars like Glen Sean Coulthard and Audra Simpson argue that Canadian sovereignty is fundamentally a settler-colonial sovereignty, citing the history of governmental relations with Indigenous populations, the reserve system, residential schooling, government-sponsored attempts at (cultural) genocide, forced relocation, and a complicated treaty regime as evidence, especially among southern Indigenous peoples.[43] In northern communities, cultural and political domination occurred through increasing intervention in Inuit lifestyles by settler-colonial political and economic powers. Early bartering encounters between Inuit and European peoples in whaling, caribou, fishing, and the fox hunt, for example, began an economic entwining of Inuit populations with European economic forces and foreign consumer goods, which contributed to widespread Indigenous starvation after the collapse of fur prices in the 1930s.[44] This economic collapse spread into increased political domination and diminishing autonomy for the Inuit through a series of federal relief programs that were implemented during the 1930s and 1940s.[45] These eventually evolved into full-scale government intervention aimed at settling permanent populations of Inuit in government-sponsored towns and municipalities, and integrating the Inuit more fully into the economy through full-time wage labour throughout the 1950s.[46] Over the next 20 years, resource development in the North became a central goal of the Canadian government, which further integrated Inuit populations into the capitalist model by encouraging the construction of sedentary communities and wage-based employment.[47] Following this model, the government's framing of climate resettlement as an opportunity for economic development can be seen as a continuation of these colonial efforts in the contemporary moment.[48]

From a perspective that centres the capabilities approach, the rapid and expansive drive for political and economic integration severed Inuit populations from many traditional lifestyles in dramatic, traumatic, and lasting ways. As Allison Crawford, Director of the Northern Psychiatric Outreach Program at the Centre for Addiction and Mental Health and assistant professor at the University of Toronto, has argued:

> In little more than fifty years Inuit people in the North of Canada have experienced sudden and sweeping change to their traditional way of life and culture. Compounding this rapid change, many of the pressures to accommodate to modern Canadian life and governance were prodded by policies and actions that have since been deemed an abuse of rights, autonomy, and dignity.[49]

The history of Canadian–Indigenous relations matters here, as it demonstrates a clear trend over time towards diminishing the political and economic autonomy of Indigenous peoples, which has yet to be adequately recognized as part of ongoing colonial practices. The last major resettlement project in the Arctic, carried out from 1953 to 1955, saw the Canadian government relocate Inuit 2,000 kilometres from their homeland in northern Quebec to the communities known today as Resolute Bay and Grise Fiord.[50] Despite having been promised abundant hunting opportunities prior to the move, these did not materialize in the new environment, which was significantly colder and harsher than their previous locale.[51] Further, these resettled families had been promised that they could return home after two or three years, should they be unhappy with the High Arctic. These promises were not kept, and migrants were separated from their families and homes for many years following the initial resettlement process, which has since been recognized as having been designed in part to stake land-use claims to Canada's most northerly borders.[52] In 1996, the Royal Commission on Aboriginal Peoples found that this relocation constituted "abuse" by the government, separating people from their traditional relationships with the land, their language, culture, and traditional belief systems (all of which would be expected under a settler-colonial frame, where solidifying authority and establishing ultimate control over Indigenous populations is the final stage of successful settlement).[53] Furthermore, recent studies have shown that these efforts in resettlement played a significant role not only in demarcating Canadian political sovereignty in the Arctic Circle during the Cold War era, but also in reinforcing Canadian political authority over Inuit autonomy.[54]

Coming out of a particularly difficult period of governmental relations in the 1950s and early 1960s, including the dehumanizing deployment of the e-numbering system to codify and track Inuit populations through the use of a dog-tagged numbering system, and the tuberculosis epidemic that relocated many Inuit to southern Canada for treatment with little to no record of their status made available to loved ones left behind, the late 1960s and 1970s saw the strong emergence of Indigenous efforts to re-establish self-governance among Inuit in the North.[55] In 1971, the Inuit formed the national organization Inuit Tapirisat of Canada (now Inuit Tapiriit Kanatami [ITK]) to lobby the government of Canada to increase their autonomy, request self-government, and process a land claim for the Northwest Territories and northern Quebec.[56] Their claims were partially recognized with the creation of regional councils to advise (not legislate) territorial governments on local issues in response to the concerns raised by federal reports and policies, including the 1966–67 Hawthorn Report and the infamous 1969 White Paper.[57] The Baffin Regional Council was established in 1977, which served as the first regional council in the Northwest Territories, and was followed quickly by the creation of six similar councils across the North.[58] The year 1982 saw the repatriation of the British North America Act, renamed the Constitution Act, 1867, and at the same time section 35 of the new Constitution Act, 1982, which includes the Charter of Rights and Freedoms, recognized and affirmed Aboriginal treaty rights in Canada. The following year the Parliamentary Task Force on Indian Self-Government (the Penner Report) picked up on the earlier recommendation from the Hawthorn Report that Indigenous peoples should be considered "citizens plus," with dual rights and a form of Indigenous "citizenship."

Yet, despite these efforts, the Inuit, and indeed the territories themselves, still lie directly under the authority of the federal government and are administered by Crown–Indigenous Relations and Northern Affairs Canada. Their claims for self-government have, in many ways, been actualized to a greater extent than those

of Indigenous First Nations or Métis, as a series of four compre-
hensive land claim agreements (James Bay and Northern Quebec
Agreement [1975], Inuvialuit Final Agreement [1983], Nunavut
Land Claims Agreement [1993], and the Labrador Inuit Land
Claim Agreement [2002]) and the relative population density of
Inuit in the North have enabled some level of autonomous
self-government through public government.[59] This is not, however, to suggest that public, consensus-based government in the
North is sufficiently organized to enable Inuit political autonomy,
merely that it enables higher levels of representation in comparison with the low representation of Indigenous peoples in the public
governments of the provinces.[60] Theoretically, then, the historical
legacy of settler colonialism and the limitations it places on
self-government and sovereign autonomy are significant to my
argument because they illuminate the ongoing potential for "loss"
as forced climate migrants under the capabilities approach.

## CHALLENGING DISAGGREGATED ETHICAL AND POLITICAL RIGHTS: CLIMATE JUSTICE UNDER SETTLER STATES

Thus far, I have argued that understanding ethically entitled climate migrants under the capabilities approach allows us to define
them as people who suffer a loss sufficient to diminish or sever
their abilities to be themselves. From here, I illustrated the way in
which the history of Canadian–Inuit relations should be recognized as fitting comfortably within a settler-colonial paradigm. The
final piece of my argument, then, explores the way in which the
legacy of settler colonialism disadvantages the ethical claims of the
Inuit in comparison to those of traditionally conceived sovereign

peoples. The distinction between Canada's Inuit, who face the brunt of climate change in Canada, and their sovereign-state counterparts can be understood as ethically similar, but politically different. Ethically, both populations face injustice because they will likely be forced to resettle away from their traditional lands and lifestyles (including the cultural ties each population has with the land) due to global environmental processes beyond their control. In this, both groups face significant loss in terms of the capabilities approach — after all, they will likely struggle to maintain their traditional way of being themselves.[61] Politically, however, this loss will function differently for each group. Where strong efforts have been made for sovereign-state resettlement to happen under proactive, autonomous terms wherever possible (for example, Kiribati purchased 6,000 hectares of land in Fiji to extend food security and hold property for future migration),[62] non-sovereign populations are largely forced to wait for their governments to choose how to act. Examples of this difference are found in the resettlement of Isle de Jean Charles in Louisiana and the Arctic resettlement of the Indigenous communities of Unalakleet, Golovin, and Teller in Alaska, where the U.S. Army Corps deemed resettlement to be a low priority based on "expert" scientific knowledge, and this delay greatly reduced the ability of these communities to resettle on their own terms.[63] While no clear resettlement plan currently exists in Canada, these concerns are certainly at the forefront of affected communities, as discussed.[64]

Here, Veracini's conceptual understanding of the way settler colonialism functions can help to explain its impacts on the political histories that complicate contemporary ethical issues in resettlement, and why this legacy matters for the future of northern climate resettlement in Canada and other states with domestic non-sovereign populations.[65] Much of my argument in this regard builds from the disaggregation of territory and sovereign (autonomous, political) authority, which is rejoined under the power of the settler society.[66] This process simultaneously disaggregates the political and ethical statuses of the affected peoples. As a result, an argument can be made for the recognition of special ethical consideration for *both* sovereign and non-sovereign climate migrant populations, as the deep-seated link between territory and political authority permeates both, despite the unjust differentiation of their political statuses.

How might this happen? Ultimately, the political differentiation in status happens because "settlers knew they were asserting *their own* as they moved across space," where sovereign authority travelled with the settler population and did not emerge from the land.[67] The North, then, was not understood as a space for "sovereign" political territory in Canada until it was colonized (before that, it was conceived of as merely land with people living on it). Indigenous peoples, therefore, never truly held conceptual sovereign territorial authority under the Westphalian paradigm, despite their ongoing cultural relationship with, and physical presence on, the land. To be clear, what I am suggesting here is that the settler-colonial paradigm complicates the Westphalian understanding of sovereignty, splitting it into two components — autonomy, and territorial authority — which would otherwise be conceptually joined. Where Indigenous people fail to hold territorial authority under the settler-colonial frame, I would argue that the same cannot be accurately said of their autonomous identity as a people who are tied to the land (as opposed to legal "territory" in Western terms). Here, while they lack political authority under the Westphalian regime, they maintain ethical authority as a people. This is why, as climate migrants, they have near-identical ethical claims to those of their sovereign counterparts, but lack sufficient political grounds — and legal standing — to actualize those claims.

This is a complex claim with significant theoretical conclusions, and so I will make some effort to further unpack it. The easier part of the claim is that under settler colonialism, as explained above, the land is not truly considered sovereign until it is claimed by the settler population. At the time of "settlement," the conceptual sovereign authority that had been carried by the settler population transferred to the land and became inextricably colonial.[68] Thus, conceptually at least, any pre-existing relationship Indigenous peoples had with the land cannot effectively be considered to be a political relationship that could have led to sovereign territorial authority in the eyes of the settler state.

The more complicated part of the claim relates to autonomous political identity, land, and the concept of ownership. Here, the conceptual disconnect between land and authority can be linked to the Lockean proviso, where — because they were not "using" the land in traditionally recognized European ways (settling, etc.) — Indigenous peoples were not seen to have the claim to territorial sovereignty that was explicitly tied to it.[69] They did nothing to change the land in any way, thus — following Locke — had no claim to ownership over it. Linking this argument to climate change resettlement ethics, there is a strong parallel to the theoretical significance of the Lockean proviso in grounding political claims for the protection of, or allocation of, special rights for potential climate migrants.[70] Under Locke's logic of landownership, the severing of sovereign land use becomes a foundational argument in constructing an argument for international liability, where the loss of use-value of the land due to climate change gives the necessary grounds for a legal breach.[71] In other words, under international law, citizens of small island states who are in the process of being inundated by rising seas can be seen to "own" their land (i.e., are territorially sovereign over it), and any loss of this ownership at the hands of another (anthropogenic climate change, in this case) becomes an issue of strict liability, just as would be the case were I to destroy your car, or your home. I am responsible to mitigate your loss and make you "whole" again, just as the international community must take responsibility for the small island state. For the Inuit, though, this logic fails to hold because of the settler-colonial paradigm *and not because there is no loss*. Here, inasmuch as the Inuit claim to sovereign territory (i.e., political land "ownership") was politically severed under settler colonialism, their ability to launch a similar claim for special protection based on loss of use-value holds no rational ground, despite the similarity in circumstances (where both small island states and northern Inuit communities are facing significant threats to traditional land-use practices of settlement and food security, as a result of climate change).[72] Thus, the splitting of sovereignty is significant: where the Inuit have no recognized claim for territorial loss under settler colonialism (the stronger claim in international law), they do hold an ethical claim to loss of cultural autonomy, as it is tied to the land (which I offer is an equally strong ethical argument rooted in the capabilities approach, despite its lack of legal standing). In this, the Inuit hold claims to normative human rights under settler colonialism, but struggle to make recognizable claims to legal human rights, as distinguished above.

From my argument, then, the territorial sovereign authority asserted by the Canadian government over the Inuit and the function of Canadian citizenship currently stand as two of their greatest barriers in staking internationally recognized claims for loss as potential climate migrants. This is problematic for Inuit communities because the rights they might expect as a sovereign people differ from the ethical recognition they might expect as citizens of Canada (their autonomy is functionally "Canadian," not "Inuit"). While sovereign peoples of small island states expecting the loss of sovereign territorial autonomy have a potential legal argument for injustice, "citizens" have a pre-existing framework for (internal) migration and are, as a result, ethically and legally normalized.[73] For example, following the devastation and resettlement caused by Hurricane Katrina, the United States government actively avoided declaring the survivors of Hurricane Katrina "internally displaced persons" (IDPs). Roberta Cohen suggests this move was made to avoid international monitoring or political intervention in the maintenance of their well-being.[74] Indeed, for IDP monitoring or international protection services to apply to a domestic population, the affected state must first declare a state of emergency and then request international intervention. IDPs have no right to this protection otherwise.[75] From traditional perspectives that view climate migrants exclusively (or nearly exclusively) as people requiring physical resettlement, the resulting injustice is easy to miss; however, from a perspective that challenges the intellectual function of sovereign authority, the injustice is remarkable.

Moreover, the 2007 United Nations Declaration on the Rights of Indigenous Peoples (UNDRIP) sheds further light on how the function of citizenship (secondary autonomous status under Canadian authority) can mask these sorts of ethical rights. Heather Nichol, for example, argues that UNDRIP should be viewed as more than merely a minority rights or human rights declaration because it "specifically enshrines the rights of Indigenous peoples as Indigenous peoples, outside of the traditional conceptual constraints of Westphalian sovereignty."[76] Through representative organizations such as the Inuit Circumpolar Council (ICC), and by using UNDRIP to frame their claims, Arctic Indigenous peoples have since sought to entrench not just their state-based right to self-determination (which has been increasingly realized over the past two decades), but also their right to be recognized as legitimate and autonomous international actors within the international decision-making regime.[77] For example, the ICC's Circumpolar Inuit Declaration of Sovereignty, issued in the wake of the Ilulissat Declaration, cited UNDRIP as the most important instrument in securing their absolute right to be directly included (and not "represented") in Arctic sovereignty deliberations: "Our rights as an Indigenous people include the following rights recognized in the United Nations Declaration on the Rights of Indigenous Peoples (UNDRIP), all of which are relevant to sovereignty and sovereign rights in the Arctic."[78] In a similar statement, Inuit Tapiriit Kanatami declared:

> We will exercise our rights of self-determination in the Arctic by building on institutions such as the Inuit Circumpolar Council and the Arctic Council, the Arctic-specific features of international instruments, such as the ice-covered-waters provision of the United Nations Convention on the Law of the Sea, and the Arctic-related work of international mechanisms, such as the United Nations Permanent Forum on Indigenous Issues, the office of the United Nations Special Rapporteur on the

Rights and Fundamental Freedoms of Indigenous Peoples, and the UNDRIP.[79]

In an era increasingly marked by climate change and resulting resettlement, self-determination could be twofold for the Inuit: first, to break the political bonds of settler colonialism; and second, to gain the ability to effectively assert their political claims as climate migrants outside of the authority of their state. As this chapter has sought to illustrate, the Inuit are somewhat uniquely positioned between the constraints imposed upon them in both contexts, where the legacies of settler colonialism further diminish their already limited capacity to achieve international recognition as climate migrants requiring special ethical considerations. This is significant because where these migrant groups currently hold sovereign status, their concerns over the loss of culture, language, and community that are likely to follow migration — especially where these points of consideration are closely tied to the land and the power to maintain political autonomy — are increasingly considered to be of legitimate international concern.[80] Yet, for the Inuit, this connection between land and loss of culture is masked under traditional understandings of territorial sovereignty and political authority in a settler-colonial state. Fundamentally, I have sought to demonstrate the ways in which this frame obscures their claims to sovereign political autonomy and the particularisms of Inuit culture as they are tied to Arctic lands. Furthermore, this distinction is significant not only for the Inuit, but also for studies in Canadian–Inuit relations and studies in climate migration, because it requests a shift in thinking about how we view the relationship between ethical burdens and political standing vis-à-vis the state. This relationship is also conceptually more complicated than what is captured by the traditional political conception of citizen–state relations as a rights-bearing category that sufficiently sustains political authority. Instead, building on the themes of this volume, it requests an understanding of citizenship as something that is deeply affected by political histories, like settler colonialism, and asks ongoing questions about legitimacy and autonomy, especially in settler states.

## CONCLUSION

Employing the capabilities approach as the foundation of its ethical frame, this chapter has sought to establish that climate resettlement efforts in Canada's Arctic are challenged to capture Indigenous claims for loss because of their political status under the legacies of settler colonialism. Beneath this claim, the chapter also challenged traditional understandings of legitimacy in (climate) resettlement studies: the legitimacy of who is recognized as being vulnerable to resettlement, the legitimacy of how the international community recognizes "loss," the legitimacy of who should have the authority to make decisions about resettlement, and the way in which these questions can affect our assumptions about political autonomy, cultural history, and their ties to land/territory. Like other chapters in this volume, these questions offer valuable critiques of traditionally conceived notions that do not sit in an intellectual vacuum. Neither are they limited in their applicability to Inuit peoples or Arctic resettlement in Canada. Indeed, the parallels between my arguments and the concerns raised by both Loo (Chapter 2) and Christensen and Arnfjord (Chapter 5) in this volume underscore deeper thematic considerations for resettlement processes in Canada and in the global context. For example,

Loo asks questions about the function of state power and legitimacy which are echoed here. Who should decide issues of mobility, agency, and autonomy? How do the power dynamics between the state and its citizens reify certain assumptions that might silence other perspectives? Where Loo revisits these questions through a lens that centres governmental relationships, this chapter has offered critique from an ethics-driven perspective that centres the capabilities approach; yet, our concerns often overlap, particularly over the issue of legitimacy. Christensen and Arnfjord raise similar questions of agency and autonomy, considering the role of "expert knowledge" in influencing the perceived legitimacy of climate change resettlement politics. Indeed, as this chapter has discussed, the role of expert knowledge also raises questions for Arctic resettlement in Canada because of its capacity to push out local Indigenous knowledge of the land and to silence the relationship between people and place that this knowledge is built on. These themes highlight this space of unresolved tension in resettlement studies as one poised for future work in the field.

In the context of Arctic climate resettlement, thinking through questions of agency, mobility, and autonomy for Canada's Inuit has led me to suggest that the history of settler colonialism will complicate the ethics involved in any policy-making process that will be undertaken as the first community-scale resettlement efforts begin to unfold. Yet, again, the concerns I have raised would also apply to other non-sovereign domestic populations currently facing resettlement due to climate change: while the theoretical frame of settler colonialism sets non-sovereign, Indigenous domestic populations as distinct — with their own special ethical considerations — it should also be remembered that *any* forced resettlement related to climate change would carry some special ethical argument because of the global anthropogenic nature of climate change. In this, the application of the capabilities approach to domestic climate resettlement would require any state to consider the agency of affected populations much more centrally than would otherwise be required under a traditional citizenship approach. Here, states like Bangladesh, the United States, and many small island nations — where domestic resettlement projects are either underway or imminent — would benefit from considering the arguments raised in this volume about agency, autonomy, mobility, and legitimacy as they seek to construct effective climate resettlement policies. Withers (Chapter 3), Côté and Pottie-Sherman (Chapter 4), and Barry and Côté (Chapter 6) all raise similar questions about the agency of domestic populations in resettlement projects.

Overall, this chapter underscores that while climate change may present new challenges to resettlement in both theory and practice, many of the fundamental themes this volume has located as underpinning resettlement studies find traction here as well. Clearly, these issues are not restricted to the specificities of their case, nor to the specificities of a single country (although these factors can make significant impacts, as this and other chapters illustrate). Moving forward, the significance of these and other areas of overlap mark important considerations as studies in resettlement shift to meet future challenges.

## NOTES

1   International Institute for Environment and Development (IIED), "Climate Change: Study Maps Those at Greatest Risk from Cyclones and Rising Seas," 28 Mar. 2007, http://www.iied.org/climate-change-study-maps-those-greatest-risk-cyclones-rising-seas.

2   Ibid.

3   Ibid.; IPCC, "Climate Change 2014: Synthesis Report," in *Working Groups I, II, and III to the Fifth Assessment Report of the Intergovernmental Panel on Climate Change*, eds. Core Writing Team and R.K. Pachauri and L.A. Meyer (Geneva, 2014).

4   IIED, *Climate Change*.

5   See, for example, IPCC, "Climate Change 2014"; Richard Black, "Environmental Refugees: Myth or Reality?" (UNHCR, Working Paper no. 34, 2001); Jane McAdam, *Climate Change and Displacement* (Oxford: Hart Publishing, 2010).

6   See especially Robert McLeman, Michael Opatowski, Betina Borova, and Margaret Walton-Roberts, "Climate Migration: What We Know and Don't Know," Wilfred Laurier University, 2016, http://www.laurierenvironmentalmigration.com/wp-content/uploads/2015/11/WLU-Environmental-Migration-Background-Report.pdf; Jane McAdam, *Climate Change, Forced Migration, and International Law* (Oxford: Oxford University Press, 2012); Jane McAdam, "Creating New Norms on Climate Change, Natural Disasters and Displacement: International Developments 2010–2013," *Refuge* 29, no. 2 (2013): 11–26.

7   *United Nations High Commissioner for Refugees Convention and Protocol Relating to the Status of Refugees: Text of the 1951 Convention Relating to the Status of Refugees, Text of the 1967 Protocol Relating to the Status of Refugees, and Resolution 2198 (XXI) Adopted by the United Nations General Assembly* (Geneva: UNHCR, 2014).

8   Matthew Lister, "Climate Change Refugees," *Critical Review of International Social and Political Philosophy* 17, no. 1 (2014): 618–34; *Ioane Teitiota v. The Chief Executive of the Ministry of Business, Innovation and Employment*, NZHC 3125 (New Zealand High Court, 2013).

9   See Wayne A. Cornelius, Philip L. Martin, and James Frank Hollifield, *Controlling Immigration*, 2nd ed. (Stanford, CA: Stanford University Press, 2004).

10  Here, one can look to the points system used to adjudicate potential immigrants that prioritizes economic value in countries like Canada, Australia, New Zealand, and the United Kingdom, or to

countries like Germany and France where a standing job offer is required for non-European Union citizen migrants. See Massimiliano Tani, "Using a Point System for Selecting Immigrants," *IZA World of Labor* (2014), doi: 10.15185/izawol.24; Cornelius, Martin, and Hollifield, *Controlling Immigration*.

11   One notable exception is in some family reunification categories, but because this category is typically pre-empted by economic value, I have not distinguished it here.

12   See Sweden's Aliens Act (2005), Finland's Aliens Act (2004), Denmark's Aliens Act, or the US's Temporary Protected Status.

13   See Roberta Cohen, "For Disaster IDPs: An Institutional Gap," *Brookings Institution* (2008), https://www.brookings.edu/opinions/for-disaster-idps-an-institutional-gap/.

14   Ursula Rakova, "How-To Guide For Environmental Refugees: Carteret Islanders' Own Relocation Plan," United Nations University (2009).

15   See the Cartagena Declaration on Refugees (1984), or New Zealand's addition of environmental degradation to the rationale of its humanitarian category supporting immigration.

16   See Keith Thor Carlson, *The Power of Place, the Problem of Time: Aboriginal Identity and Historical Consciousness in the Cauldron of Colonialism* (Toronto: University of Toronto Press, 2010).

17   See Margaret Moore, *A Political Theory of Territory* (New York: Oxford University Press, 2015).

18   Diane C. Bates, "Environmental Refugees? Classifying Human Migrations Caused by Environmental Change," *Population and Environment* 23 (2002): 465–77; Craig Johnson, "Governing Climate Displacement: The Ethics and Politics of Human Resettlement," *Environmental Politics* 21, no. 2 (2012): 308–28.

19   Johnson, "Governing Climate Displacement"; Martha Nussbaum, "Capabilities and Human Rights," *Fordham Law Review* 66 (1997): 273–300; Martha Nussbaum, *Women and Human Development: The Capabilities Approach* (Cambridge: Cambridge University Press, 2001); Amartya Sen, *Development as Freedom* (New York and Oxford: Oxford University Press, 2001 [1999]).

20  Sen, *Development as Freedom.*

21  Nussbaum, "Capabilities and Human Rights"; Sen, *Development as Freedom*; Johnson, "Governing Climate Displacement."

22  Johnson,"Governing Climate Displacement," following Sen, *Development as Freedom.*

23  Johnson, "Governing Climate Displacement."

24  Simon Caney, "Cosmopolitan Justice, Responsibility, and Global Climate Change," *Leiden Journal of International Law* 18, no. 4 (2005): 747–75; Simon Caney, "Human Rights, Climate Change, and Discounting," *Environmental Politics* 17, no. 4 (2008): 536–55; Sujatha Byravan and Sudhir Rajan, "Providing Homes for Climate Exiles," *Climate Policy* 6, no. 1 (2006): 247–52; E.A. Page, "Intergenerational Justice of What? Welfare, Resources or Capabilities?" *Environmental Politics* 16, no. 3 (2007): 453–69; E.A. Page, "Distributing the Burdens of Climate Change," *Environmental Politics* 17, no. 4 (2008): 556–75; Mathias Risse, "The Right to Relocation: Disappearing Island Nations and Common Ownership of the Earth," *Ethics & International Affairs* 23 (2009): 281–300; Mathias Risse, "Immigration, Ethics, and the Capabilities Approach," United Nations Development Programme Online Human Development Research Paper Series, 2009, http://hdr.undp.org/en/reports/global/hdr2009/papers/.

25  Cara Nine, "Ecological Refugees, States Borders, and the Lockean Proviso," *Journal of Applied Philosophy* 27, no. 4 (2010): 359–75; Lister, "Climate Change Refugees"; Nicole Marshall, "Forced Environmental Migration: Ethical Considerations for Emerging Migration Policy," *Ethics, Policy & Environment* 19, no. 1 (2016): 1–18.

26  IPCC, "Climate Change."

27  F.J. Warren and D.S Lemmen, eds., *Canada in a Changing Climate: Sector Perspectives on Impacts and Adaptation* (Ottawa: Government of Canada, 2014), 286; Camille Parmesan and Gary Yohe, "A Globally Coherent Fingerprint of Climate Change Impacts across Natural Systems," *Nature* 421 (2003): 37–42.

28  Warren and Lemmen, *Canada in a Changing Climate.*

29  Ibid.

30  Tristan Pearce, James D. Ford, Amanda Caron, and Bill Patrick
    Kudlak. "Climate Change Adaptation Planning in Remote, Re-
    source-dependent Communities: An Arctic Example," *Regional
    Environmental Change* 12 (2012): 825–37; Chris Furgal and Terry D.
    Prowse, "Northern Canada," in *Impacts to Adaptation: Canada in a
    Changing Climate 2007*, eds. Donald S. Lemmen, Fiona J. Warren,
    Elizabeth Bush, and Jacinthe Lacroix (Ottawa: Government of
    Canada, 2008), 57–118.

31  Warren and Lemmen, *Canada in a Changing Climate*; N.J. Couture
    and W.H. Pollard, "Modelling Geomorphic Response to Climatic
    Change," *Climate Change* 85 (2007): 407–31; L. Alessa, A. Kliskey,
    and P. Williams, "Perception of Change in Freshwater in Remote
    Resource-dependent Arctic Communities," *Global Environmental
    Change* 18 (2008): 153–64; Peter H. Larsen, Scott Goldsmith,
    Orson Smith, Meghan L. Wilson, Ken Strzepek, Paul Chinowsky,
    and Ben Saylor, "Estimating Future Costs for Alaska Public
    Infrastructure at Risk from Climate Change," *Global Environmen-
    tal Change* 18 (2008): 442–57; F. Zhou, A. Zhang, R. Li, and E.
    Hoeve, "Spatio-temporal Simulation of Permafrost Geothermal
    Response to Climate Change Scenarios in a Building Environ-
    ment," *Cold Regional Science and Technology* 56 (2009): 141–51;
    Pearce et al., "Climate Change Adaptation Planning."

32  Henry Huntington and Shari Fox, "The Changing Arctic: Indige-
    nous Perspectives," *Arctic Climate Impact Assessment* (Cambridge:
    Cambridge University Press, 2005), 77–78.

33  Ibid., 78.

34  Timothy R. Leduc, *Climate Culture Change* (Ottawa: University of
    Ottawa Press, 2010); Kenyon Bolton, Martin Lougheed, James Ford,
    Scot Nickels, Carrie Grable, and Jamal Shirley, *What We Know,
    Don't Know, and Need to Know about Climate Change in Inuit
    Nunangat* (Ottawa: Inuit Tapiriit Kanatami, 2011); Pearce et al.,
    "Climate Change Adaptation Planning."

35  Inuit Tapiriit Kanatami, "The Climate Change Bind for Inuit: The
    Double Burden of Impacts and Campaigns," *Unravelling the Arctic
    Panel Discussion* (Ottawa, 22 Apr. 2015).

36  Ibid.

37  Ibid.

38  See Loo, Chapter 2.

39  Moore, *A Political Theory of Territory*; Heather Nichol, "Reframing Sovereignty: Indigenous Peoples and Arctic States," *Polar Geography* 79 (2010): 78–80; Lorenzo Veracini, *Settler Colonialism: A Theoretical Overview* (London: Palgrave Macmillan, 2010); Laura Valentini, "Human Rights, Freedom, and Political Authority," *Political Theory* 40, no. 5 (2012): 573–601.

40  Veracini, *Settler Colonialism*, 54.

41  Lauren Benton, *A Search for Sovereignty: Law and Geography in European Empires, 1400–1900* (Cambridge: Cambridge University Press, 2010).

42  Indeed, Veracini, *Settler Colonialism*, 70, suggests that the interplay for autonomous independence in Canada went on far longer than in most countries, where "developing settler isopolitical nationalisms and imperial commitments continuously co-defined each other in reciprocal tension for a very long time." It is worth noting, as well, that this is not a clean recreation of sovereign authority, but rather one that plays out in deep tension with traditional colonial responsibilities to the homeland, especially those related to resource extraction. See Benton, *A Search for Sovereignty*.

43  Glen Sean Coulthard, *Red Skin, White Masks* (Minneapolis: University of Minnesota Press, 2014); Audra Simpson, *Mohawk Interruptus: Political Life across the Borders of Settler States* (Durham, NC: Duke University Press, 2014). Also see, for example, Truth and Reconciliation Commission (TRC), *Honouring the Truth, Reconciling for the Future: Final Report of the Truth and Reconciliation Commission of Canada* (Winnipeg: TRC, 2015); Arthur Ray, *An Illustrated History of Canada's Native People: I Have Lived Here Since the World Began* (Montreal and Kingston: McGill-Queen's University Press, 2011).

44  Erik Anderson, *Canada's Relationship with the Inuit: A History of Policy and Program Development* (Ottawa: Department of Indian and Northern Affairs, 2006).

45  David Damas, *Arctic Migrants/Arctic Villagers: The Transformation of Inuit Settlement in the Central Arctic* (Montreal and Kingston: McGill-Queen's University Press, 2002), 192–93.

46  Ibid.

47  Inuit Tapiriit Kanatami, "Backgrounder on Inuit and Housing for Discussion at Housing Sectoral Meeting" (2005), http:// www.itk. ca/roundtable/sectoral-housing-backgrounder.php; Damas, *Arctic Migrants/Arctic Villagers*, 192–93; R. Quinn Duffy, *The Road to Nunavut: The Progress of the Eastern Arctic Since the Second World War* (Montreal and Kingston: McGill-Queen's University Press, 1988), 16–17; Patrick Gerald Nixon, "Eskimo Housing Programmes, 1954–65: A Case Study of Representative Bureaucracy" (PhD diss., University of Western Ontario, 1984), 90–134.

48  Inuit Tapiriit Kanatami, "The Climate Change Bind."

49  Allison Crawford, "The Trauma Experienced by Generations Past Having an Effect in Their Descendants: Narrative and Historical Trauma among Inuit in Nunavut, Canada," *Transcultural Psychiatry* 51, no. 3 (2014): 340.

50  R. Dussault and G. Erasmus, *The High Arctic Relocation: A Report on the 1953–1955 Relocation*, produced for the Royal Commission on Aboriginal Peoples (Ottawa: Canadian Government Publishing, 1994).

51  Crawford, "The Trauma Experienced by Generations Past," 339–69; Dussault and Erasmus, *The High Arctic Relocation*.

52  Dussault and Erasmus, *The High Artic Relocation*; Daniel Soberman, "Report to the Human Rights Commission on the Complaints of the Inuit People to the Human Rights Commission" (1991).

53  See Veracini, *Settler Colonialism*; Soberman, "Report to the Human Rights Commission"; George E. Marcus, "Ethnography in/or World Systems: The Emergence of Multi-sited Ethnography," *Annual Review of Anthropology* 24 (1995): 95–117.

54  Nichol, "Reframing Sovereignty"; Michael Byers, *Who Owns the Arctic? Understanding Sovereignty Disputes in the North* (Vancouver: Douglas & McIntyre, 2009); Soberman, "Report to the Human Rights Commission"; William R. Morrison, *Under the Flag:*

*Canadian Sovereignty and the Native People in Northern Canada*
(Ottawa: Research Branch, Indian and Northern Affairs, 1984).

55  Anderson, *Canada's Relationship with the Inuit*; Soberman, "Report
to the Human Rights Commission"; Inuit Tapiriit Kanatami, "The
Climate Change Bind"; Soberman, "Report to the Human Rights
Commission."

56  Gabrielle Slowey, "The Northwest Territories: A New Day?" in
*Transforming Provincial Politics*, ed. Charles Smith and Bryan Evans
(Toronto: University of Toronto Press, 2015).

57  Anderson, *Canada's Relationship with the Inuit*, 104–05. The
two-volume Hawthorn Report, so named after the head of the
research inquiry, anthropologist Harry B. Hawthorn, is titled *A
Survey of the Contemporary Indians of Canada*; the 1969 White Paper,
titled *Statement of the Government of Canada on Indian Policy*, was
withdrawn by the government the following year after widespread
backlash and condemnation from Indigenous leaders for its
assimilationist assumptions.

58  Anderson, *Canada's Relationship with the Inuit*; Slowey, "The
Northwest Territories."

59  David Brock and Alan Cash, "Is There a Confidence Convention in
Consensus Government?" *Canadian Parliamentary Review* (Autumn
2014): 10–16; Barrett Weber, "'Government Closer to the People':
On Decentralization in Nunavut," *Polar Geography* 37, no. 2 (2014):
177–92.

60  Brock and Cash, "Is There a Confidence Convention."

61  Of course, it must also be recognized that cultures are alive and
adapt to their changing environment. The loss here, then, is not one
of culture, but one of access to traditional/historical cultural ties.

62  Mereseini Marau, "Kiribati to Buy Land in Fiji," *The Fiji Times
Online*, 2013, http://www.fijitimes.com/story.aspx?ref=ar-
chive&id=224285; "Kiribati to Follow Maldives and Buy Land for
Survival," *Miadhu News*, 2009, http://www.miadhu.com/2009/02/
local-news/kiribati-to-follow-maldives-and-buy-land-for-surviv-
al-9269/. More than a decade ago the Maldivian government
pursued land purchases in Australia for relocation, but more

recently it has aimed at protecting the islands — and the islands' tourist-based economy — by land reclamation and other geoengineering projects. It remains to be seen whether these efforts can be enough, especially given the dying coral reefs that provide some protection. See, for example, Nenad Jare Dauenhauer, "On Front Line of Climate Change as Maldives Fights Rising Seas," *NewScientist*, 20 Mar. 2017, https://www.newscientist.com/article/2125198-on-front-line-of-climate-change-as-maldives-fights-rising -seas.

63 See Robin Bronen, "Climate-Induced Displacement of Alaska Native Communities," *Brookings Institution* (2013), https://www.brookings.edu/wp-content/uploads/2016/06/30-climate-alaska-bronen-paper.pdf.

64 Inuit Tapiriit Kanatami, "The Climate Change Bind"; Huntington and Fox, "The Changing Arctic," 77–78.

65 Veracini, *Settler Colonialism*, 70–72.

66 See Benton, *A Search for Sovereignty*

67 Veracini, *Settler Colonialism*, 73

68 This conceptual path follows the principle of *terra nullius* (no man's land), where Indigenous populations were not considered sovereign nations by colonizers at the time of colonization. See Simpson, *Mohawk Interruptus*; Coulthard, *Red Skin, White Masks*; Benton, *A Search for Sovereignty*.

69 Veracini, *Settler Colonialism*.

70 See Nine, "Ecological Refugees"; Moore, *A Political Theory of Territory*.

71 Nine, "Ecological Refugees."

72 See, for example, Huntington and Fox, "The Changing Arctic."

73 Nine, "Ecological Refugees."

74 Cohen, "For Disaster IDPs: An Institutional Gap."

75 Ibid.

76 Nichol, "Reframing Sovereignty"; also see Roger Normand and Sarah Zaidi, *Human Rights at the UN: The Political History of Universal Justice* (Bloomington: Indianan University Press, 2008).

77 Nichol, "Reframing Sovereignty."

78 See point 1.4 of Inuit Circumpolar Conference, *Circumpolar Inuit*

*Declaration on Sovereignty in the Arctic* (2009), http://www.inuitcir-cumpolar.com/files/uploads/icc-files/PR-2009-04-28-Signed-Inuit-Sovereignty-Declaration-11x17.pdf.

79  See Point 3.13 of Inuit Tapiriit Kanatami, *Circumpolar Inuit Declaration on Arctic Sovereignty* (2009), http://www.itk.ca/circumpolar-inuit-declaration-arctic-sovereignty.

80  Especially see Nine, "Ecological Refugees."

# INDEX

migration. *See* rural–urban
migration
mining, 7, 56, 59
mobility: cost of, 104, 118; as
a facet of socio-economic
life, 115; of Greenlanders,
145, 146; versus immo-
bility, 115, 117–18, 208; of
Indigenous peoples, 17;
and migration, 116–17;
and rural places, 115–16,
185
modernism. *See* high modernism
modernization theory, 80–81
Monkstown, 99
Mushuau, 6, 17
Muskrat Falls hydroelectric
project, 7
Nain, 6
'Nakwaxda'wx peoples, 17
National Film Board of Canada (NFB), 64, 66, 79, 98
Natuashish, 6
natural resources, 24–26
neo-liberalism, 10, 12, 71, 123
Newfoundland and Labrador:
and colonialism, 6; gov-
ernment of, 44, 49, 81;
government resettlement

policies of, 44, 45, 46,
48–49, 81; and poverty,
47; and religion, 92–93;
resource geography in,
121; and rural communi-
ties, 4; waves of resettlement in, 121–23; "ghost
villages" of, 118; *see also*
names of specific com-
munities
Newfoundland Fisheries
Development Committee
(1953). *See* Walsh Report
Newtok, 11
Nippers Harbour, 112–13, 134
n. 4
non-governmental organizations (NGOs), 13, 28, 162,
168, 169
non-state actors, 20–21, 47,
182
Northern Canada, 11, 18,
56–57, 244, 247
Northern Coordination and
Research Centre (NCRC),
57
Northern Ireland, 185
Northwest Territories, 16, 237
Nova Scotia, 17, 29 n. 13, 103
Nutak, 6, 7

savings incurred from,
48, 112–13; in Newfound-
land and Labrador, 4–5,
10, 121; in Quebec, 59,
60; in United States, 2,
18; internal migration,
187; neo-resettlement,
123; of isolated communi-
ties, 1–2; political economy of, 12–13; popular
culture and, 43–44; re-
sistance to, 22–23; versus
relocation, 4; as a tool
of human territoriality,
15–16; voluntary, 2, 20, 24,
119–20, 126; "people-cen-
tred approach," 14, 20; *see
also* displacement
residential schools, 17, 134
resistance, 15, 22, 100, 117, 206
Resolute Bay, 17–18, 236
resource development, 24,
235; *see also* fisheries;
extractive development
Round Harbour, 112–13
Royal Commission on Aboriginal Peoples, 18
Rural Resettlement Ireland
(RRI), 21, 182, 188–89,
192–210

rural–urban divide: in Greenland, 148, 157, 160–61,
165; rural "staying" as an
active process, 116–17,
132–33
rural–urban migration, 149,
159, 171
Salvation Army, 80
Sayisi Dene First Nation, 16
Shishmaref, 11
Shubenacadie (Nova Scotia),
17
slum clearance, 9, 29–30 n. 13
small island nations, 11, 19,
25, 243, 248
Smallwood, Joseph R.
("Joey"): and attacks on
centralization, 94; and
clerics, 93; and coercion
tactics, 103; and media,
86; and resettlement
plans, 5, 48, 65, 82
Snook's Arm, 112–13, 134 n. 4
Snowden, Donald, 61–64, 67,
69
social cleansing, 10
social sciences, 56, 59
Southern Harbour, 83, 86–88
sovereignty, 2, 11, 16, 18, 230,
232–34, 240, 242